Hey, Day!

Super-Amazing, Funk-da-crazing,
Ultra-glazing Things to Do, Make
and Ponder Every Day of the Year

The Appreciation Section

XO Keva—Hunka hunka love of my life Tim, lovie sissie Aimee, Mom and Dad and Alfie, my loving and adorable fam & Clea.

XO Clea—My Gorgeous gaggle of girlfriends, my wacky grandma Ruth, Keva, Georgia, & hubba hubba Jeff.

We also want to say merci, gracias, domo arigato and danke schoen to our fave pub chicks—Ginee, Jody, Amy & Jen.

Hey, Day!

Library of Congress Cataloging-in-Publication Data
Hey, day!: super-amazing, funk-da-crazing, ultra-glazing things to do, make and ponder every day of the year.
    p.   cm.
  ISBN 0-06-446241-2 (pbk.)
    1. Handicraft for girls—Juvenile literature.   2. Amusements—Juvenile literature.
3. Games for girls—Juvenile literature. [1. Amusements. 2. Handicraft.]
TT171.H48 2001
745.45'083502—dc21   00-054211
                                                                              CIP
                                                                              AC

1 2 3 4 5 6 7 8 9 10
❖
First Harper Trophy edition, 2001

Visit us on the World Wide Web!
www.harperchildrens.com
Printed in Canada

la la la la

Here's the scoop:

ha! lalala

Hi, clea

♡keva x°

ha!

Hey, Day!

Super-Amazing, Funk-da-crazing,
Ultra-glazing Things to Do, Make
and Ponder Every Day of the Year

clea*

mucho gusto.

XXX

007
"poop"
K+T♡
t.L.f.

ha!

chi-hua-hua

Super Clea and Keva Marie

mini jupe

ha!

lalala

HarperTrophy®
An Imprint of HarperCollinsPublishers

CLEA AND KEVA PRESENT THE COOLEST DAYBOOK EVER

CLEA

KEVA

Welcome to the craft-wacky book we call Hey, Day!

"Hey, Day!" is:

A handbook for the ridiculously cool-cool girl.

A road map to living a badass life.

A reference for school (not).

A directory of all things crafty.

An inspiring diary thing that stokes you out.

Or just think of it as the punk rock Girl Scout guide.

The Coolest Daybook Ever provides you with the answers when you are bored, in love, hungry, bored, tired, antsy, bored, in a bad mood, bored, or feeling badass and, well, you know, all that stuff.

We wrote it for the pure sake of spicing up your life and for the sake of a cooler cool-girl world. And, well, we wrote it for fun!

It's everything to every girl. OK, well, maybe not, but it is a handy little book written in an effort to make your life funner. And, well, to make our lives funner, too...

Clea: Funner is soooo NOT a word.
Keva: Is too!
Clea: Is NOT!!

WHOA!

That way your life can be full of zip and zing! And you can do lots of neat things. And you will never, ever be bored again. And you will always be boss. And love thyself till you can't stand it no more.

There are 365 days' worth of exasperating, relaxating, rejuvenating, exclamating, complicating, super-amazing, ultra-glazing, funk-da-crazing things to do, make and ponder.

Yes, we said ponder.
So get crackin'.
And welcome to...

Hey, Day!

YO!

♡ keva xo clea ★

Yo. You know and we know that some holidays fall on different dates each year. So, when we say, "Today is Easter," we know it may not actually be Easter. In other words, not all dates are exact. Go with it. Read ahead, read behind, read upside down. But go with it. Merci.

JANUARY

HOLA CHICAS

Have you made your resolutions yet? (get crackin'!) Clea*'s fave day this month is the one about her dog. This is George, her girl doggy.
Say hello to

GEORGE!

Keva has a dog, too, Alfie. Well, it's her mom's, but she borrows him lots. Oh, and Keva*'s favorite day is Wednesday. Any Wednesday. (Don't ask.)

OK, bye, xo us

ADÍOS CHICAS

The mornings suck.

You know the drill. Alarm goes off, you make grumpy noises and resist the temptation to fall back asleep as you push yourself or (like Keva used to do) make yourself fall off the bed and stumble to the bathroom to pee and haphazardly wash face, brush teeth and apply deodorant.

Then you stumble back to your room, bump into a few walls here and there, lazily throw on the first items of clothing you can find, pull hair in pony, grab backpack and mosey off to work or school, whichever the case may be.

Either way, you know you don't wake up to the world for at least 45 minutes and even then, you're a bit foggy in the eyes.

WELL, NO LONGER! From this day forward make a new pact:

"I will spend at least five minutes every morning in bed thinking about my day before I stumble off to the bathroom."

After you try this for a few days you will find that this relatively painless little exercise will make for a clearer head, a sharper mind, a better outfit and perhaps even a more thought-out life. Now pick your ponders.

Things CLEA ponders before leaping out of bed: what to wear (duh!), what Georgia (my dog) will do today, how much the old feet STINK, what CD to grab for the car 🎵 and if eating scrambled eggs 🍳 for the 14th day straight is bad for me! Oh + I wonder what the heck KEVA will be wearing today....

Things Keva ponders before leaping outta bed: The meaning of last night's dreams, if I snored, what face cleanser to use for today's face wash ☑, what shoes 👟 to wear if there are any clean socks left and if they match and what I was doing last year.

January 2

YO.

So you're reading a magazine. **LA DA DA.**

LUKE I AM YER FATHER

Read read. When all of a sudden you spot a picture, photo, drawing, sentence, word, article that grabs you by your shirt collar...

and all but says WHOA!

"makeup"

You want to try white lipstick eventually.

You might soak it in, this picture, photo, drawing, sentence, word or article, and then move on to the next. But three days later you won't have any recollection of that very thing that grabbed you so. And if you can't recall it three days later, do you really think you can remember that particular "cool thing" when you need it weeks or months later? Hence, the (said in a booming Darth Vader-like voice):

future files

Really just an elaborate way to hold on to magazine clippings and, therefore, your thoughts. Today you create a couple of basic files. You get your system up and running. And then throughout the year, we'll give you more ideas for additional files.

"fashions"

(Said in a French accent.)

Sure, you could use a filing cabinet with hanging folders and files, if you've got one already. Or you can create your very own with things you've got around the house, such as shoe boxes or old record jackets. The principle is all the same. They should be easily accessible, sorta organized and labeled clearly enough so you can tell which is which.

Today, start by creating THREE Future Files. These are utterly trivial and we're proud of that fact. You should be too.

"hair"

For the 'dos you want to do.

It's also great to have a box (adorned in glitter, of course) as your "weigh station." This is where you can drop your clippings when you don't have time to actually file them away. This way, they won't get lost. And when you've got a moment or three, you can go and file those weigh station pictures, photos, drawings, sentences, words and articles away.

more future files to come...next month

TO ODE IS DIVINE

Odes are nuggets de appreciation.

Little poems all wrapped up in dedications.

Words that become proclamations

...of your respect, love, lust or friendship.

Clea & George in the Nevada desert. They look happy, huh?

To show your friends, your colleagues, your family and your idols how much you in fact appreciate them (it's so easy to forget and take them for granted), we suggest you get in the habit of scribing the occasional ode to let them know you care.

No need to craft a life-size artistic representation of, say, Clea's dog George out of butter, just do it with words. In an ode.

Odes are the easiest of poems because they are from the heart. They are snippets of feelings directed at one person and one person only. They don't have to rhyme (although it IS fun to rhyme). They just need be your interpretation of why that person is so great. It's about appreciation. And appreciating people is a simple, pleasing, basic good habit to come by.

CLEA's ODE to GEORGE

george is a girl dog with a masculine name
...but everyone loves her just the same
she doesn't know how to bark (even a bit)
and no dog is cuter as they jump, beg or sit
she wears baby socks so her feet stay warm & snug
when you see her you'll fall for her cute li'l mug

Now go and write up an ode of your own.

January 4

The Spellcaster
today's spell?

ANIMAL COMMUNICADO

Yes, that is right, learn to chitty chat with your kitty kat (or dog or bunny or pony, too).

Here is what you will need

a radio
a cotton tablecloth
a cup of pet food
a picture of your pet
a clump of cotton stuffing from a pillow

The best time to cast this spell is on a Friday night during a new moon directly after sunset. Take all your supplies and head for a place where no one will bug you (e.g., the bathroom, bedroom, garage). Lay the tablecloth on the floor and sit down on it. Be sure to have a wee bit of space left over. Next, place the picture of your pet upside down on the tablecloth. On top of that, place the cotton stuffing, and then on top of that dump the food. Now spend the next five whole minutes (time yourself, if necessary) saying your pet's name over and over again. Then turn on the radio. Whatever song comes on instantly becomes you and your pet's song (if you get commercials, wait until you get music). Continue to listen to the song and pay attention to the words. Try to sing along by adding your pet's name into the lyrics whenever possible. Once the song is over, turn off the radio. Put the food back into the cup. Take the stuffing and put it into your pocket. Feed your pet. From now on, whenever you are hanging out with your pet, sing that song to them and they will slowly, but surely, begin to understand you.

You need a tradition. Something that is all you. Now, here's how to make your own. Spend some time alone and think of stuff you find extra special cool. Celebrating the anniversary of the day you got your pet? Watching cartoons every Saturday morning? Going to the park every third Tuesday just to smell the flowers? Renting "Valley Girl" every Fourth of July? Whatever your funny quirk is, make it special by deeming it, from this day forward, your tradition. Name it and share it with all your best friends. Think: a few years from now when someone asks you, "What the heck did we do two years ago on Elvis's birthday?" you can say: "Well, every year on Elvis's birthday I wake up early and read my favorite book from front to back before everyone wakes up!" Make your tradition today and stick with it forever.

traditions are rad

Clea always watches
"Willy Wonka + the
Chocolate Factory"
and eats deli platters
on Xmas day.
　　　It's a tradition!

Keva invites a few pals
over to la bodega on
July 4th to lounge
about in the sun and
test out all the latest
beauty tips in the
teenie mags!
　　　It's a tradition!

January 6

Clea here, time to share.

My parents almost named me Pandora. My great-grandmother's name was Dora and they were gonna name me after her but then thought, well, Pandora was cuter. But when I was born I was apparently very hairy and wrinkly and they changed their minds and decided I was a Clea. Which I like quite a bit. But I digress. My parents told me that story when I was about seven. Ever since then, I have been a little obsessed about the world of Pandora, her choices and her story. According to Greek mythology, Pandora was the very first woman created by the gods.

See, Zeus was all mad at Prometheus (a Titan) for stealing the power of fire and giving it to the mortals. To get Prometheus back for his indiscretion, Zeus fashioned the beautiful Pandora out of clay. He sent her off as a gift (oh, brother!) to Prometheus. With her came a dowry, or rather a box and a message to never open it. (I never said the gods were fair, just or politically correct peoples.) Anyway, Pandora simply couldn't resist opening that secret box. Only problem was that it was supposedly filled with the evils of the world...which subsequently were then released. Bummer.

Pandora quickly put the top back on but everything had escaped— everything, that is, except for HOPE. That is why, even in the darkest times, even when evil rears its ugliest head or people are just plain mean, there will always be hope for a better tomorrow.

remember this, for it is true...

WHO SAYS A PANDORA'S BOX HAS TO BE EVIL! *NOT US.*

SECRETS CAN BE DELICIOUS

good stuff

memories

junque

secrets

special stuff

wind machine

Pandora's Box (or yours)
(originally a bottle)

with secret stuff in them are definitely cool.

The point is to really focus on how you're feeling right here, right now. That way, some day, light-years from now, you can be transported back in time to this particular moment. ("Why, look how much I've grown," you'll say.) So, make a dedication. Get a box—any box will do. Line the inside with fabric in your most favorite color. Write a poem about how you are feeling right at this very moment. On a separate piece of paper write down the date and time underneath it and include a photo of yourself. Spray your favorite perfume into the box, three times. And then promptly close the box and tape it up. Find a secret place to hide it away. (Um, the back of your closet is good, or in the far east corner of the attic.) And do not (no way, Jose) open it up until at least one year from now.

Boxes

January 8

12 things you can live without:

Styrofoam
A day planner
Bad rap music
"Whatshisface"
Curse words
Spreading gossip
Microwave energy
Nagging
Yelling at Mom   i ♡ alfie
Hatred of people
Fear
Questioning yourself

Sometimes we get so used to using all of
everything we got that we forget
to stop and think:

"Do I need this in my life?"

That's what today is for. Ask yourself,
"Is this good for our dear mother earth?"
"Will this make that person happy?"
"Is this really me?"

We made a list of things to think about.
Now make yours.

DUMB JOKES ARE THE BEST.

Where do you find elephants? **IT DEPENDS ON WHERE YOU LOST THEM.**

Try some of ours, Or make up your own. (We're pretty partial to elephant jokes. So sorry.)

Do you ever laugh so hard that snot comes out your nose?

Gosh, that's great.

Go ahead and make someone laugh today. It makes you feel all warm and fuzzy. And maybe snot will come out of their nose.

Why do elephants float on their backs? **SO THEY DON'T GET THEIR TENNIS SHOES WET.**

What goes clomp, clomp, clomp, squish, clomp, clomp, clomp, squish? **AN ELEPHANT WITH A WET TENNIS SHOE.**

Why did the elephant stand on the fluffy marshmallow? **SO SHE WOULDN'T FALL IN THE HOT CHOCOLATE.**

What's gray, yellow, gray, yellow, gray, yellow, gray, yellow, gray? **AN ELEPHANT ROLLING DOWN A HILL WITH A DAISY IN ITS MOUTH.**

January 10

You should never part with your favorite pair of jeans. Never. They're like your favorite photo: they can conjure up terrific moments from your past. Getting rid of them would be sacrilegious and you know it. But maybe they're thrashed. What's a girl to do?

Make a Bag Out of 'Em

1. Zip up the jeans and then turn them inside out. With a pair of decent scissors cut off both legs about 3" from the crotch.

inside out

3"

CUT

oh, bells are so out

just cut 'em off, babe

2. Keeping them inside out and flat, now sew each of the legs shut. Sew this part on a machine or do it by hand, but if you choose the latter, your stitches need to be tight and small. OK? OK. Cut off the extra material below the stitched seam. (Leave about one inch of material behind.) Turn your bag right side out.

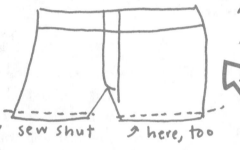

sew shut *here, too*

a needle

P.S. If you don't have a pair of jeans that you're ready to stop wearing, go to your favorite house de thrift and buy the cheapest. But we didn't need to tell you that, did we?

3. You can sew purse straps on (with just a few good stitches) or just weave a ribbon through the belt loops and tie, cinching the top tight. You can carry it around by the excess ribbon. Make sure to put secret stuff in the pockets, like your breath mints. Or a superspy note. Or a photo of your pooch. You get the drift, now dig the picture if you can.

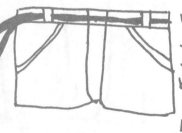

weave a ribbon through the belt loops and carry like that!

✛from the very official desk of Miss Keva Marie ✛

Women who influenced my life.
Part One. By Keva Marie. Betsey Johnson Rocks.

When I first heard of Betsey Johnson, I was fifteen. Fifteen sucked. I was depressed, frustrated, upset all the time and thought that I was wasting my youth wallowing in depression. I was so worried about not having fun that I wasn't having any fun. I constantly worried that when I got just a little bit older I would have to be an adult, and I was scared of everything I thought went with that: bad jobs, drudgery, boredom. I thought the fun times were over.

That made me scared. Scared and sad. Scared, sad and, well, more depressed. Then I saw an article about Betsey Johnson and as if in an instant my fears were erased. There she was, in a hot pink leopard tutu, crazy dreads and neon fishnet tights looking so cute and talking about her designs and her loft and her office and how she was 40-something and I just kinda went gaga.

I felt like I got a bang on the head. Then I had an epiphany. It occurred to me for the very first time in my life that I don't have to be boring when I grow up. In fact at that moment I decided that when I get older I ain't gonna grow up, I'm gonna grow better. Better and cuter and sillier and no one will stop me. It was from that day forward that I vowed to myself that as I grew older, I would still be young at heart and goofy as I wanted to be.

Betsey Johnson gave me the strength to make my vow just by being herself. She inspired me like no other and I haven't even met her...yet!

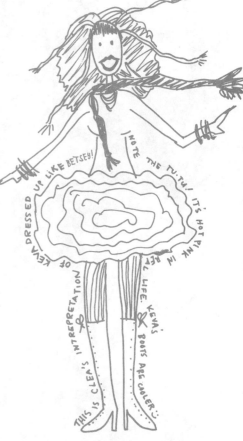

She's the wild child who made hot pink punk.

By the way, Betsey Johnson is a world-famous designer of fabulously bright and crazed women's clothing who owns her own shops across the country and lives in NYC.

IMagine you're a boy.

Be a VEGAN for a day!

Or a vegetarian for a day!

Vegetarians come in all shapes and sizes. Most don't eat beef or fowl but will partake in the dairy stuff. Vegans don't eat meat or any other animal products, including dairy like milk or eggs. Whatever your beliefs, it can't hurt to abstain from meat, or even dairy, for a single day. So expand your horizons and try something new.

*If you are already one, celebrate your veganness with these fabulous recipes.

You can enjoy these SNAX any day, vegan or not. But they do happen to be meat and dairy-free.

Tofu Tacos

Scrape the corn off one cob. Slice 4 mushrooms. Cut up a green or red bell pepper. Chop half an onion and a couple cloves of garlic. Slice up a half slab firm tofu. Heat up a little oil and add everything plus a couple shakes of chili powder and cumin. While that is cooking slice up an avocado and squeeze a little lemon juice on it. Buy either hard taco shells and heat them in the oven for a few minutes or soft tortillas and heat them up in a hot frying pan (no oil!) for just a few seconds. Stuff filling inside, top with avocado and devour, hungrily.

It's a taco. honest.

Famous Vegetarians: Liv Tyler, Madonna, Claudia Schiffer, Michael Stipe, Michael Jackson, Shania Twain, Louisa May Alcott, Mister Rogers, Fugazi guys, Morrissey, Ahmet Zappa, Carmen Miranda, Ellen Degeneres, Drew Barrymore, k.d. Lang, Cher, Natalie Merchant, David Duchovny, RuPaul, Lisa Simpson, Eric Stoltz, Vanna White, Raffi, David Bowie, and Brad Pitt.

THIS IS A COOKIE. SWEARS.

*Did you know Oreos contain animal by-products but Hydrox cookies (the ones that look suspiciously like Oreos) don't? All hail Hydrox!

Kevq: So, do you think they all get together + have lunch?
Clea: Oh. yeah. I'm sure.

Oh, piggy piggy piggy.

We all know that saving money is good and I'm sure we all try to do it. Girls are smart. But is the cash sometimes floating around...stuck in a pocket, in a drawer, in the back of last year's diary? If you're at all like us, the answer is "YES yes yes, how did you know?"

When you're sitting around and thinking about Mom's birthday prez or a spring break trip, it is time to reinspire and recalculate your plan. That's right, recalculate. As in stashing. As in getting all the extra coins into a safe place where you know you won't spend it, at least for a little while.

The best safe place is sometimes the obvious place: The Piggy Bank. The reason: You feed it with cash and coin and nope, you cannot grab that handful of change for your trip to the flea market. You can't because the piggy bank has it. Which means that if you have a goal the piggy will help because of one pure and easy fact: Once you deposit, it's in for the long haul.

When the piggy bank is full or you decide (long, hard thinking leading to painful decision) you need the cash for a certain plan o' action, then wrap a towel 'round piggy and take a hammer to the underside of his cute rotund belly and crack. Unwrap towel. Stuff coin into paper change rolls (banks give these to you for free!) and count, count, count.

Go shopping. Return. Superglue piggy. And start all over again.

*Oh, and no removable rubber stopper piggy piggys allowed.

SEIJIN NO HI

LET'S PARTY!

Seijin no hi, otherwise referred to as Adult's Day or Coming of Age Day, is a national holiday in Japan to celebrate all who turn 20 years old that year. In Japan, that is when you are considered an official adult. It's the age when you can vote, drink and smoke in that country. C'mon, this is very interesting, no?

Parents spend enormous amounts of money to outfit their 20-year-olds in elegant, formal clothes like kimonos and ritzy suits. And a lot of people play archery on this day. Why? Couldn't tell you. But they do. So go tell someone who is turning 20 or someone who just turned 20, happy Seijin no hi! And ask them if they wanna go put on a fancy kimono and play archery with you.

clea's dog is twenty... in people years though she's almost 3! dog years are weird. twenty is an even number but you knew that. do you like even or odd numbers better? we like odd because we like anything that is odd. odd is good. still, twenty is a magical number. but do you think that is the official adult age?

will you be studying when you're 20? what will you be studying when you're 20? will your very best friend be your very best friend when you're 20? who will you be when you're 20? will you be in school when you're 20? the # the 20: will you be in school when you're 20? questions @ the 20

YO! OPEN A BOOK!

You're bored.
You don't know what to do.
You don't have a car.
Or gas.
Or money.
Or energy.
Or whatever.
Play this game.

Grab the nearest book (besides this one) and sit down with it in a big ol' comfy chair. Now close your eyes, open the book and take your right index finger and place it somewhere in the book.

It's so random. Now open your eyes and look at what word your finger landed on.

Spend the next five minutes contemplating the simple beauty of that word. That and nothing else. Meditate on the word. Think of all the things that it reminds you of, good and bad, happy or sad, and when you are good and done, repeat the game.

play the game. read a book. be yourself. just not bored! xoxo

COLLECTING COOL JUNK IS FUN.

(WE KNOW. WE COLLECT A LOT OF JUNK.)

Everyone should have something they collect. It makes thrift stores and garage sales and swap meets that much more fun when you are looking for some trinket to add to your collection at home.

When deciding on what to collect, pick something that's an extension of you. Like Clea collects poodle stuff. Poodle bookends, ceramic poodles, poodle jewelry, poodle pictures, stuffed poodles, poodle purses, poodles. Sure, she likes dogs. But that's not why she collects poodles. They're the prissiest, most femininely bizarre animals on the face of the earth. They are always unnaturally portrayed as pink. And she loves pink. And her boyfriend hates pink. And poodles always look confident, unlike bulldogs which look mean or hounds which look sad or Chihuahuas which look helpless. Poodles!

And remember to take time out throughout the year to simply enjoy the beauty of the individual items, and don't just get caught up in more, more, more. That part is fun, but remember to enjoy the goodness of each thing.

Oh, in case you were racking your brain, wondering what Keva collects, here you go: faux gold gilded frames and weird kiddie art and old straw hats, the kind you would garden in, and shoes.

Oh, does she collect shoes.

January 18

The Real Deal on Hot Guy Martin Luther King, Jr.

You'll begin to see there are real connections from the seemingly "little actions" you can accomplish on your own to the big changes the world needs as a whole.

In honor of Martin Luther King, Jr., and his day, we're going to dream (all right!). Dream of what would make our lives betta, our friends' lives cooler and our little baby sisters' lives super-dupa fly.

Martin Luther King, Jr., delivered his famous speech at the Lincoln Memorial in Washington, DC, in August 1963. Man oh man, could that guy write speeches. In that speech, he said people asked him, "When will you be satisfied?"

Ask yourself the very same question. Think: When will YOU be satisfied? Get a book. Start with: "I have a dream..."

What kinds of things would you like to change in this world? It may seem daunting to think about, but all BIG actions start with little actions.

So, make two columns.
On the LEFT write down all the things that you think would make this world a better place...for all people. Think big, think grandiose. Write down as many things that you can dream of.

On the RIGHT side of the page write down things you yourself can actually do to contribute. Clean up the park on Friday? Collect used clothing? Write a meaningful letter to someone in charge?
(See tomorrow!)

So one day you find yourself walking down the street, and you come across your old elementary school (as Keva does every Sunday morning when she walks to the coffee shop). So there you are, gazing upon your old school. You feel happy as you reminisce about first-grade crushes when all of a sudden you notice this vulgar, disgusting, super nasty graffiti all over what used to be your four-square court. "YUCK!" you yell, but no one is around.

You feel angry and sad. You feel like something should be done about this. But you don't know what . . .

Write a letter!

To whom, you ask? Why, to someone who has the power, such as a government official. Letters, when written well, can be a very powerful thing. They are a call to action, a plea for help, a real voice from a member of the community. And who knows, hopefully you will get a response or, better yet, a solution!

First you must find out who those powerful people are, so grab the tele. To reach your local congressman or woman, call the Congressional Switchboard in DC (that's District of Columbia, Washington style) at 202-224-3121 and say something like, "I want to know who the congressperson is in my area, please." They will then ask you for your zip code and then connect you directly to that office.

Just like that!

Ask for their mailing address. Now that you have your contact, get ready to voice your concern. Here are a few things to keep in mind:

1. Only talk about ONE thing. You're more effective this way. 2. Ask for a response. 3. Be nice. 4. No threats allowed. 5. Shorter is actually better, it's more succinct. 6. Use a typewriter or computer, for neatness counts. 7. Spellcheck! 8. Ask someone, a friend or parent, to proofread it. And don't forget to include your name, address, and telephone number or email address for your response back. Good luck,

Keva xo

SICKY SURPRISE IS A SUPER SILLY SINGSONGY SOUNDING NAME. BUT THAT'S WHAT WE'RE GONNA MAKE.

It's cold out almost everywhere in the country these days, so it's inevitable that someone you know has been sneezing like mad or has the winter ache. Bring them a Sicky Surprise. It's nice and it just might make 'em feel betta.

Stuff you can buy:

Plastic bears filled with honey

A big teacup (scour the halls de thrift for a fancy but cheap one)

A hanky

Tea bags

Stuff you can make:

The sore throat recipe.

Gather three small, roughly chopped garlic cloves and 1/8 teaspoon cayenne pepper and put into a small bag. Write down these instructions and tie them on to the bag o' garlic and stuff: "Mix these together with a tablespoon of honey. Take a spoonful when needed. Chew well. Swallow. Don't take a swig of water. Yes, it's hot. But it works."

all. better TEA! xo

Now go find someone who is sick and in need of the Surprise.

greased lightning

hey, babe, what's your sign?

stickers rock

i don't think so!

whatever

STICKERS

VIVA ROCKS

•:•SUPERCLEA•:•

are fun, that's sort of a given. Don't know what it is about them, but they are innately happy. You go to the store and you're often just swept up in the glitter and the cuteness of it all. We suggest making your own.

girls kick ass

A.
You can buy sticker paper from the office supply store. They have your basic white and they can be either printed via your computer or simply drawn directly on with pencils, pens and crayons. This is cool because it comes with the peelable backing paper. Oh, and you can also photocopy on this paper at the copy shop.

TWO WAYS

B. Or you can go the cheap-gal way and draw or print up your designs and then glue-stick them to things. Problem with option B is that you cannot easily hand them out to friends and family unless you give them your glue stick, too. But it still works, so there.

go team!

stickers rock

Some possible sticker crafts include: Making your bizness cards on stickers... Simply writing out your name or, better yet, your secret superhero name...Making photo stickers of your favorite picture of you and the gals. Or of that cartoon character you've been doodling for two years now...

...The record store wants three bucks apiece for those band stickers? Make your own, they'll be way craftier. Make stickers for your own band. Duh...Rally excitement for your girls basketball team with stickers, stickers and more stickers. We just love stickers. And frankly, who doesn't? (Besides maybe dads.)

oh goddess

i love unicorns

i luv jeff

cats are people, too

pacey & joey - tlf

i love dogs

January 22
Does your bra ride up your back?

Are the edges of the cup loose or wrinkled? Do you have red and/or indent marks on your shoulders? Does the front of the bra pull away from you?

CROSS YER ♥

Do all these questions about your bra make you squirmylike?

If you answered yes to any of these questions, chances are no one ever showed you HOW to buy the right bra. (Shame on you, Ma.) While it is not the most fantastic of topics, it will make a difference in so many ways, like for one, they are more comfortable when you get one that fits. Not to mention the stunning silhouette you'll be cutting when you pick out one that actually supports you!

Keva style...

fancy!

Clea likes cotton.

We contacted the Victoria's Secret headquarters for our top secret B.R.A. formula: to get your correct size, measure your rib cage with a tape measure under your breasts. Write that number down and add five inches to it. That is your back size, as in 32 or 34 (always round up to the nearest even number).

1 rib cage measurement + 5" = bra back size

jans cute, 32 B!

2 Then measure around the fullest part of your breasts. Now, subtract that number from your bra back size:
bra back size – breast measurement= X

oh pretty!

So, for sake of argument, Jan's measurement is 27, we add five to that for her back size = 32. The measurement around the fullest part of her breasts is 30 inches, so we subtract that from 32 and we get two inches, which means she's a 32B! Lucky Jan!

3 Now if,
X = ½" you are an AA cup
X = 1" you're an A cup
X = 2" you're a B cup
X = 3" you're a C cup
X = 4" you're a D cup

Bare

keva likes leopard.

OO

ones!

INTRODUCING THE FABULOUS HAIR SALAD!

Today it's all about guacamole for the hair AND for the body.
So get ready to get slimy.

WHAT YOU WILL NEED...One very ripe avocado. One large egg. One fine blender. A go-for-it attitude. That's it.

Cut open the AVO, remove pit & scrape insides into the blender. Add egg and whirl. In the bathroom make a part in your hair. Slather some green goop into your scalp and roots. Then make another part and slap on more green goop. Keep making parts and pouring the stuff on until you've covered most of your head or you used up all da goop. Leave on for 20 minutes.

While waiting, wash the blender so this stuff doesn't harden and get brown and crusty. Go scare your little brother or cat.
Take a Polaroid and send to Grandma.
And eat some chips and guac...

A BOWL OF GUAC. Quarter one plum tomato, throw out the seeds and tomato snot, and chop. Scoop avocado insides into a bowl and mash with a fork. Stir in tomato, add a splash of lime or lemon and even some chopped red onion if you dare. Don't forget the salt and peppa. Eat with chips. Yum. Guac is like fruit salad in that there are no hard, fast rules. Wing it. Add peppers. Add jicama. Add scallions. Whatever.

Your hair should be dry by now. Wash out the gunk with lukewarm water. You might need to shampoo afterward, but if you do, choose a mild one. End result? Intensely shiny and soft hair. Hooray!

January 24

We, Keva and Clea, have recorded a few of our most silly and random email conversations. Why? Because they speak to our relationship, because they are funny to read days later, because they provoke thought. Read 'em if you dare (down below). And then email your friends. About bullfighting and Spain and bad books and more. Keep a few of your emails

Keva: And, like, why in the world are you suddenly concerned, Mizz Clea?

Clea: Not suddenly. I like the art part of bullfighting but I never liked the fighting part. Bull-admiring from afar with a red cape would be more like it.

Keva: What if your boyfriend decided he wanted to go to a bull fight, what would you do?

Clea: I would lecture him on the cruelties of the game. And then I might buy him his own red cape. He can chase George, my dog, around with it. That would be fun actually. Would you go?

Keva: Yeah. In Spain. I would go in a minute. Plus, I just read this really bad book. It was in Spain and the chick was a model turned CIA agent and she went to see the fights all the time. Do you like to read bad books? Sometimes, just because?

Clea: Oh, yeah. Bad books are good. And good books are good. But bad books are good in the bathroom and in the bathtub and under covers with a flashlight.

Clea: While I love bullfighting paintings (and I do love them) and I love the color red, I still cannot get over how ugly & barbaric the whole actual bull-fighting thing is. I would really like to keep the outfits but not hurt or torture the bulls.

DISCUSSION QUESTIONS. BULLFIGHTING...AN ART? A SPORT? A TRAVESTY? IF CLEA'S BOYFRIEND ASKED YOU TO GO TO THE BULLFIGHTING, WOULD YOU GO? WOULD IT MAKE A DIFFERENCE IF YOU WERE IN SPAIN? WHERE DO YOU READ BAD BOOKS? YOU DO READ BAD BOOKS, DON'T YOU?

Today we wanna just focus on a word. A beautiful, pulsating, exciting, otherworldly word. That word is...

Why do we cherish this word so? It means a revelation. Often it means a quick snippet of a revelation. Like you just discovered the whole meaning of the world, but, oops, lost it. But for that second, you had it and held it and knew it.

That's why we love the word "epiphany."

That, and the fact that the miniword "pip" is contained in the word "epiphany." In fact, you can just call those revelations, those moments of clarity, you can just call them "pips." As in "Oh, I just had a pip! It's so clear now, I want to be a drum major!" Like that.

We just want to remind you to keep track of your pips. Take note of them. Write them down. Tell a friend. Revel in your pips. Grasp their inspiring meaning. Hang on to their mystical divinity. Cherish that moment of being so darn sure of something, anything.

Make a page in your diary or notebook or scrapbook. Title it PIPS. And add to it whenever the pip strikes.

January 26

Hey Chicky, it's Australia Day.

Australia Day is sort of like Columbus Day here in the U.S. It's the day Europeans "discovered" Australia, but little mention is made of the fact that tons of people already inhabited the country. In the U.S., it was the Indians. In Australia it was the Aborigines. But, hey, it's still a great day to celebrate the things we know and love about Australia. Like, like, um, Crocodile Dundee.

And it's a good day to practice your Australian accent. Remember to say "mate" lots. And pronounce Australia like this: "Stray-a." Forget that stupid shrimp on the barbie routine. And instead of saying "Bye," simply say, "Ta." It's really much cheerier.

Speak 'Strine (that's Australian for Australian!). These words and phrases are so very Australian. Work them into your speech as much as possible today (or, heck, any day).

Aussie
pronounced "Ozzie," Australian

Bush telly
a campfire (get it? you sit 'round the campfire and watch it.)

Not full the quid
um, dumb

Fair dinkum
genuine and true

Chuck-a-sickie
to take the day off even when you're totally healthy

Pash passionate kiss

Oldies parents

Australia!

CLEA'S BEEN DOWN UNDER! HER HEIDI LIVES THERE!

Sydney

Melbourne

Tasmania!

Wowser an uptight spoilsport

or because they're super foxy but maybe they're not

It's the future honey wish list!

Grab your fave pen and a nice clean plain sheet o' paper. Shut your door, don't answer the phone, do a few quick breathing exercises... now date & sign the top of the sheet and number down 1–12, leaving plenty of space between each. Think (think hard and think deep) of all the things that you REEEEEEEEALLY want in a future cutie pie. The things that may be super petty or duper deep but important all the same. Personality traits that maybe you like in your mom or dad or brother or best friend that you absolutely must have in a KISSABLE form in the future. Don't worry about order of importance because they're all important, right? Now be sure to keep this in a secret-safe place but remember where that place is because the idea is to pull it out the next time you find yourself CRUSHING over someone. Take it out. Read your list. Are they all the things you dreamed about? Or are they more like three outta twelve? If it's the latter, you need to think:

EVERY GIRL must have one. It's the ultimate date guide to be used, referred to and never abused or lost or forgotten about in your wacky, kookie girl-meets-boy world.

Have fun and try to do this once a year. Yeah! xoxo

"Maybe I only like them because I heard they like me" "or because they're super foxy but maybe they're not what I would really like and I'd prolly get sick of them so..."

* Or maybe they score a 100% and you know it's quite possibly a GOOD THING.

January 28

URBAN LEGENDS ARE MODERN FAIRY TALES.

They are also known as "college stories" as in, I swear this happened to my brother's roommate in college. It's always the person's roommate. We contacted our friend and confidante Lisa B. to tell you all about Urban Legends. Why? 'Cause she's an Urban Legends freak! Take it away, Lisa.

Urban Legends appear mysteriously and spread spontaneously in varying forms. They contain elements of humor or horror, so they make for good storytelling. They do NOT have to be false, although most are. ULs often have a basis in fact, but it's their life after the fact that gives them particular interest. Here is one of my faves: Supposedly, at one or another college, a girl was studying late but went back to her dorm room to get a book she left behind. So she wouldn't disturb her roommate, she didn't turn the light on when she went in. She just got her stuff off of her desk and dashed. Later, when she went back to her room, she found her roommate dead as a doorknob and a note written in bloodred lipstick on the mirror. It read: "Aren't you glad you didn't turn on the light?"

Why do you think Urban Legends were created and retold if they aren't true? You could try making one up. Remember to make it about a cousin's friend at college or some such distant person you don't really know. Then gather some friends, turn off the lights, bring out the candles and spook away.

LISA'S INGENIOUS ANALYSIS© THIS LEGEND IS A HAIR-RAISING CAUTIONARY TALE ABOUT THE DANGERS OF LIVING AWAY FROM HOME.

WE WERE FIRED!

We were once very angry and sad and mad and crazed, and now we aren't. You see, we were both fired. On the same day, by the same donkey, but that's a whole 'nother book.

I, Keva, and my pal Clea were both truly miserable in our own ways. We felt like we lost the biggest game of our lives. We were defeated, angry and, maybe most important, ashamed. We were fired. Fired from jobs we loved. Then one day I got a call.

CLEA: Hey, it's Clea.

keva: What's up?

CLEA: I've been thinkin' we should write a book together.

keva: Really?

CLEA: Yeah, I have a few ideas and I know that if we put our heads together we can make something happen.

keva: OK, let's do it.

Actually, it wasn't that simple, but pretty darn close. **We knew** how to make ourselves happy, we knew what we wanted to write and we decided, together, that we didn't necessarily need other people to hire us or fire us to accomplish our dreams. **So** we started getting together on the weekends at 9 a.m. to work all day and then again on weekdays after work. **We wrote pitches,** sent packages out to publishers, mailed follow-up letters, and lo and behold, we got offers! **We** quit those jobs that were not fulfilling enough and now we work together exclusively on projects that bare our heart and soul, and none of this, none of it we say, would have happened if that donkey hadn't been so dumb as to fire us and ignite the flame within. So there. **Moral of the story:** Getting fired is sometimes the best thing that can happen to you. And losing isn't always bad. Because when things are taken away from you that you want or need or love, you are forced to dig a little deeper inside and come up with the stuff that means the mostest. So don't be scared, worried and, most important, ashamed. It happens to the best of us and sometimes it's the best thing that could've happened. And it's not like it was before.

IT'S WAY, WAY BETTER!

SWEDISH IS FUN TO SPEAK!

The accent is so wildly different from American English.
Call up the spirit of the Swedish Chef from the Muppets.
Fix yourself a plate of herring. And practice, practice, practice.
(Or just wing it.)

You know how to whistle, don't you? Put your lips together and blow.
Vill du veta hur till vissla? Rättvis putte din läppen tillsammans och slaget.

Yeah, the Thin Mints were my favorite, too.
Ja, Thin Mints var kock jag likt bäslikaledes.

My favorite candy is Swedish fish.
JAG lik söt svensk fisken bäst.

I was a Girl Scout.
Jag var en flickan spanaren.

I can tie your legs into a knot with my bare hands!

JAG slipsen din ben inne till en knyta med mig bar handen!

What's your sign?
Vad' din horoskopen tecken?

Mine is... "hello cute guy."
Min er "hallå skarp pojken".

It's 2nd Semester!

IT'S TIME FOR AN OVERHAUL...

Yeah, you already know how to decorate the inside of your locker. You sure don*t need us to tell you how. We*re sure it*s covered with your favorite pictures of your favorite stars and your favorite boys and your favorite friends. But maybe there is room for one or two more things. Like some furry wallpaper. Or suction cups and clothespins to hang up your favorite objects du jour. Or pockets. Pockets are good. They*re secret storage compartments of the most basic kind. First off, you should name your locker. Think about it for a moment and we*re sure that the perfect name will reveal itself. Clea*s locker was without a doubt a Pippy. It just sort of had that devil-may-care, I*m-a-kid-with-no-parents-and-yet-I-love-gingham vibe. Once you and your friends name your lockers it becomes easier to meet at the correct time and place.

it's like shorthand:
Pippy, 2:05

Lining the interior walls of the metal locker is easy if you take the time to make a pattern. You need tracing paper or another lightweight paper that is bigger than the space you wish to cover. Now push the paper against each wall. Take your pencil and trace the shape onto the paper. Wrap this paper up and take it home where you will have sharp scissors and fabric waiting.

A FEW SUGGESTIONS: ASTRO TURF (YOU CAN FIND IT AT HARDWARE STORES), FAKE FUR, DENIM, YOUR OLD AND FRAYING THUNDERCATS BEACH TOWEL

Once you*ve cut the fabric to the approximate size via the pattern, bring it back to school, along with that gum type glue that is sticky but removable at the end of the semester. Tack up your new wallpaper lickety-split, before anyone notices.

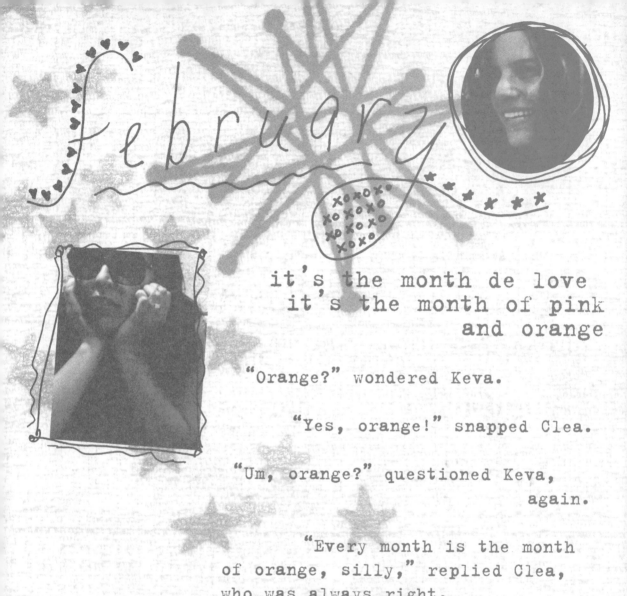

February

XOXOXO
XO XO XO
XO XO XO
XO XO XO
XOXO

it's the month de love
it's the month of pink
and orange

"Orange?" wondered Keva.

"Yes, orange!" snapped Clea.

"Um, orange?" questioned Keva,
again.

"Every month is the month
of orange, silly," replied Clea,
who was always right.
Well, not always.

Regular Style

WHAT'S IN THIS YEAR? HAPPINESS ☺
WHAT'S OUT THIS YEAR? DEVILS 😈

On the first day of spring in Japan those kooky folks throw roasted beans to drive out the bad luck and bring in the good luck.

sardine head

THE HOLIDAY IS CALLED SETSUBUN.

As you toss your beans out to the world, it is customary to shout:

"onj wa soto, Fu ku uchi" = "Devils out, happiness in."

(Which sounds to us like a fabulous thing to shout out on any day, really.) But wait, there's more. Many people also place a broiled or dried sardine's head and a small branch of holly on the front door. **Yum**. They do this because they believe that the thorny leaves of the holly and the fishy smell of the sardine drives away evil spirits (called oniyarai or tsuina). Oh, there's still more. In Japan, you're supposed to throw more beans around your house to protect the family from misfortune. Afterward, everybody is supposed to pick up and eat the number of beans that corresponds to their age, plus one. We know this may upset you, but thankfully you don't have to eat that many sardines. So toss some beans around and enjoy a happy, peaceful year, free of evil.

beans thrown on floor ward off bad mojo.

*We know what you're thinking, Whoa, another Japanese holiday. And there are more. We love them. They are random and odd and fabulous.

FEBRUARY 2

Alert.
Alert.Alert.
VALENTINE'S DAY
IS APPROACHING!

Making and giving and getting Valentine's cards are some
of the best things ever. Better than those other holidaze because
no one says you have to give cards. It's totally your prerogative.

1. WRITE CUTE THINGS IN THEM
2. COPY SAYINGS FROM AN E.E. CUMMINGS POEM
3. MAKE YOUR THUMBPRINTS INTO HEARTS BY DIPPING
YOUR THUMBS IN RED FOOD COLORING OR EATING
A BUNCHA RED PISTACHIOS, AND PRESSING ON PAPER
4. PAINT CANDY HEARTS AND GLITTER I-LOVE-YOUS

And best of all give them to everyone you know...even your dog.
It's amazing how many smiles you'll get when you give valentines.

Valentine's Day cards are all love love love.

Chinese New Year

Chinese New Year is the biggest of all holidays in China. It ushers in a new year, but more than our own New Year, it celebrates the passing of winter, the dawn of a fertile new cycle of farming. It is steeped in all sorts of traditions and mystery and fortune.

People celebrate the holiday over four days of eating and playing and more eating. But basically it is a great excuse for a party and, heck, that's the best kind of holiday. (Sort of like a Thanksgiving in February, but without the turkey.)

We think you should take full advantage of this excuse and throw a party. But first you need to know what all the symbols of the holiday stand for. Then get ready to celebrate. Make a flyer inviting all your pals. Tell them to bring red punch and green tea and to don their luckiest of charms. Decorate your house or room like mad. Serve boiled eggs and yellow popcorn and peanuts. And make your own fortune cookies.

The Deal with the Food:

YELLOW FOOD *gold and money*
PEANUTS *life*
SCALLIONS *cleverness*
FISH *abundance*
PEACHES *immortality*
NOODLES *longevity*

The Deal with the Decor:

RED *the fire of life*
CHERRY BLOSSOMS *feminine beauty*
LOTUS FLOWERS *creative power!*
TRAY OF DRIED FRUITS *togetherness*
PAPER LANTERNS *protection from wind*
WIND MACHINE *ha ha, just kidding*

*Most of these items can be found at the regular old store but if you have a Chinatown nearby, hit the streets and you'll see all sorts of great decorations, food and more. Or try looking up Chinese grocery stores in the yellow pages—you might find cheap paper lanterns or incense or dried duck feet.

A LONG TIME AGO...

Supposedly, a Chinese emperor invited all his little forest friends to a Chinese New Year party. But only 12 animals came. The **RAT** was first, followed by the **OX**, who was trailed by the **SNAKE**, who let the **DRAGON** enter first, and then came the **TIGER**. Next came the **PIG** with the **RABBIT** on his back. The **DOG** followed close on their heels. The **GOAT** came in so quietly that many thought it was actually a **SHEEP**. The **ROOSTER** entered next, cock-a-doodle-dooing so loudly that the **MONKEY** almost turned back and left, but in the end, the **HORSE**, who was last, talked the monkey into staying. That horse can be mighty persuasive. The emperor honored these 12 animals by naming the years after them. Many Chinese believe that the year of a person's birth determines that person's personality traits, physical and mental attributes and degree of success and happiness throughout his or her lifetime. Do you agree?

*Remember, if you were born in January, you are the sign of the year before you were born. Got it?

Rat:
1972, 1984
Charming, aggressive, talkative yet unrevealing. Quick-witted perfectionist.

Ox:
1973, 1985
Hardworking, self-confident yet quiet and patient. Great friends.

Tiger:
1974, 1986
Fearless, unpredictable and magnetic. Loves excitement, work and money.

RABBIT→
1975, 1987
Delicate, sweet and popular. Loves clothes and peace.

Dragon:
1976, 1988
Lucky, feisty, powerful and yet inflexible and stubborn.

Snake: 1977, 1989
Charming, popular
seducers who hog the
spotlight and hate
to be ignored.

HORSE:
1978, 1990
Hot-blooded, confident,
energetic fools. Selfish and sexy
(a lethal combo).

Monkey
1968, 1980, 1992
Fun-loving, cheerful and energetic,
talented and creative.
The center of attention.

DOG
1970, 1982, 1994
Faithful, serious, sincere
and righteous. Hates gossip.

goat→
1967, 1979, 1991
Elegant, charming, artsy,
gifted and fond of nature.
Oh, and lazy and vain, too.

Rooster:
1969, 1981, 1993
All-knowing, straightforward,
cautious dreamers who
love flattery.

PIG!
1971, 1983, 1995
Caring and giving, admirable,
intelligent and romantic.

FORTUNE COOKIES

ARE ONE OF THE PURE JOYS OF LIFE. IT'S A DELICIOUS COOKIE AND YET IT'S ALSO
A DOOR TO MYSTERIOUS POSSIBILITIES. IT'S THE VERY BEST REASON TO EAT
CHINESE FOOD. AND THE GAMES. OH, THE GAMES. AS YOU READ THAT LITTLE
STRIP O' PAPER, ADD A FAUX ENDING TO THE NUGGET DE FORTUNE.

SUCH AS "WITH _____" (INSERT FAVORITE HEARTTHROB).

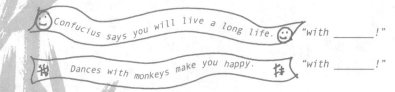

Confucius says you will live a long life. "with _____!"

Dances with monkeys make you happy. "with _____!"

This recipe makes 50 cookies, so write 50 fortunes on pieces of
paper six inches long and a little less than a half inch tall.

You'll need:

5 tablespoons unsalted butter
4 large egg WHITES
1 cup sugar
3/4 cup + 1 tablespoon flour
a pinch o' salt
3 tablespoons heavy cream
1/2 teaspoon vanilla extract

FORTUNE COOKIES
WERE NOT
INVENTED IN
CHINA. THEY WERE
INVENTED IN SAN
FRANCISCO, AS IN,
CALIFORNIA. AND
THEY ARE NOT
PART OF THE
TRADITIONAL
CHINESE NEW YEAR
FEST EITHER. BUT
TO US, THERE IS
NO BETTER COOKIE.
SO WHY NOT
INCORPORATE
THEM INTO YOUR
CELEBRATION. PASS
THEM OUT TO ALL
YOUR FRIENDS. AND
THE BEST PART IS
YOU GET TO CREATE
THE FORTUNES.

BE CREATIVE.

Heat oven to 400 degrees. Melt the butter (microwave works
well). Mix together egg whites and sugar and beat till frothy.
Add flour and salt. Beat till combined.
Add melted butter, cream and vanilla extract and beat another 30
seconds. Grease cookie sheets—better yet, use nonstick ones. Drop
on the sheets a heaping teaspoon of batter, spacing the dollops
five inches apart. Using the back of a spoon, spread the batter
of each dollop to a four-inch circle. Bake until the edges
darken just a tad, about five minutes. Make chocolate ones by
adding 3 tablespoons Dutch cocoa to flour.

Now, you gotta work quickly when they come out of the oven. Work
one by one. Grab a thin spatula and flip the cookie over. Roll
the cookie into a LOOSE tube and insert your fortune through the
tube so both ends stick out. Make an indent with your finger in
the center of the tube and then fold each end inward, forming
the traditional fortune cookie shape. Repeat with all the
cookies. And let cool. Store them in an airtight container.
(They'll last about a week.)

Imagine...

you are the first female president.

Clay Mask 101 Night.

oH i have a zit!

You can make your own clay and mud masks pretty easily, but you do need to hit a health food store to buy the clay. The stuff in your garden simply isn't safe. And it could have animal poo in it. Most health type stores and even some drugstores have what's called French Clay or Fuller's Earth. It's a clean, loose clay used in science experiments, it's not too expensive and it keeps for a while if you don't mix it with water. Start with clean skin, though. Put on some calming, soothing chick music. Pull your hair off your face. This is the simplest clay mask you can make. You need just 1 tablespoon of French Clay or Fuller's Earth per application. Now, what you mix it with depends on the quality of your skin.

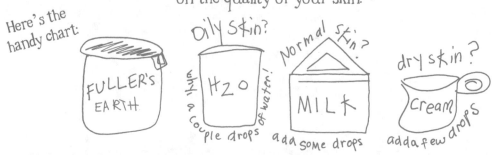

Here's the handy chart:

FULLER'S EARTH

Oily Skin? with a couple drops of water! H2O

Normal skin? add some drops MILK

dry skin? add a few drops Cream

Add just enough liquid to make it a spreadable pastelike consistency. Slather it on your face and neck and lie down. Breathe. Dream of faraway places and faraway boys. When your face feels like it will crack, rinse. Finish with a light moisturizer.

ZIT ZAPPING TIP

Mix a tablespoon of the clay with a couple drops of water. Dab onto zit with Q-tip. Sleep. In the a.m. rinse off any left over. Science explanation: The clay absorbs excess oil in the zit, speeding along the healing process. Neat, huh?

Have you been adding **THINGS** to your (remember, Darth Vader)...**FUTURE FILES?** If not, oh well. We're certainly not going to scold you or anything. Or guilt you out just because you didn't partake in our **CRAFTINESS**. Or rummage through your things. No. We'll just move on as if nothing happened. And talk about where you want to live. Have you thought about where in the world you want to carry out the remainder of your days when you are financially **INDEPENDENT** and can go where you like? When you get a job as head producer for some fat agency, getting $100,000 a year + a **PARKING SPACE**!!?? Would you stay in your **HOMETOWN?** Or move halfway across the world? **BIG CITY?** Small town? As you flip through your magazines and catalogs you might catch a **GLIMPSE** of a beautiful city. Or read about an amazing music scene. Or note a city's incredible weather in the middle of January and think, hey, I could **RIDE MY BIKE** year-round there.

All these clippings can now be collected and placed in your new file, marked:

PLACES TO LIVE.

Don't hesitate and think, "Yeah, but will I really ever have the opportunity to live in Alaska?" Just clip it and file it. The file is by no means a stone-carved map of everywhere you will ever live, ever. It's just to mark at this time in your life, you've thought, "Wow, Alaska is so very bitchin'." You like those husky dogs. And you like Eskimo pies. And you love the rhythm of the word: Al-ask-a. Us, too.

In Clea's PLACES TO LIVE Future File:
Minneapolis, Chi-town, San Francisco, Indonesia, Australia, Boise, as in Idaho.

In Keva's PLACES TO LIVE Future File:
San Francisco, Puget Sound in Washington, London, somewhere like the Hamptons but not, beach-side North Carolina.

FEBRUARY 9

Hey, we're gearing up for Valentine's Day.

See, Valentine's Day is a particularly good day to play the part of a freshly bitten vampire. It's a good day to walk around saying,

"I vant to suck your blood."

To get the look, all you need is a little blood—fake of course. Here are two recipes that you can concoct quickly and, more important, painlessly.

jar of fauy blood

Older, Cakier Blood.

Get the large tube of Close-Up Clear Red toothpaste. Mix it with 1/2 ounce of red food coloring. 1-2, easy as punch. This blood is thicker and good for fake scabs. Make two little fang marks on your neck and let dry.

Fresh-Looking Blood.

Mix 1 cup white corn syrup with 1 tablespoon red food coloring and 1/2 teaspoon yellow food coloring. If it needs to be thinned a bit, add a little water (no more than a tablespoon). Take a little bit and drip it out of the corner of your mouth.

Keva: Clea, this one is weird

Clea: I know, but its all in good fun

Keva: OK, but I still think its weird

THERE ARE MANY SOAP OPERA-WORTHY
STORIES SWIRLING AROUND ABOUT THE
ORIGIN OF VALENTINE'S DAY. BUT OF COURSE
NO ONE REALLY KNOWS HOW IT ALL STARTED.

AN EDUCATED GUESS...

In ancient Rome, the Romans liked to have these big feasts
where people just ate and ate and drank and drank and
had a rousing good time. Now, fierce wolves used to roam
the woods, and the Romans were a little worried wolves
would ruin the various feasts by barging in and stealing
the food. So they called up a god by the name of Lupercus
and asked him, very politely, to keep the wolves away.
He did so and the Romans, who were happy, hungry, thirsty
people, decided to throw another big party, this time in
honor of Lupercus. They called it Lupercalia. One of the
bizarre but interesting Lupercalia customs went like this:

On the eve of the big festival the names of all the Roman
girls were written on slips of paper and placed in a jar.
Each young man drew a slip. The girl whose name was
chosen was to be his sweetheart for the rest of the year.
We think this is rather cheesy and quite unfair.
We have rewritten this custom—now it goes as follows:

On the eve of the big festival all the boys put their names
on slips of paper and throw them in a big fishbowl.
The girls, one by one, come up and choose a name.
They look at it. If they don't like that guy, they throw it
back in the fishbowl and just randomly pick whichever
boy they want. And those boys have to worship them as
Roman goddesses for all eternity.

THE END.

Countdown = 2 days till V-day.

Valentine's Day is the perfect excuse to sit yourself down and write a whomping good love letter. Better than email, more seductive than ordinary mail, more creative than a card. Don't be scared of this ancient format, it's really quite simple and we'll talk you through all ten glorious steps. And if you don't have a love interest, by all means take this opportunity to write one to…yourself. Yes, that's what we said, YOU. LOVE THYSELF.

Step 1:
Choose your paper and an unleaky pen. You're not looking to get your message across with flowery stationery but with words, so choose something simple.

Step 2:
Find yourself a quiet, remote place to write. NO DISTRACTIONS ALLOWED. If you don't have that at home, find a corner at the library or coffee shop. Once there, close your eyes and take in the moment with a couple of deep breaths.

Step 3:
Date your letter. This is important because it will mark this day in history for ever and ever. If the recipient opens this letter again twenty years from now, they should be reminded of exactly when this fantabulous offering was given to them.

Step 4:
Contemplate your opening. You want it to have meaning and power and romance. Some possible beginnings are:

HONEY   Sweetie

hey Stud guy   YO MAMA

WHAT UP, CHUCK

Step 5:
The first line is often the hardest so we suggest making this first sentence about WHY you are writing.

"I am writing to tell you I can't stop thinking of you, even during chem and that's my favorite class..."

If the WHY part is just too heavy for you, how about writing an opening sentence about the time you met. Or something you two have in common.

Step 6:
Now comes the heart of the love letter. It doesn't have to be long but it should be succinct. Words are very powerful, so don't underestimate their ability to transcend paper and pen. Perhaps tell your amor why they are special to you. What is it about them that actually makes you tingly? Note a favorite shirt or a great smile.

Step 7:
Close with style. End your letter on a positive note, summing up your feelings and reason for writing in one entrancing farewell sentence.

Step 8:
Like the salutation, you must also be careful in choosing a valediction (that's the ending). You could simply sign it Adieu. Or try any number of these...

Step 9:
This is where you add something extraspecial that is all you. Do you love the scent of gardenias? Add a few petals or a small photo or drawing. An acronym is good, too, so make up one. Like this.

dream of me, THINE,
farowell, Stud Guy, farewell

F.A.A.D. = forever + a day
L.I.P.S. = Love is Pure Sweetness
B.A.M. = Bust a move

Lastly, Step 10: Address it. And affix the stamp upside down. It's an old custom that means "I Love You." Now drop it in the mail and go have yourself a good time.

FEBRUARY 12

Countdown ... **1** day left till V-day.
So let's plan a Valentine's Day brunch!

Here's la Menu for...

Zee Valentine's Day Brunch:

fill a pitcher with hibiscus, lemon + straw-berry juice. Slice limes, toss in. fill w/ crushed ice mmm...

serve in tall glasses

Passion Juice

Get a heart-shaped cookie cutter. And four slices of bread. Cut a heart out of the center of each slice of bread. (You can save those little hearts and toast them and put a dollop of jelly on each one and use as garnish. But the part you are really interested in is the full slice, crust and all.) Grab four eggs. Melt a little butter over medium heat in a skillet. Put two slices of bread down in the butter. Crack an egg over each heart-shaped hole. When the egg gets firm, flip over. Cook for a minute or two more, till the yolk is no longer runny (unless you like it a little runny). Repeat with other two pieces of bread and those leftover eggs. **Eat.**

egg

Heart Toast

Countdown - 1 day left till V-day Countdown - 1 day left till V-day Countdown

Dessert of Love

Combine 1/2 cup sugar with 1/2 cup water and the zest of 1/2 lemon in a medium saucepan. Stir until the sugar dissolves. Then stir in 3/4 pound of pitted cherries. Bring to a boil, reduce heat, and simmer for 10 minutes. Stir in two pears that have been peeled and sliced and simmer for 5 more minutes. Spread two big, fat slices of pound cake with butter and toast till they are golden brown. Generously spoon with fruit and juices over the cake. Serve warm, topped with a big ol' dollop of whipped cream. **Yields 2 servings.**

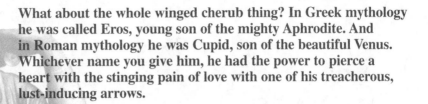

What about the whole winged cherub thing? In Greek mythology he was called Eros, young son of the mighty Aphrodite. And in Roman mythology he was Cupid, son of the beautiful Venus. Whichever name you give him, he had the power to pierce a heart with the stinging pain of love with one of his treacherous, lust-inducing arrows.

Here's the scoop: There was this really beautiful babe, a mortal named Psyche. Venus, Cupid's mom, was super jealous of her fair looks and ordered Cupid to punish this gal. But when Cupid met her, he fell in love. They married, but because she was mortal and he was a god, she was not allowed to look at him. (That is so, so wrong.) Psyche's obnoxious and evil sisters convinced her that she should look at him. She did and, well, Cupid punished her by leaving and taking their home and gardens away with him. Psyche really loved Cupid and was so heartbroken that she went wandering aimlessly, trying to find him so she could make it up to him. She went to the Temple of Venus. Now remember, Venus, her mother-in-law, hated her. Venus said she'd help Psyche but only if she performed all these dangerous tasks. Well, Psyche finished 'em all until the very last one. Venus gave her a little box and told her to go and capture some of Proserpine's beauty (Proserpine was the wife of Pluto) and take it to the Underworld. Of course, she was told not to open the box. But Venus knew temptation would overcome Psyche. Sure enough, it did. Psyche opened the box and she instantly fell into a deadly slumber. Well, in the end, Cupid found her and couldn't stay mad at her and woke her up (he could do that, he was a god), and the rest of the gods were really moved by her do-anything-for-love attitude and they made her a **goddess.** Now, what does this story teach us? Nothing. They were freaky in goddess times and you can't obsess over a boy, god or not, and expect him to come and, um, wake you up just because "you'd do anything for love." Lust is fun, love is fun, so is soccer and painting and hanging out with your friends. So is winning poker with two pairs, dancing until dawn, rolling with your dog on the lawn. You get the point. Life is bigger than any boy.

(But boys are definitely a fun part...)

happy Valentine's day, Keva

HAPPY VALENTINE'S DAY, CLEA

AND NOW FOR THE ACTUAL PAR-TAY.

1. Get some butcher paper. **2. CUT OUT BIG HEARTS AND USE THEM AS PLACE MATS.** 3. Tie roses to the ends of your silverware. **4. THROW ROSE PETALS ALL OVER THE TABLE.** 5. Cut more paper hearts, punch a hole in their tops and tie some string to them. **6. TAPE THE ENDS OF THE STRINGS TO THE CEILING ABOVE THE TABLE IN A CIRCLE (BE SURE IT'S NOT THE KINDA TAPE THAT TAKES OFF PAINT).** 7. Play Mazzy Star and Mozart. **8. AND DON'T FORGET THE CANDLES.** 9. Handwrite menu items on paper in calligraphylike script. **10. DRAW LITTLE BORDERS AROUND THE PAGE.** 11. Copy menu onto vintage-looking sheets of paper & place on plates. **12. INVITE A SMALL GROUP OF BEST FRIENDS. HAVE THEM DRESS VERY NICE. PAY YOUR SISTER TO HELP SERVE FOOD IN A WAITRESS OUTFIT.**

Serve the recipes

from yesterday and make sure to take pictures of everyone looking fabulous and romantic. You will need these pics for a project that lies ahead...
(Have them developed by the 20th!)

P.S.

Clea says, "Hey, if this falls on a weekday, by all means make this a dinnertime Valentine's Day Brunch . . . and serve in the evening hours!"

In honor of Presidents' Day we are going to dispel some myths about the two gentlemen who were presidents of this country and whose birthdays are the very reason we celebrate Presidents' Day:

George Washington & Abraham Lincoln.

First off, Washington did not cut down no cherry tree. Total myth. In celebration of the falseness of this, you could down some Ben & Jerry's Cherry Garcia. We wouldn't care. While wigs were definitely the fashion for men in Washington's time, he in fact did not wear a wig. Which really upset us because we wanted to make George Washington's birthday Wig Day and suggest that you wear a wig around today if you have one. Well, then we thought about it and decided that even if George didn't wear one, it sure looked like a wig and by golly we don't really need reasons to declare a day Wig Day, so there, it's Wig Day, wear one if you got one. (George did powder his hair, though, to make it more wiglike. You could do this but believe us, it's not nearly as fun as wearing a wig. In fact, it's not fun at all.) The father of our country was a stepfather, but not a biological father. Washington never fathered any children of his own. He did, however, raise Martha's two children from a previous marriage. (Yes, George was her second! Ooh la la.) Who was the taller president? Well, yeah, Abe was, but only by two inches. George was 6'2" and Abraham was 6'4". You would have guessed Abe was taller by a few more inches than two, huh? A young girl living in New York suggested to Abe that he grow a beard while running for president because his face was so darn thin. He did and now he is famous for it. So today, suggest to someone he grow a beard. Lincoln didn't write the Gettysburg Address on the back of an old envelope on the train to Gettysburg, as some books say. It was way too bumpy on trains back then to write. He wrote it on official stationery, mostly before leaving. And if all this silly stuff is just too trivial for you today, might we suggest pondering what **you would do if you were president?**

FEBRUARY 16

Shh. Don't tell anyone. Keva reveals secrets.
About...Love Potion #9.

OK, so a long time ago my mom had this friend. She was French. She was hot. She had an accent and wore lotsa makeup and her name was Celine. She also had lotsa men. Always. The woman was like a man magnet. That was her. Now me, on the other hand, was sorta (um, totally) a big dork. My perm was starting to grow out, I had braces, I wore the wrong kind of eyeliner. Like purple. Oh, it was icky. OK, in comes Jimmy Goode. Was he a dream. Skinny. Blond with that little spike of hair in front. Converse. Jeans. Old ratty tight tees. He was hot. He was funny. His last name was Goode. I mean, it doesn't get any better, it gets worse. You see, I had it bad for Jimmy, and seeing as I was a major dork, but a smart dork, one day I pulled Celine aside and told her of my troubles:

"Celine, you have to help me."   *"Oh, cherie, what is zee matter?"*

"I'm a big dork."   *"What is a big dork?"*

"Never mind. I don't feel pretty."   *"Oh, dear, now Celine understands."*

Celine went ahead and fixed my hair and picked out some cute outfits for me. Stuff I had, but she kinda put them together differently. She showed me the right kind of makeup (light touch!) and told me to get a few decent bras, and just when I thought it was all over, she got real quietlike and said: *And now I have a secret for you.*

And out of her bag came this bottle with what looked like maybe oil in it. She started to tell me some crazy story about pheromones and how they attract animals and that humans have pheromones and that there is an ancient Egyptian oil that drives the men crazy.

"But, cherie," she said, "be very careful, the pheromones must be only a hint, the rest must come from you, your je ne sais quoi, ah certain mood, certain attitude." What she meant is that I had to not only wear the perfume but **be** the perfume. I got the stuff, I wore better bras and I asked Jimmy Goode to go to the Sadie Hawkins Dance with me and he said, "Yes," and that night I had my first kiss. Braces and all. Good story. Now what's the moral? That the famous Love Potion #9 ain't no potion at all. It's an attitude. Don any perfume that makes you feel powerful. Channel your own je ne sais quoi. And then find your own Jimmy Goode. This one's taken.

MEMORY MAKER JAR

Mayonnaise

THE HANDY-DANDY MIRACLE MOJO MEMORY MAKER FOR QUOTES + OTHER SUCH FUNNY REMARKS.

Do you have a friend or three who say the most hilarious things? They just sort of naturally pour out of their mouths, perhaps at truly inappropriate times? Or maybe your dad says the cheesiest things, like calls you and your friends "Swing Cats" or some other such nonsense. You say to yourself, **"That was the funniest thing, can't forget that one"** ...but then you do. *Forget it, that is.* Introducing the **HANDY-DANDY MIRACLE MOJO MEMORY MAKER FOR QUOTES AND OTHER SUCH FUNNY REMARKS.** (It's actually an old mayonnaise jar, but don't tell anyone.) You see, every time your friend or dad or grocery clerk says something brilliant or ridiculous or amusing you write-it-down. You grab the nearest pen and the closest scrap of paper and you write it down, like this:

"I feel like such a Rudolph, you guys never let me play in your reindeer games."
—Clea 2/17

If you're out 'n' about just stick the scrap paper in your purse till you get home. Then unload all the scraps into your **HANDY-DANDY MIRACLE MOJO MEMORY MAKER FOR QUOTES AND OTHER SUCH FUNNY REMARKS.** At the end of the year, decorate your Memory Maker Jar however you please (we'll remind ya later), pop a bow on it and give it to whomever is most deserving of a good laugh as a Christmas gift or Chanukah present or in honor of Mozart's birthday or just because.

it's the best
6400×1798323

FEBRUARY 18

KEVA: Hey, Clea, my sister wants to go to the zoo but I feel like if I go it will be against my religion.

CLEA: Understood. But there are good zoos. Aren't there? And what about endangered animals and how the zoos rebuild their populations. And what about petting zoos. I love petting zoos. I love baby piglets. And baby goats.

KEVA: Well, like, I think goats are, cool, too, but must people see them only in goat pens? I mean, whatever happened to the goat farm or the neighbor Bob with the billy goat?

CLEA: You proved my point...see, that's exactly why zoos can be cool. Who has a neighbor Bob with a billy goat anymore? Not I. I think zoos can be fantabulous as long as the animals aren't cramped in some smelly cage. And as long as no dastardly evil zookeepers work there and hit the animals, which you do hear about from time to time, which is so absolutely disgustingly gross I don't know how people live with themselves. But when I was young, my mom would take us to the zoo and we'd watch the monkeys frolic and throw stuff at one another and I just remember that as one of the best things I ever did with my family. **And I love baby piglets.**

KEVA: I think I wanna get a goat and call her Missoula.

CLEA: Where will you keep her? You think that is better than a zoo? What if goats need other goats?

KEVA: But I have a dog. I mean, my mom has a dog. Alfie. Goats and dogs hang out, don't they?

CLEA: But how about if you're gonna get a goat for your garden, you get two, so they have each other. Then if Alfie joins in, that's cool, but if goats don't like dogs, you're still covered.

KEVA: Now, that's a plan.

CLEA: Stan.

DISCUSSION QUESTIONS

ARE ZOOS GOOD OR EVIL? DO YOU HAVE FOND MEMORIES OF THE ZOO? CAN YOU PICTURE YOURSELF AS A FARMER? DO YOU HAVE A NEIGHBOR BOB? DO YOU LOVE PIGLETS? AS MUCH AS CLEA? DO GOATS AND DOGS GET ALONG? WHO IS STAN? DOES HE OWN A GOAT?

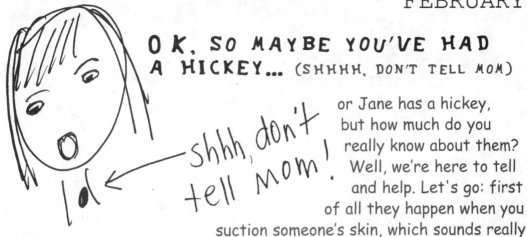

O K, SO MAYBE YOU'VE HAD A HICKEY... (SHHHH, DON'T TELL MOM)

shhh, don't tell mom!

or Jane has a hickey, but how much do you really know about them? Well, we're here to tell and help. Let's go: first of all they happen when you suction someone's skin, which sounds really gross but we're told it can be nice. Ahem. Weird, huh. Um, so it is defined as a "temporary red mark on the skin from biting or sucking." Whoa. Anyway, as someone is there at your neck, sucking away, he is in fact breaking little blood vessels in your precious skin. Owie. Doesn't sound so romantic now, does it? If you end up with one, here's the scoop.

HOW TO COVER ONE UP:

80's style

a turtle-neck?

a scarf?

WHAT TO TELL PEOPLE:

You missed with the curling iron. You slept in your rhinestone dog collar. It's the latest trend in makeup. It's a tattoo. What of? The island of Maori.

P.S. When Keva was younger, she was so all about hickeys that her mom used to get real real mad at her. But now she doesn't know what all the fuss is about. She avoids those hickeys like the plague.

Be good. Make presents.

By now you have your photos back from the fabu
V-day Brunch you threw. They are cute, aren't
they? Glad you think so, because chances are
so will your friends or your family. Which is
why today you are going to make cheap and easy
V-day frames for the pictures from the brunch.

Just nab some cardboard. And some tape, scissors
and maybe even some candy. Oh, and a string or
ribbon, too. Cut a shape out of your cardboard,
one big enough to view the picture through.
Instant frame. Proceed to decorate any way you
please. Use: glitter, nails, pennies, matchbooks,
pics from magazines. At the top of the frame you
could paste cutout letters (from more magazines,
silly) that spell out a word that best describes
the recipient, such as "lovely," "handsome"
or "flame."

Tape the photo behind the frame. You could
even secure the photo with an extra piece of
cardboard and some more tape. Then attach the
ribbon or string as a loop for hanging. (More
tape, we like DUCT tape. It's neat. And
powerful.)

And there ya go, frame number uno! Shake off
any excess glitter. Wrap in tissue. Write a
nice letter. And give to a pal the next day.
Now repeat with other pictures. Presents Rule!

there
was a red
hot here but
Keva got
hungry

Women who influenced my Life part ONE by Clea

You may have already read about how Keva was a depressed child because she feared getting old at a very young age. I never had that fear. And it wasn't because I met Betsey Johnson when I was five or any such thing. It was because I had my own Betsey Johnson in Ruth.

Ruth is my grandma. My kooky, crazy, silly, wacky grandma. I've known her my whole entire life and she's never been old and she's never been adult in the sad sense of the word. She's always seen life through big, bug-eyed, rose-colored glasses.

she was a pretty thing when she was a lass

Ruth would put bananas in the meatloaf because it was fun to run bananas through her old-fashioned meat grinder. So, it didn't taste so good. It was fun. And she did it for the sheer funness of it all.

Ruth would constantly repaint every inch of her house a different color. The garbage cans? Bright gold! The floor in the kitchen? Metallic glitter silver! The fireplace? A mélange of reds and grays! The refrigerator? Russian royal blue!

Ruth would start singing and dancing every time she got an audience. We had this little outdoor amphitheater near where I grew up and she would take us there and make us all get on stage and sing for strangers. Show tunes were her favorite.

And Ruth would always listen to my problems, big or small, and impart nuggets of advice that always came accompanied by silly, laugh-inducing endings.

she's still quite glamourous!

Because of Ruth's goofy, loud laugh, because of Ruth's love of all things bright and colorful, because of Ruth's generosity (she taught English to the entire Cuban Jai Alai team of Miami!), because of Ruth's daring and drive (she took flying lessons at age 72!), I have always known that growing up isn't about becoming more sedate or being more serious. It's about enjoying life, every day. It's having fun and helping others have fun, too. And maybe, just maybe, that's why I still have a costume suitcase (coming your way in December) and why I write odes to my dog George daily and why I called up Keva that one fateful day and said, "Hey, you and me, we should write a book."

FEBRUARY 22

Yo. There is this great movie called "Say Anything" and in it John Cusack's best friend Corey, played by extreme cool girl Lili Taylor, announces at the graduation party that she "wrote 63 songs this year and they're all about Joe and I'm going to play every single one of them tonight." You really need to watch this movie if you have not done so. We cannot stress that enough. Corey works out her obsession with her ex, Joe, by singing horrid punk rock odes to his poor taste in girls.

Do you need any other reason besides this classic movie moment to pick up a guitar and start a band? In case you do, here's 13 more.

1. FAME. 2. You love music but the school marching band just isn't cutting it. 3. Yet another excuse for you and your girlfriends to get together on a regular basis. 4. You want your poems heard but you aren't into the whole boho coffeehouse slam scene. 5. Looks great on future college applications (well, it IS an extracurricular activity). 6. F – U – N (DUH). 7. Putting those music lessons your parents forced down your throat to good use. 8. Guys dig chicks who rock. 9. Excuse to be obnoxious (and get away with it). 10. Or conversely, to get over that shy thing you got going on. 11. A great excuse to wear pleather & feather boas. Or wear your hair differently. Or change your style 360 degrees. 12. As Madonna once said, "Express Yourself!" 13. You need yet another hobby.

The following week is dedicated to igniting you, inspiring you, encouraging you to

start a band.

Grab a few of your musically inclined friends, find a sympathetic parent with a soundproof garage to use as a practice space, start by covering a few of your favorite songs and don't worry if you suck. Just go-go-go.

Now rock on.

LET'S PLAY GUITAR.

The C chord

PUT YOUR FINGERS WHERE THE BLACK DOTS ARE.

NUMBERS HERE
CORRESPOND WITH HERE
Left hand
3 2
4

NOW STRUM! (WITH YOUR RIGHT HAND, SILLY.)

We'll start with the C chord. That's it, over there. Your fingers are now numbered. Feel free to write the numbers on your hand with Magic Marker. The washable kind. Then match up your numbered fingers with our handy-dandy chart. It's understandable if you just picture those vertical lines as strings on the guitar and the horizontal lines as the frets. They are the bumpy things that run down the neck of thee geetar.

Practice the magical C chord. Then move on to A and D.

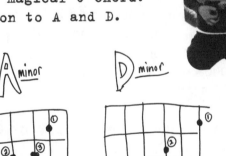

A minor

D minor

Start by practicing those three chords. After you get comfortable with each of them, play them faster and faster together... A C D A C D A A C A D C C D A D D C A ...and work it till you can effortlessly switch between the different chords. Hey, you're playing.

FOR THOSE SHY FOLKS WHO MAYBE DON'T HAVE THE APPARENT CONFIDENCE TO START A BAND...

OK, maybe you are already halfway to starting a band. No, you say? Well, do you play clarinet or violin in the school band? Did your mom force piano lessons on you at a sickeningly young age? Or maybe you're just like supro-stud-geek on the computer. See, all these instruments (and many more!) can play a tremendously gigantic role on your road to punk rock (or punk rap or sugar pop or electronica country) stardom. Bands do not have to be made up of your basic drums, guitar & bass. In fact, adding any instrument (and we mean any) can give your band that added extra uniqueness that makes ya stick out in the lumpy, bumpy landscape that is rock 'n' roll. And if you can't find someone to play bass, simply eliminate bass from the whole idea of a band. Just a few examples of bands that have incorporated other instruments besides the classic guitar, bass, drums threesome:

Violin: P J Harvey, Modest Mouse, Björk
Cello: Three Mile Pilot, Built to Spill, Björk
Piano: Tori Amos, Ben Folds Five, Rufus Wainwright, Björk
Saxophone: Rocket from the Crypt, Big Bad Voodoo Daddy, Björk
Trumpet: Rancid, Lauryn Hill, Björk
Organ: The Artist Formerly Known As Prince, Jewel, Björk
Computers: Fatboy Slim, Madonna, Eminem, Will Smith, Björk

(Now do you see why we love Björk so much?)

HOW TO WRITE SONGS

Go get your favorite CD with your favorite song on it right now. Grab a notebook or a scrap piece of paper or a napkin, and while you're groovin' to the song, write down the lyrics. If you can't quite figure out the words, fill in the holes with stuff you make up. Grab another tune and repeat.

Now examine these wordy works of art as if you were in English class and your teacher had you dissecting the postmodern versus the traditional meaning of the iambic pentameter. No, don't do that. But look at it. Does it rhyme? What is the pattern? Has the musician used similes? Or clichés? Painted a picture with the words or just been straight up about it? Why does this song do it for you right now? Is it because it sounds like the words were written just for you? Or because you can dance around your room to it till your hair is wild, crazy and big.

Use this song as a model for your first very own song. No, you're not going to copy every song, but this once, to get ya started, try imitating the flow or the rhythm or the pattern of this song. As for subject matter, well, that's another story...

Ask yourself some questions, like what consumed your every thought today? The answer is the subject of your new song. It doesn't have to be profound or earth-shattering, but it does have to be something you know, something you think about and something that, good or bad, you care about. Once you write one or two, you'll be surprised how naturally the songs can flow from your inner being.

name your band.

The most important ingredient to a band's success? Why, the name, silly. Even if you decide, nah, starting a band's not for me, you can still pretend and choose a name for you and your band of friends and refer to it whenever speaking of the gaggle of gals as one. Like "the Super Big Gulps are hitting the slopes at high noon." A good band name can also often mask, at least for a short while, the fact that the music sucks. So here is a pocket guide to naming your first very own band. The following are the primary categories from which band names are most commonly (or at least most easily) chosen.

Movies and television. Many band names come from obscure (and the not so obscure) references to the big screen and/or the telly. Think about your favorite movie or TV show and ponder the names of various characters and names of places they hang.

Food and/or foodstuff. Your favorite food is Maple Donuts? Why, that's a great name. Scalloped Potatoes? Not bad. Green Jell-O? Taken. There are also bands named for Cake, Red Hot Chili Peppers, Little Debbie's, Salt 'N' Pepa, Ice T, Lemonheads, Tater Totz and, um, Vanilla Ice.

A play on another person's name. Nat King Cole becomes Nat King Kong. Thelonious Monk becomes Thelonious Monster. Elvis becomes El Vez. Evel Knievel becomes Midevel Knievel. And of course Marilyn Monroe and Charles Manson combine to be the wealthiest guy with boobies the world has seen.

Another hint: Use Super or Big in your name. Like Big Star, Big Drill Car, Supersuckers, Superchunk, Supernova. Heck, just add Super or Big to an existing name and you too can avoid lawsuits. The Big Beatles. Super Green Day.

Bonus game: Combine band names to make bigger, longer, bad-arse new names. We'll get ya started...

Luscious Jackson 5
Elton John Spencer Blues Explosion
Grateful Dead or Alive
Veruca Salt 'n' Pepa
Girls Against Boyz II Men Without Hats

Your turn now...

You want to get the WORD OUT about your band.
But how?

→ FIVE STEPS, plus the Downlow

1. You can usually get about 500 **stickers** made for around 50 bucks. But remember, this expensive step is so not necessary. Because you can get the word out with homemade stickers. (See January 21: Sticker Day!) Plaster your junk, your friends' junk, your bike, your notebooks, your car bumpers, your friends' car bumpers, your backpack, your friends' backpacks (OK, you get the point).

MY BAND ROCKS

2. You can also **poster** the heck out of your local telephone poles, but more on that later.

3. You can create a **website** for your band. Link it to other websites about like-minded bands.

4. Or craft a **zine**, touting the members' likes and dislikes ("Clea likes Bonne Bell Lip Smackers, Clea dislikes gossipy people").

5. Create your **band bio** and have a friend with a camera take your photo. You've got an instant **"press kit."** Now send that to your local paper—maybe they'll run it.

D.L. Feel like we've gotten ahead of you? Here's the **downlow**. See, if you like jumping around the house while blasting your favorite songs, you won't believe the rush you get from playing music with your friends. It's better than ice cream. **BETTER THAN BOYS.** Better than most everything. And who cares if only two people ever hear you—you can be legends in your own minds.

FEBRUARY 28

Postering 101

To get the word out about your new band and perhaps even your upcoming show, you gotta make posters. Why? Well, posters rule. Posters rock. You rule. You rock. You make posters. You have show. 1,2,3,...here we go.

FUN FOR ALL — DON'T MISS OUT

THE FLYBABIES

With special guests: BATS!, NO MANS LAND, HILL BILLIES, + Miss Lucy the amazing singing bird. MARCH 5th at THE ROADHOUSE 7PM 3rd + Lincolna

(bring your own snacks) B.Y.O.S.

ALL AGES FREE SHOW

Grab some paper, any kind, and paint or markers and go. This is the best way to advertise your band. Yippee!

MARCH

WE decided that MARCH is just about as good as any other ole month to be dubbed PRINCESS MONTH. So there it is! HOORAY for MARCH! Now, all you gals out there, take heed. Grab your PRINCESS accoutrements, gee - tar (you are practicing, right?) and good-luck charms (this one here is Keva's) and get ready to reign!

March 1

REJECTION CAN BE COOL.

P.S. Keva was rejected from cheerleading in junior high. Go Go Go Keva!

Take it from us, we've been rejected plenty of times. Occasionally by boys, often by publishers (ha!) or magazine editors (double ha!) or the swim team (um, well, Clea has been rejected by the swim team).

But, see, we're still on top. Woo hoo, yeah, we are. Why is that? Because rejection is just a part of attempting.

So, what do we do? Get a little bummed (sometimes). Think about if the rejector was right to reject that idea or thought, and then figure out how to make it better. Occasionally we just chalk it up to idiots in charge. But sometimes—often, even—the person in charge has insight that we don't. Like that Clea is a terrible swimmer. Or that a whole book dedicated to Vanilla Ice's career was indeed a real lousy idea. Or that with many a tweaks, nips and cuts this book is all the better (our editor made us say that).

Anyway, rejection is cool because for the most part, you're one step closer to success. Really, it is true. You have to get rejected sometimes. It's physics. Law of averages.

Rejection is cool because sometimes you do actually learn from it. (Cruddy thought, ain't it?) But it's true.

Rejection is cool because those who are rejected in high school are often the successful ones in their adult years. It, too, is physics. If you don't believe us, go ask Tori Amos, Ben Folds Five and Clea Hantman aka Super Clea (she's always been super, but people just didn't know it).

So go out there and try something new, and if rejection comes your way, revel in it.

Because rejection is cool.

HOW TO MAKE:
BIZNESS CARDS

CALL THEM SOMETHING SAPPY, LIKE FRIENDSHIP
CARDS. OR SOMETHING BOLD, SUCH AS
INTRODUCING...ME! CARDS.

The point is to have something to give to new friends, old friends, incredibly cute boys, your neighbor Mrs. Neidermeyer (in case of an emergency), the guy with the overgrown lawn (you can mow!), or the lady down the street who needs a dog walker.

Some possible options of things to say on your cards: Your name (duh). A nickname or even your superhero name. Email address. Phone number. Your birthday (always good to remind people!). Things you collect (always good to remind people!). Current talents such as "excellent dog walker." Future job description: "professional poker player to be." Or just some random title you award yourself, like "The Enchanted One." Or you could add messages. "Email me or else!"

Classic bizness cards are 1 1/2" X 2 1/2", which is a pretty good size because they will fit conveniently in your wallet. You can make each one a little different or you can make a standard card and photocopy it down at the neighborhood copy shop. (Card stock is good.) Then make sure to have them on ya at all times... you know, just in case.

DOLL DIY

In Japan there is a festival all about chicks. It's called the "Hina-matsuri" or the Girl's Festival. (And sometimes Doll Day, but more on that later.)

On this day, families with daughters invite over relatives and friends and host a special feast. They serve fabu drinks and eats and everyone toasts the girls in hopes that they grow up to be healthy and fabulous. We think this part rocks.

A girl's first Girl's Festival is called her "hatzu-zekku." It is very popular for the girl's grandparents to present her with her first set of "hina" dolls. (Hence that dumb Doll Day name.) These are super elaborate (and pretty expensive) sets of dolls that are displayed in tiers. On this day, girls display all the dolls that have been given to them for Hina-matsuri. Originally this wasn't about expensive dolls, it was actually an ancient purification ritual.

See, back in the Heian Era of Japan (that would be 794 to 1191, natch), you'd start by making a paper doll of yourself. Then you'd decorate it (Glitter? Neon paints? Sequins?) and play with it. Then, and this is the pretty cool part, you'd rub the paper doll on yourself, which supposedly transferred your own impurities (the little white lies you've been telling, the "impure" thoughts about Jimmy, that sort of thing) to the doll. And then, to wash away all your bad stuff, you'd throw the doll in the river. Now, if you're gonna try this at home you might want to rethink the whole glitter part because that would be bad for the little fishes. Instead you could make the doll out of veggie dogs, decorate her with peanut butter and raisins and set her free. The fishes would thank you.

"Hina-matsuri"

JOLEN *Lippy Bleach*

You've seen the stuff. You know what it does. Yes, we're talking about Jolen. Or hair bleach,

Hint hint. Feel free to add a slim stripe of Jolen to your hair for a handy-dandy easy bleach stripe. Don't leave on too long. But hey, if your folks don't dig that sort of thing, best to heed their laws. Or…just plant that stripe on an underside strand, that way when your hair is down, you look all norm, but put your hair up and it's bad girl time. Um, we didn't say that.

Check out your own lip. Get a mirror and walk outside. Natural light is best. Hold the mirror close to your upper lip and examine if there are any hairs darker than your skin. If so, then today is the day.

Now get thee to a drugstore. Head for your favorite aisle, (besides the makeup and hair dye and tampon aisle, of course). Go directly to the beauty skin cream aisle and look for facial hair bleach. We love Jolen because it's sensitive and it's been around forever (it's a blue box with white lettering) but by all means, experiment with other brands.

Now head home and wash your face. Hello, with gentle stuff.

Anyway, follow the instructions. Usually there's a cream (that's the bleach part) and a powder and you mix 'em up and then with a little plastic spatula, you slap it on, baby.

Wait a few minutes. When it starts to tingle, remove with warm water and head back outside to examine hair more closely. Repeat the next day if you need more lightening.

Don't fret. It's normal. It's natural. We all have it. Some more than others. Feel oh so womanly.

Ooh la la.

March 5

TIM'S TIPS

JUST IN CASE YOU'RE IN A BIND, STUCK IN A SMALL DARK PLACE OR IN JAIL (EGADS, NO!), WE (WITH THE HELP OF KEVA'S HUNKY BEAU, TIM) CAME UP WITH SOME TIPS. STUFF TO GET, THINGS TO OWN, JUNK TO BE AWARE OF... BECAUSE SOMETIMES, YOU JUST NEVER KNOW.

Gum is great for sticking in a doorjam if you wanna make like the door's locked but it's not, or you need to sneak back in later.

A miniflashlight fits in the purse and sometimes you can use it to bang on the head of a jerk.

Mini Swiss army knives are very handy. Keep one on your key chain.

Screwdrivers (Tim says it's preferable to have both Phillips and flat head) can double as a can opener. Some screwdrivers can even open doors.

Rubber bands make great slingshots. Or fudge a lock with one to keep your sister out.

Safety pins are grand in case your button pops off or you have a blackhead. (Oh, that's gross, we know we are gross.)

Small sewing kit What if you get a rip?

Duct tape (good for shutting up loud ones) can also fix leaky drains, defuzz sweaters and tie up your shoes if you, um, lost your laces.

it's national procrastination day.

we're not sure who exactly came up with this fabulous idea of giving everyone an excuse to be lazy, but we're all for it. today, you will do not much of anything. if you've got things like a job or homework, well, we can't tell you not to do those things. we'd get in trouble.

but layoff the crafts. forget about going that extra mile. don't clean. don't make your bed. put it all off till tomorrow and just loaf. as in lay around. and let your mind wander.

*or you could catch up on some sleep and simply take a catnap. meow.

March 7

IMAGINE YOU COULD CHOOSE ONE PERSON (imaginary or real), without judgment or bias, to read your diary. This person would surely find the real you through your writings and words. IN A PERFECT WORLD, WHO WOULD THAT PERSON BE?

Yuck. YOUR PERIOD. We know. IT SUCKS. Sucking all around. *Amen!* So hey, let's make super kick-ass tampon cases! Let's be proud of our periods. (Or at least have a cool new accessory to tote 'round.) Hooray!

March 8

get DOWN with your T·A·M·P·O·N·S *

Get your hands on a pencil case. Any pencil case. Glue a small bottle of Advil to the side of the case. (Or inside.) Decorate. Think: glue & pictures & glitter. Go graffiti style. Go mad. Make cases for all your friends. Decorate the inside with your handy-dandy personalized li'l flowchart.

Go ahead and copy this chart and then decorate it up. When your period rears its ugly blood-spurtin' head (um, yuck!), mark the date down in the first box. When it's over, make a note in the second box.

Stash the chart inside your new tampon/pain-meds case and voila! You are one organized, prepared & stylish menstruating babe. Power to the posse!

*Oh, and if you're lucky enough not to have gotten your period as of yet, make one of these as a present to yourself, a sort of future Hooray, I Got My Period, Oh Joy, Day gift.

It should look something like this:

Jan.			July		
Feb.			Aug.		
March			Sept.		
April			Oct.		
May			Nov.		
June			Dec.		

the end.
period.

This is clea when she was younger

INDIAN PRINCESS

When you're in need of being transported to a different time and place, turn to your makeup bag. (Or a good book.) Become an Indian princess and feel the earthly beauty within you arise and awaken. Be a big, bad, earthy American Indian chick. While you're at it, give yourself an Indian princess name. Like Moon Glow Dave (oops, we mean Dove).

Part hair down the middle. If you got short hairs pin them down because as long as they're parted the effect will still work. Get bronzer (the kind that's loose in a pot is best) and a brush and dust all over face until the sun-weathered goddess look is achieved. Apply a tad heavier on cheekbones. With a rust-colored lip pencil, line lips and then fill in. Take some Vaseline or lip gloss and a pinch of the bronzer and mix together in the palm of your hand. Apply to lips with finger. With a dark brown shimmery eye shadow, brush upper lids and into the crease of your lids and under your eyes as well. Then use an exotic eye pencil like turquoise or green or yellow and line your upper lid along the lash line. Apply colored mascara, like green or purple or blue, to top and bottom lashes. Attach a headdress.

WEAR LOOSE CLOTHES, LEATHER TASSELS, MOCCASINS AND WARM COLORS OF THE SUNRISE.

COOL ACCESSORIES EVERY INDIAN PRINCESS MUST HAVE:
Walking stick decorated with bit of fur and feathers. Dream catcher. OK, no, no dream catcher. Turquoise jewelry. Rock garden tiara. Little leather sandals. Toe rings.

IT'S MARDI GRAS SEASON.

New Orleanians (people from New Orleans) are always either planning a party, having a party or recuperating from a party. We think that rules. But then again we're kinda like party freaks. Nonetheless New Orleans is like a magic city lost in time with bluegrass and oysters and blues and nightcrawlers and ancient buildings and women with blue hair and cauldrons and French Quarters and old cobblestone streets and the funniest accent from the most mysterious people ever.

Here is a primer on Nawlin-speak. Use freely over the next few days.

Dem. The plural pronoun "them." Use it in a sentence: *Dem donuts are good.*

Der. "There." Use it in a sentence: *Dem der donuts are darn good.*

Flyin' Horses. A carousel. Even if the horses don't move. Even if it doesn't have any horses on it. Use it in a sentence: *I met Leo at the flyin' horses—he was on a rhino, I was on a camel.*

Lucky Dog. That's hot dog to you Yankee folk. Use it in a sentence: *We went down to Bourbon Street and had us a couple of lucky dogs. Now I feel ill.*

Nutria. The very, VERY large rodents with big, orange teeth that populate the city's canals. Use it in a sentence: *I hear lucky dogs are really just fried nutria.*

Po-Boy. The sandwich of Nawlins. You can put anything in a po-boy. Use it in a sentence: *That sloppy tofu po-boy wasn't quite Taco Bell–quality but it was delish.*

Toolin' Around. Killing time. Use it in a sentence: *Betty, Jane and I had a bad-arse time just toolin' around Friday night.*

keva in the french quarter with lisa b.

clea in a bad neighborhood in new orleans sitting on a sidewalk couch, umm...

March 11

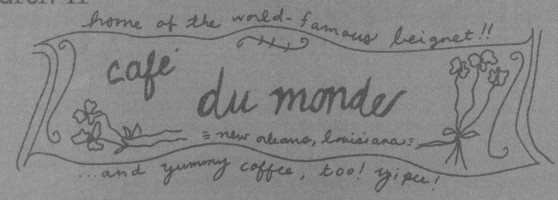

home of the world-famous beignet!!

café

du monde

= new orleans, louisiana =

...and yummy coffee, too! yipee!

You say what? BEIGNETS (ben-YAYS) BEIGNETS (ben-YAYS)!!! Beignets are really just chichi donuts, but, darn, are they good and very Nawlins, chérie. They come from the Café du Monde in the French Market in the heart of New Orleans, which is just the most fabulous place. BEIGNETS, BEIGNETS, BEIGNETS, BEIGNETS, wonderful, devilish, delightful little donuts with a sexy French name and all that powered sugar. It is your mission to make sure that everyone you know will soon know the love of the BEIGNET! If you cannot find the lovely BEIGNETS, then here is what you need to do: get plain, airy, fluffy fresh donuts and stick 'em in the toaster oven for a few minutes. Just till they get oh so hot. Then pull 'em out and pour tons of powdered sugar all over them. Pile on to a plate and, yum, you got yourself some insta-BEIGNETS, ma chérie.

BEIGNETS!!

BEIGNETS!!

¡beignets! beignets!
¡beignets! beignets!

Channel that burgeoning artiste in you. Because self-portraits totally and absolutely rock, we came up with three silly ways to document your bad self. Here's the first—more coming your way later, skater.

Five-bean Art.

(Or six- or seven- or twelve-bean art.)

Head to the health food store or some super grocery that has bins and bins of different dried beans. They are pretty cheap. Now pick up a small bag of every kind of bean imaginable because this is your color palette. The more colors the better. Get some sturdy cardboard or an old piece of wood or some scrap metal with dull edges (by all means, recycle). And you'll need some strong glue. Before you crack that seal on the glue, start arranging the beans to form the image of your face. Use red beans for your lips and black beans for your hair or eyes. When you are happy with the likeness, move a few beans at a time, spread the glue and slap down the beans. Keep going till your image is complete. Give to your best friend or to your mom or hang it up in your room.

adzuki

black beans

pinto

canelini

red lentils

March 13
It's WAR

Despite its scary name, War is a card game originally designed for children. But we like to play it because it's simple and fun and takes no effort, just perfect for

THE HUMP MONTH OF MARCH.

In its most basic form, all you need is two players and a deck of cards. Aces are high (meaning they beat everything) and suits (as in hearts and spades and such) don't count. Deal out all the cards so that each player has 26. Don't look at your cards, just keep them facedown in a pile. The object of the game is to win all the cards. Both players now turn their top card faceup and put it on the table. Whoever turned the higher card takes both cards and adds them facedown to the bottom of her pile. Then both players turn up their next card and so on. If you turn up cards that are equal, there is a war. Leaving those two cards on the table, both players play the next three cards of their pile facedown and then another card faceup. Whoever has the higher of the faceup cards wins the war and adds all 10 cards facedown to the bottom of her pile. And if by some dumb luck your new faceup cards are equal too, then the war continues.

* Keep playing until one player has all the cards and wins. Believe us, though, it can take a long, long hump-month time.

KEVA: ME AND AIMEE USED TO PLAY THIS ALL THE TIME WHEN WE WERE BORED.

Kinda like teatime,
bath time is just as neat.

Baths are relaxing and calming and soothing and peaceful
and you can put stuff in baths like herbs and rose petals
(organic, of course) and oils that make you smell
all good and that spice you up!

BATHS ROCK!

So, hey, if you're itchy, take a bath.

If you're stressed, take a bath. If your psyche is bruised,
take a bath. If it's Tuesday, take a bath. And even if your cat
is in an extra good mood, take a bath! **BATHS ROCK!**

Did you know you can make your own bath oils? Get some castor
oil (sold at drugstores) and pour some into pretty bottles.
Add an ounce or so of an essential oil (try the health food store
or a Body Shop type shoppe) and label with cool tags. But what
kind of essential OIL to get? **LAVENDER** smells deeeeelish and
works for achey heads and acne, too. **ROSEMARY** smells spicy,
foresty, deep, dark and woodsy and it clears you up if you're stuffy.
TANGERINE oil is used for anxiety—apparently that sweet citrus
smell is universally relaxing. For dry skin try **YLANG-YLANG**,
which smells kind of like Asian jasmine but not.
CHAMOMILE is terrific to clear out your pores right-like.

P.S. OATMEAL is just about the best thing if you have poison oak
or ivy or are covered in bites from Spot's resident fleas or you get
the itchy eczema like Clea. Just dump some in your bath.

DARTH VADER ASKS,
HAVE YOU BEEN KEEPING UP YOUR FUTURE FILES?

Grab a new record jacket, bright red folder or shoe
box. Write across the top, around the sides,
anywhere you can write:

THE COOLEST JOBS (Ever!)

And don't just look for the obvious when thinking
about future potential career moves. Say you look
through a catalog and see adorable models vamping
it up on some way-old college campus.
Model is the obvious choice. But instead think:

stylist extraordinaire. Or copywriter.
Or location scout. Or catalog mogul
(you can run the show).
Question the fun but otherwise
overlooked parts of your life.

Who decided to call this particular color of red
lipstick, VAMP? (Product consultant and/or in-house
creative director.) Who came up with the Rubik's
Cube? (Inventor.) Who comes up with the new flavors
at Baskin-Robbins? (Chef.) Who picks the movies
that show at your local cineplex? (Movie distributor.)
And even if you know you want to be a doctor
because your mom was a doctor and your grandma
was a doctor and medicine and science is without a
doubt the most fascinating Rice Krispie of life,
do you know what kind of doctor you want to be?

Look for clues while you read about anything
and everything. Cut out words and pictures that
make you think about the job behind the product
and shove them in your FUTURE FILE.
(You will indeed thank us later.)

Inside Keva's JOB Future File:
* High-paid "personality"
* Dog walker
* Hotel owner
* Clothing shop owner
* Party planner
* Party girl
* Professional partier

Inside Clea's JOB Future File:
* Casting director
* The person who picks out music
for a movie's soundtrack
* Farmer Clea has a nice ring to it
* Skillful French-trained chef
* Famous sexy rock star
* Political speechwriter

STAIN REMOVAL CAN BE FUN. HONEST.

By the way, we don't know how to get out banana.

Every gal (and guy, but we're not concerned with them here) should know how to lickety-split remove stains from their clothes. It's not a chick thing and it's not a boring home-ec '50s thing, it's common sense. And it comes in handy, believe you me. You want your clothes to last longer, you want to save your favorite jeans from that accidental nail polish spillage, you want to salvage that vintage blouse with the yellowed underarm stains. Here is your handy-dandy guide to stain removal.

BLOOD (Been scratching them flea bites, haven't ya?) If the blood is fresh, sponge with cool salted water and rinse with clear water. If that don't work, dilute hydrogen peroxide (1 part to 9 parts water). Sponge it on. Rinse well. If the blood ain't fresh, go directly to the hydrogen peroxide part. Repeat if necessary.

CHOCOLATE First, scrape off as much as possible with a butter knife. Hot soapy water will then remove fresh stains from washable articles. If a brown stain remains, look in the laundry aisle for something called diaper wash. It should contain sodium percarbonate. You can soak the stain in this and follow it with a good rinse in warm water.

DEODORANT Ick, that white residue is nasty. Sponge with a laundry presoak (spot stain remover) and warm water. Rinse. Sometimes deodorant messes with the color of your clothes. Try sponging with ammonia (diluted with equal amount of water). Rinse well. P.S. Look for our upcoming bestselling book, "Help, I Cannot Decide What Deodorant to Use!"

PEN First, saturate material with an alcohol-based hair spray. The alcohol content in the hair spray will break up the ink. Be sure to place an absorbent paper towel or rag under the stain to catch the excess. You then need to blot the stain with a rag. Repeat the process until the stain is removed, then wash normally. Some fabrics can be damaged by the hair spray. Test it out on an inconspicuous area first.

NAIL POLISH Apply acetone or nail polish remover, but take care with synthetic fibers, as both of these dissolve some types of rayons. Wash or sponge with your usual laundry product after treatment. Remove any remaining color by using a chlorinated laundry bleach for whites or hydrogen peroxide for colors.

SWEAT STAINS (OH!)
If they are new stains, they should just be washed normally. But if they are older (like on your vintage clothes), try sponging with a mixture of 1 tablespoon vinegar and 1/2 cup water. This treatment also helps to remove sweat smell! Yippee!

March 17

IT'S ST. PATTY'S DAY

oh, hooray! Will you wear green today?

A great holiday because you get to pinch people simply because of their failure to partake in fun and don green, which by the by is an exceptional color and should be worn regularly anyhow. Yes, it is an Irish holiday. But whether you're Irish or not you too can celebrate all that is St. Patrick's Day. It's a good thing to do because as legend has it, St. Patrick banished all the snakes from the island of Ire. And while snakes aren't all bad, that's kinda cool. But wait, the legend gets better. After Patty died, they kept his jawbone around and supposedly you could reverse the evil eye if you touched it. So, if life has not been going your way of late, perhaps you should concentrate today on St. Pat, his jawbone and eliminating your curse.

Six things to do on St. Patty's Day

1. Watch "In the Name of the Father" and "The Commitments."
2. Listen to the Pogues.
3. Add green food coloring to all your meals (especially at school!).
4. Look for lucky four-leaf clovers and their marginally lucky brethren, the three-leaf clover.
5. Learn a jig.
6. Reread "Green Eggs and Ham."

beware! this is an evil eye.

You're a curious girl.

You want to understand why people do the things they do. Analyze their handwriting... to find out about their personality. Or so say graphologists, the people who study other people's handwriting for a living.

In handwriting analysis you break up letters into zones.

The UPPER ZONE is tall letters: t, h, k, l
The MIDDLE ZONE speaks of basic letters: c, e, a, o
The LOWER ZONE is the dip-down letters: p, g, y, g

UPPER ZONE

This is supposed to represent your beliefs, goals and aspirations.

Large Loops = active imagination
Extra tall loops = a dreamer
if loops don't extend very high = BIG EGO!

MIDDLE ZONE.

This, they claim, speaks of your personal habits.

itty bitty letters = NO CONFIDENCE
Oversized letters = big ego!
if the letters run together = no (outward) emotion
if the letters are spread out = SHOP·O·HOLIC!

LOWER ZONE.

Finally, the lower zone is about how you relate to primal things such as money, survival, body issues and gunk like that.

little loops = not ready to get physical
Big old loops = a romancer
slanty loops = dependent on others

March 19

It's National Frozen Food month, a holiday thought up by some poor sap at Birds Eye or Ore-Ida or some other frozen food company that's trying to spice up sales of frozen succotash and/or turkey pot pies.

Baking with TOTS

← NOT BONGOS! they're TOTS!

So why do we care? Because those little plunks of potatoes, otherwise known as Tater Tots, come frozen, 128 to a bag. And frankly, we'll use any cruddy excuse to incorporate Tater Tots into our daily lives. Hence, the following recipes that could, if you were feeling oh so adventurous, make up one fabulously pro—Tater Tot dinner party, from start to finish. That's right, Tater Tots are not just a side dish anymore.

Sloppy Tots

Bake your Tots like normal. Brown a pound or so of ground beef with some chopped onion and garlic (as much as is to your liking). Add in 1 8-ounce can of tomato sauce, 1/2 cup ketchup, 1/2 cup water, 3 tablespoons brown sugar, a dash or two Worcestershire and a splash of salt. Pour mix over cooked Tots and add 2 cups shredded cheddar. Bake in a 300 degree oven for 10 or 15 minutes and then pile the gunk on top of toasted buns. Double yummy!

Tot Stir-Fry

For all you vegans! Heat 2 tablespoons peanut oil in a skillet. Add a couple tablespoons soy sauce and some ground ginger, plus cut veggies like bell peppers, green beans, onions, mushrooms, snow peas, maybe even a can of water chestnuts. Toss in the Tater Tots. Cook for 5–10 minutes. Add a few dashes of a store-bought stir-fry sauce and voila! Dinner is served.

Tot Pudding

You heard me right, Tots for dessert! Bake up your Tots like you would anyhow. In a bowl mix 1 cup sugar, 6 tablespoons soft butter, 4 eggs, 1/2 teaspoon each cinnamon and vanilla extract and 1/4 teaspoon nutmeg. When blended, mix in your cooked Tots, 1 cup drained pineapple, 1/2 cup dried cranberries and a handful of pecans. Pour into a greased 11" x 7" baking dish and cook for 45 minutes in a 325 degree oven. Let it stand before serving. Offer delicious whipped cream—in case this isn't how your guests envisioned dessert, they can mask the flavor with processed cream in a can.

ah the first day of SPRING ~ you do KNOW, it's time to clean!

thee rules are:

1. Get three boxes. Name 'em: **"Funk Up." "Set Free."** And **"Kick Out."**

2. Play your favorite CD now and loud.

3. Psyche self out.

4. Walk around your room looking for items. Sort of like **"I-Spy."** "I-Spy questionable green sweater on the floor that has underarm stains but super dope glitter buttons."
*This applies to all things in your room.

5. Ask yourself the following questions (out loud, of course):
* When was the last time I wore or used said item?
* Does it hold sentimental value?
* Is it fixable? Redeemable? Recyclable?
* DOES IT LOOK GOOD ON ME?
* Is it itchy and/or scratchy?

6. Sentence your stuff to the following destiny:
If it is a keeper, hang it up or wash it, NOW. If it's got untreatable stains but the buttons are cool, throw in the **"Funk Up"** box. If it's totally wasted, it goes to the **"Set Free"** Box. If you're not wearing it simply because you've now got boobs and it no longer fits, toss into the **"Kick Out"** box—it is banished.

7. The **"Funk Up"** box goes into a craft corner for future makeover project.
The **"Set Free"** box gets taped up and put in Mom's car to tote to the nearest Salvation Army or other local charity, church or thrift store. The **"Kick Out"** box gets taped up, dated, labeled with contents and stored in garage till future garage sale. Or you could just pass these goodies out to your friends.

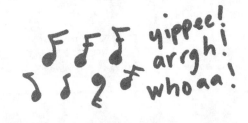

yippee!
arrgh!
whoaa!

March 21

Whatever do we mean? We mean this: Go out and look for oh, say, only record albums with tropical covers (because you're redoing your room with a tiki theme this week). Or only things that have owls on them (see collecting, January 17). Or maybe you're on a mission to replace the glassware you keep breaking when you go for those midnight juice runs half asleep. Pick a theme, any theme. Romance novels. Retro bathing suits. '80s punk rock wear. DOGGYs. Office and/or school supplies under $2.

GO THRIFT STORE SHOPPING... WITH A MISSION!

Your mission, should you choose to accept: to concoct a theme of the day and only purchase things that are both cheap and related to said theme.

this doggy's head nods!

Think of it as a scavenger hunt. Hit as many stores as you have in your neck of the woods. Spend the whole day rummaging.

Honestly, the whole experience of shopping is increased tenfold when you mandate the proceedings with a random and silly quest. Plus, since we are shopping the halls de thrift, it's not going to break your piggy's back. Now get thee to a house of thrift pronto.

This is a pillowcase.

A wrinkled old pillowcase. It needs another job besides covering Clea's pillow. And besides, we bet your laundry is piling up in the corner of your room. Maybe it's stuffed in some cute little laundry basket that you've had since you were seven? If so, make yourself a brand-new, portable, compact and all-new disgustingly cute laundry bag. With a pillowcase.

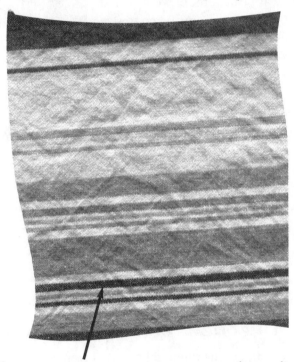

All you need is one of these, some yarn or string and a needle, thread and a tad bit of sewing knowledge (the most basic kind). Sew on string in the upper corners and hang on doorknob. You could decorate it, though, you know. Appliqué shapes of other fabrics, write on it or add a sock puppet head to the top. To do that, stuff a sock, sew it shut, add button eyes and yarn hair, and you got yourself a little princess bag. Or, if your laundry is sorta smelly mostly, maybe skip the sweet dollface and just stick to basic, utilitarian ex-pillowcases. They're good, too.

March 23
PERSISTENCE IS KEY.
A little tale of a frustrated girl up at 4 a.m., by Keva.

YOU SAY WHAT?
I SAY PERSISTENCE.

When I was 15 years old I was obsessed with fashion — the way clothes hung on the model, the way red looked with purple, the way the photo was shot, the color of her hair, the color of her dress, the style of her shoes. Most important, I was obsessed with the visions in my head and my total inability to draw them. Argh, was I frustrated! I would come home from school, grab food, run to my room and go to sleep. At 4 a.m., when the world was not awake to bug me, my alarm would go off and I would spend the next four hours drawing. Oh, did I drive myself nuts. Each piece of paper would get smashed into a little ball and thrown across the room. Nothing was right, nothing was good enough. I sucked, I was terrible, a disgrace!

per·sist·ence n. [U] the quality of being persistent; steady pursuit of one's goals.

I was experiencing such beautiful, colorful, amazing visions in my head. But when it came to executing such images, from brain to hand to pen to paper, I was a failure. How? How? How?! It went on like this for months. Every night more visions: a tulle skirt, a fur puff coat in neon purple, a skintight black-sequin bikini. I saw it all. I continued to draw. I just couldn't let it go, I couldn't abandon my visions. I bought tracing paper and pencils. I began to make body shapes. I studied hairstyles and replicated them by the thousands.

And then it happened: One night I was there, alone in my room, and it happened. Just like that. I was drawing what I saw in my head. This ingenious outfit, all suede and leather and Parisian. It was there on paper in front of me. The very same outfit. Drawn by none other than me.

"wow!" i yelped though no one heard

I was so happy I think I even cried. And the funny thing is that from that day forward I was a changed girl. A new Keva. I had confidence. I mean, not every drawing after that was good and they certainly still weren't amazing, but I had done it. My drawing came close to matching my vision. I guess I knew that if I could break through the wall just once, I would be OK. And I was. From that day forward I became unafraid to do a bad job. And I have a greater appreciation for every work of art because I know what that felt like, to create my vision with tears in my eyes. I then realized that it was persistence that was at work. With persistence, you can do anything if you just keep at it. **Persistence is key.**

makes good gift!

PLANT FLOWERS IN A POT!!

PLANT FLOWERS IN A POT. (AKA "Stumped for what to give Aunt Nancy for her birthday?") Yep, that's right, flowers in a pot. Planting flowers is fabulous and you know it. You take a seed, you put it in the earth and you nurture it. You water it. You care for it. You love it and talk to it and then it grows. It becomes something you've helped it become. With love, you did it. It's good for nature and you feel closer to the earth. Here's what you do: Get a pot with a bottom tray. Get some soil. Get some seeds (ask the guy at the nursery what's good for this season and will grow indoors easily) like marigolds. Easy so far, huh? Get some paint. Get a paintbrush. On the outside of the pot, paint a poem or a cool girl quote or maybe just doodle. Dump in the dirt. Water it a bit. Make sure the soil is loose with a lot of air. Then plant your seeds. Three or four seeds and no more (no cramping allowed). Put them in the dirt about two fingers deep. Cover the seeds with more dirt. Pat down gently. Water a bit more. Sit back and relax and wait for your flowers to grow. Or give to Aunt Nancy with a smile.

March 25

The Oscars are upon us!

We know, they can be kinda lame...

But checking out the celebrities' fancy ball gowns is kinda fun. So why not invite a few friends over and have a little Oscar night party. Make invitations. Cut out pictures of your favorite movie stars and adorn the invites with these. Ask everyone to dress up fancy.

See if it's OK if you move the furniture around the TV movie-theater style, in rows. If you want to sweeten the pot, write down the nominated movies and nominations for best actor and actress on scraps of paper and put them in a hat. (They list this stuff in "TV Guide.")

Make every guest take one scrap of paper when they arrive, and if their "pick" wins they get to take home a fabulous prize you found or made. Such as a pair of old tube sox. Or a bottle of bubble bath covered in gold paper. Maybe a thrift store trinket you no longer need.

The sillier the "prize," the better.

IMAGINE YOU'RE ON A DESERTED ISLAND.
NO, REALLY, A DESERTED, DESOLATE, EMPTY ISLAND.
WHAT FIVE THINGS WOULD YOU WANT TO HAVE WITH YOU?
WRITE THEM IN YOUR DIARY...TODAY.

March 27
CELEBRATE your inner dork.

It's better to come to terms with the dorky side of yourself, because there ARE dorky sides of yourself. There are embarrassing, awkward, freaky sides to everyone. Just remember, this is but one side of your multidimensional, fantabulously rich personality. So, our suggestion... (say this in a deep, doomful voice) "THE MOBILE OF HUMILIATION" (dun dun DUN).

Get your mitts on... a hanger. A good ol' fashioned metal one. Some wire and/or string. Regular ol' craft glue. Cardboard (feel free to cut up an old box or lift from neighbors recyclable pile.) Ten really embarrassing pictures. No editing allowed. These are the pix you wanna tear up but NO, get a hold of yourself. Make them art.

Cut five pieces of cardboard about the sizes of your photos. Glue a pic on each side of the cardboard. Punch a hole at the top of the picture. Tie your string (or hook your wire) through each hole and attach to the bottom of your hanger. Make the pieces of string varying lengths so that the pictures hang down at different levels. Hang the mobile up from your ceiling, like over your bed. Voila, room decor of the most shameful kind.

(If you haven't rounded up ten, by all means draw some reenactments of mortifying events!)

All your photos should be pretty close in size.

If you don't wanna cut or glue the pix, make color photocopies of them and use those.

KEVA: YEAH. I HAVE THREE PHONE NUMBERS, TWO EMAIL ADDRESSES, A FAX NUMERO (WELL, TWO), A WEBSITE, TWO ADDRESSES AND GOSH, I THINK I'M AN ADDICT.

Clea: Cell phones rock. Walking and talking, talking and walking. It's just the best. And I love my phone. It's blue.

KEVA: NO WAY, I HAVE THE SAME PHONE. I BET MY BILLS ARE HIGHER THAN YOURS!

Clea: I know they are, you talk talk talk like no one else I know. What noise does your phone make when it ring a ding dings?

KEVA: IT GOES "DA DA DA DA DA DAAAAAAAAAA." DO I REALLY TALK MORE THAN ANYONE YOU KNOW?

Clea: Yes, you talk more than anyone I know. You get like 67 calls a day. How many calls do you make a day? I make about three. Pretty exciting, huh? Oh, my phone rings like this, "dum dum da dun dum, bump bump."

Clea: Oh yes, you be an addict of the techno kind. I am addicted to coffee with real sugar in it. Which is not a good addiction like technology. What else are you addicted to?

KEVA: GUMMI BEARS. OH, MAN, I WISH I HAD SOME NOW, I MEAN THE DISCO IS ON BUT I COULD REALLY USE SOME GUMMI BEARS TO MAKE MY FINGERS JUST FLY ON THE IMAC KEYBOARD. SPEED BOOK WRITING!

DISCUSSION QUESTIONS★

Do you believe it's OK to talk on a cell phone in the grocery store? In a car? If you're driving? Are you a technology addict? Do you think Keva spends too much time on the phone? Are bears really a German icon?

Clea: That's what sugar does to me. I like Gummi Bears but Bit-O-Honey and Chic-O-Stick are my favorite. I wonder who thought up the idea to make them bears. It's so random. Fruit shapes would be so much more logical.

KEVA: AREN'T BEARS LIKE GERMAN ICONS?

Clea: Why, Keva, that is, maybe, correct.

KEVA: COOL! I MADE THAT UP.

WE DEEM TODAY HAPPY DAY.

FORGET ALL YOUR TROUBLES. THINK ONLY CHEERFUL THOUGHTS. CONVERSE WITH ONLY PEPPY PEOPLE, AVOIDING YOUR DARK AND DEPRESSIVE FRIENDS FOR A DAY. (IF YOU ARE ONE OF THOSE DARK AND DEPRESSIVE FRIENDS, PERK UP, JUST FOR TODAY. COME ON, IT WILL TOTALLY FREAK EVERYONE OUT.)

Smile lots. (Even if you don't mean it at first.)

Hum. Play with a puppy or a kitty if you can.

Walk with a bounce. Or dare to skip.

Find the happiest guy at school, sit down next to him at lunch and share your sandwich with him.

WEAR YELLOW, IT'S THE HAPPIEST OF COLORS.

Drink lemonade, it's the happiest of beverages.

Jot down any thoughtful, momentously happy thoughts for future perusal when you're feeling low and cruddy.

DRAW HAPPY FACES AND SUNFLOWERS IN THE MARGINS OF ALL YOUR PAPERS TODAY.

watch "happy days" reruns.

Wear a little pink on your cheeks.

SKIP WHENEVER POSSIBLE.

LISTEN TO THE B-52'S.

*AND...IF FOLKS DON'T THINK YOU HAVE LOST YOUR MARBLES, THEY MIGHT JUST SMILE BACK, AND THAT, MY FRIEND, IS COOL.

Everyone should know a little Italian!

It's the language of love. It's the bee's knees.
It's the only way to communicate with foxy Italian
foreign-exchange students. And besides, you can use this
as a "secret-agent" language between you and the gals.

You say: Hai un bellissimo culo. He says: Whatever.

Where can I get a great bowl of spaghetti?

Dove posso avere un favoloso piatto di spaghetti?
pronounce it like dis: Doe-vey poe-soe ah-VEH-ray oon
fahv-ah-LOW-zo pee-ah-TO dee spaw-GET-tee?

Would you like to join me, like "Lady and the Tramp"?

Vorresti avere con me come "Lady and the Tramp"?
pronounce it like dis: Vor-es-tee ahh-VEH-ray
con me ko-may "Lady and the Tramp"?

You have a fabulous butt.

Hai un bellissimo culo.
pronounce it like dis: Hi oon bell-EES-ee-moe coo-low.

Go away, smelly guy!

Vattene ragazzo, puzzocente!
pronounce it like dis: Vah-tent-eh rah-gat-so, poot-so-chen-tay!

Peel me another grape, Antonio.

Pelami un altro grappolo, Antonio.
pronounce it like dis: Pel-ah-me oon all-tro
grah-PO-low, Ahn-toe-nee-oh.

March 31

TIME TO:
CREATE-A-TREND.

You know how magazines are always coming up with these bizarre combinations of influences and declaring them a trend? It often seems so very arbitrary. Like someone spun a big wheel until it landed on aerodynamic western wear and VOILA! That's the new look of the season. Now showing on all the runways of Paris and Milan.

Well, you too can play big-time fashion editor with your own handy-dandy CREATE-A-TREND generator. Cut out three circles and divide them into your basic pie shape. On one write adjectives. On another write sports. And on the third write places. Pin together in center. Spin. See how they line up? Use this to formulate the latest "look" and then go directly to your closet and concoct an outfit that will illuminate this new trend. You are the trendsetter of the school. Work it, flaunt it, be it. Go!

Create-a-trend wheel o' style!

Preppy · Utilitarian · field track · bicycling · Dressy · Sloppy · Nerdy · fifties · Soccer Rodeo · motorcross · wrestling · Youthful · Goth · Boxing · break dancing

Parisian · Asian · Yugoslavian · Jamaican · Mid West · SoCal · NYC · New Orleans

Cut 3 circles, different sizes, write your own categories. pin together.

=:Spin!:=

Clea: Why, Keva, that boxing Asian Goth thing you got going on is hot!

Keva: Thanks. You look pretty chichi in your retro Tibetan break dancing garb!

Clea: Oh, tomorrow I think I will wear sloppy, Midwestern motocross!

Keva: Ooh la la!! Maybe I will wear New Orleansian youthful wrestling clothes! This create-a-trend wheel thing is fab!

LET THERE BE LIGHT.
SPRING FORWARD. FALL BACK.

APRIL

K: we love eggs! C: yes, we sure do!

CLEA: April is sorta one of those months that has little and lots of meaning all at the same time.

KEVA: Well, Clea, you are a strange girl.

APRIL 1 OUR CALENDAR OF THINGS TO DO, MAKE AND PONDER FOR THE MONTH OF APRIL.

APRIL 1
Dig through trash in kitchen and dig out old coffee grinds for future projects.

APRIL 2
Buy a box of toothpicks.

APRIL 3
Call up old boyfriend and tell him you forgive him.

APRIL 4
Call him back and say you were dared to do it.

APRIL 5
Spring nose cleaning.

APRIL 6
Wear leg warmers over your stretch jeans.

APRIL 7
Only speak when spoken to.

APRIL 8
Burn this book.

APRIL 9
Give away your favorite clothes to the Salvation Army.

APRIL 10
Run away.

APRIL 11
Call home from a pay phone and say you've stepped out for a few days.

APRIL 12
Tie a yellow ribbon round an old oak tree.

APRIL 13
Show up for school wearing a cap and gown.

APRIL 14
Play with your food.

APRIL 15
Balance checkbook.

APRIL 16
Get rosebed ready for second generation soil.

APRIL 17
Call your dad "Mom" and your mom "Dad."

APRIL 18
Begin new collection of "sands of the world."

APRIL 19
Plan your next trip to Aruba.

APRIL 20
Bring your dog to school. Tell them your doctor can give you a note.

APRIL 21
Rename your best friend.

APRIL 22
Dump laundry basket on floor, roll around on top of clothes for five minutes to reduce static electricity in the air.

APRIL 23
Announce to everyone you know you are now, officially, a breatharian.

APRIL 24
Make a Jell-O mold for your teacher. Tell her it's packed with vitamins.

APRIL 25
Remove the color orange from your life. It creates artistic chaos.

APRIL 26
Sign your name "Sally" on all school papers.

APRIL 27
Pack a bag, tell the units your catching the next plane to SF to see the Pixies reunion show.

APRIL 28
Start a golf club.

APRIL 29
Get to know your friendly telephone operator by name.

APRIL 30
Crawl out the bedroom window and then crawl back in to reintroduce yourself into your environment.

Ha! April Fools. Please disregard all the above, except for April 12th, 23rd and 30th, those are good to go.

☀ Let there be Light *

spring forward ← fall back

daylight saving time is, to us, one of the best holidays of the year, even though it isn't a holiday, really. but we love it and celebrate it as one because finally, after a long dark winter, we get an extra hour of sunlight as a reward. yippee.

dst is actually a law, but isn't adhered to in Hawaii, American Samoa, guam, puerto rico, the virgin islands, the eastern time zone part of indiana and most of arizona. which can get sort of confusing, especially if you live there or some close relatives do. oh and dst, as it is often referred to, is observed in like 70 other countries.

keva: How do you know all this to be true?
clea: i'm smart.

it begins for most of the u.s. at 2 a.m. on the first sunday of April. time reverts to standard time at 2 a.m. on the last sunday of october, which we hate, save for the pretend extra hour of sleep.

dst was devised to save energy, or so they tell us. the powers that be say that energy is directly connected to when we go to bed and when we get up. when we go to bed, we turn off the lights and tv. by moving the clock ahead one hour, we can cut the amount of electricity we consume each day. whatever. all we know is we like this day, lots. and we think it is the perfect day to be outside after 5, because it's still light out. so, in honor of the fabulous holiday (work with us here) we say, no tv watching till it gets dark. you must go outside and enjoy the extra hour of daytime.

go onto your back porch and yell, "Let there be Light!" and have a bar-be-que.

we don't care how cold it is. get your family together. get other families together. grab your friends. and party like it's dst!

P.S. This doesn't really have to do with DST, but once on Christmas Eve, Clea was flying on a plane to Australia to visit her papa, and because of the time difference and all, when she arrived in Sydney, it was the day after Christmas. So Christmas never happened! Spooky.

This is Aimee, Keva's adorable "lovie sissie," sleeping. We say, wake up and get outside!

NEED A BREAK FROM THE MONOTONY OF LIFE? PAINT A CHAIR. (DUH!)

It's one of our all-time favorite pastimes. Painting stuff. And, hey, no one gets in trouble, provided you stay away from your mom's antique wingback. This is the perfect way to express those inner color dreams without getting a slap in the bootie. Here's what you need:

A wood chair (The cheaper the better—keep those eyes peeled toward the curb on trash morning.)
Sandpaper
Paintbrushes
Gloves (Or be bold.)
Old clothes (For wearing, silly.)
An old sheet or plastic stuff for the floor
Paint (*Use old leftovers or scour the "oops" section at Home Depot.)

Do not, we repeat **DO NOT**, spend massive moola here. Trust us when we say that you'll love your chair that much more when it cost you like a buck twenty four.

And well, OK, 1, 2, 3...paint.
I mean, do whatever you want.
Flames, names, leopard prints, poems, faces, your dog Georgia or whatever.

*Here's an artistic rendering of the one we made.

A few words about bothersome boys (and men) who should really know better but often don't.

OK, so you're walking along the street, minding your own business, grooving to the song in your head, when some guy, maybe you know him, prolly you don't, says something lewd or whistles or catcalls or clicks his tongue or whatever.

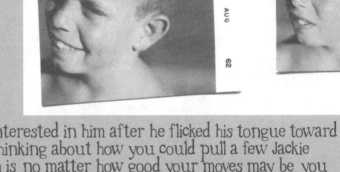

You become heated. Grossed out. Can he possibly think you'd be interested in him after he flicked his tongue toward you? In your mind you may be thinking about how you could pull a few Jackie Chan moves on the dude. Problem is, no matter how good your moves may be, you could seriously be asking for trouble if you took such a route (like namely, he could get physical back. Can we have a "YIKES"?).

So, what do you do? There are as many answers to that as there are catcalls in the world. We've talked to those who laugh pitifully at the caller, those who hock loogeys, those who call up the nastiest belch they can find within. And then there are those who subscribe to the ignore-them approach. This is probably the safest path to take. And that can't be all bad.

Oh, one more word on the subject.

Icky boys who whistle and click their tongues at your breasts (or your legs or your backside) are not flattering you. They are not impressed with your breasts (however lovely they may be), they are just impressed with breasts, period. So, do not take this as flattery, please. Flattery is when someone compliments your style or your taste or your intelligence.

KNOCK, KNOCK.
WHO'S THERE?
GIN!

Getting started:

Grab yourself a partner and learn how to play Gin. Why? Because card games rock and roll. Because when you're stuck in an airport or riding on a bus or waiting at the hospital, it's a great way to pass the time. Because grandmas love Gin. And grandmas are right on.

Rules:

You start with a basic deck of cards. Hopefully your deck means something to you. Like you got them on vacation in the Grand Canyon. The object of the game is to arrange as many of your cards into "sets" as possible. There are two kinds of sets. Sequences & Groups.

Sequences are three or more cards in the same suit (all hearts, for example) in a consecutive order (4, 5, 6).

Groups are three or four cards of the same rank or the same number like a 7 of hearts, 7 of clubs and a 7 of spades. (Works for picture cards, too.)

A card can belong to only one set at a time. Two or more people. 52 cards. (No jokers.) Someone should be dealer. The dealer deals 10 cards to each player FACEDOWN. The next card gets turned FACE UP. This is the discard pile. The rest of the deck gets placed next to the discard pile, FACEDOWN. This is the stock.

Now you can look at your cards.
Time to play.
A turn consists of two steps:

1. The DRAW.
2. The DISCARD.

You must begin by taking the top card from either the discard pile (the face UP stack) or the stock pile (the FACE-DOWN stack). Add it to your hand. You know what card you're getting if you pull from the discard pile but it's a secret what you get if you pull from the stock pile. And remember, you're looking to make sets. Next step is to discard a card. (You can have only 10 cards at the end of each turn.) You can discard any card you don't think will work in your set(s). Discard it faceup into the discard pile (hence the name!).

How to win:

Keep doing this till one of the players is ready to show his/her completed sets. The player then knocks on the table and says "Gin!" if they aren't lyin' and they really have their sets and sequences in order, well, then they win. And you start all over again. Now, go find Grandma.

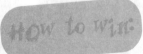

Earth Day is approaching. Now, first off, every day should be Earth Day. Or at least most days. There's all sorts of boring stuff you should kinda be doing already such as running the washer and dryer only when you've got a full load, recycling your cans, avoiding using disposable plastic items. Basic blah-blah you already know. So in honor of Earth Day maybe you should take your neighborhood under your big 'n' bright wings. Come up with a project that will ignite the fire in your neighbors' bellys and benefit the earth. Meanwhile, here are our favorite Earth Day slogans to be repeated today and every day!

STOP AND SMELL THE ROSES. LOVE YOUR MOM.

Go Earth. NATURE ROCKS. ROCKS ROCK.

Revolt against the oppressive fascists that spill chemicals and kill endangered species and generally disrupt the beauty that is this planet.

Keva takes a walk through the Garden of Eden.

Eating food by Color Day

Sometimes it's fun to do stuff that you think is really silly. Silly and simple. Really easy, too. For instance: Slip 'n Slides. Now that's cool. And movies in the daytime. And popcorn with M&M's and, well, today we're gonna talk about a simple fun thing that is oh so easy: Eating Food By Color Day. What?

Allow us to illustrate. Keva ate red stuff all Saturday, all day. Beets, tomatoes, red cabbage (it's purple but still), strawberries, a sun-dried tomato bagel with red pepper crème cheese, red snapper and salmon with red potatoes, V8s, Hot Tamales, and Dentyne between meals.

She had a strawberry smoothie with a red straw and told the girl behind the counter she wanted a shot of beet juice and none of that green stuff 'cause today was her red day not her green day. The girl thought she was super wacko, but that didn't matter to Keva.

No way, Jose. When she got home from a long day she wore a red muscle tee and red spandex pants and red platforms and, well, of course, red lips (MAC, Russian Red) and she went into her redroom (AKA: her bedroom) and took a nap. While she napped she dreamt of more food and more snax and the color blue. Blue? Yikes.

She woke up right away. "Blue?!" she yelped.

OK, blue it is. So the next day she went to work in blue capris with blue butterfly clips in her hair and ate blueberries by the dozen-so you do it. Pick a color. Tell everyone. Laugh at your bad self, wink, wink, change colors whenever you want.

A SLAMBOOK IS A PERFECTLY GOOD WAY TO KILL A LUNCH BREAK.

devil

Get a spiral notebook or one of those black-and-white composition books. Number each page down the side 1 through 25. Then at the top of every page write a question. Dig deep here—pretend you're some interviewer on the telly asking celebrities truly **PERSONAL** questions about their lives. Then pass it 'round to your friends (and random cute strangers). They each pick a **SECRET** number and write in their answers to each question, on each page, on that particular line. Don't forget to fill in your own answers, too, but wait till some others have done so, that way you're not the first (and obvious) not-so-secret writer.

SOME SAMPLE QUESTIONS...

Do you like SPAM?

Deserted island. You and who?

At what age do people become old?

Barber, salon or Mom?

Baggy or tight?

What nickname would you like people to call you that you've never been called before?

Who was the last person who was rude to you?

Who was the last person you were rude to?

Are you sorry?

At heart are you a devil or an angel?

Ever said "I love you" to a non-family member?

just call her 'Boo Boo'

APRIL 9

we deem today honesty day

just like that, poof, it's honesty day.

That means today you shall tell the truth. You shall also get in touch with your inner feelings and remind people whom you love and care about that you love and care about them. You must listen to your insides today: that's what honesty is all about. Could you really have studied more? Do you really even like that boy you've been crushing on or do you just like the way he smiles at you? Hum Billy Joel's "Honesty is such a lonely word" song... even if you hate Billy Joel. Watch "Johnny Dangerously," a movie about a really honest gangster. Or "Liar, Liar," about a guy who can't help but tell the truth. Wear blue, because blue is the most honest of colors. Avoid foods with preservatives today— preservatives are dishonest. So are fat-free foods. Don't cheat, lie or steal today. Well, any day, but 'specially today. Be Wonder Woman and force the truth out of various and sundry liars with your powerful lasso.

AIRMAIL RULES.

And what better way to send a note of love or to divulge a super
spy girl secret than in a handy-dandy, easy to make paper airplane.
Plus, you can be earth girl, too, and use like an old map or the Home Depot
catalog or some such thing. Follow the instructions below and when you're all
done, hold up your airplane in your right hand (unless you're left-handed), just
slightly above your shoulder. Breathe. Spy your girlfriend or love interest.
Squint for aiming's sake and then with a slight tip backward of the wrist and
a little push of the arm, release the paper airplane into the air.

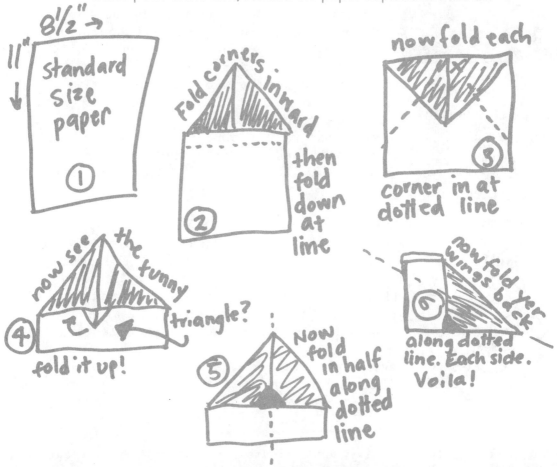

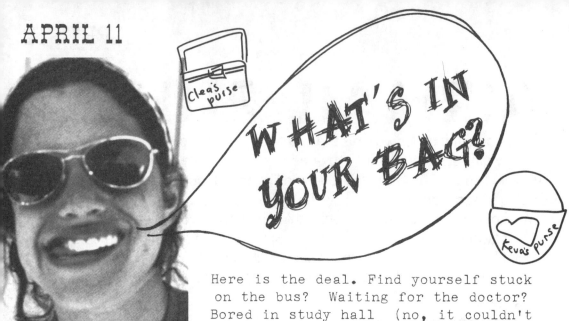

WHAT'S IN YOUR BAG?

Clea's purse

Keva's purse

Here is the deal. Find yourself stuck on the bus? Waiting for the doctor? Bored in study hall (no, it couldn't be true!)? We say DUMP IT! Grab a pal, get your bag and do the overturn. Your backpack or your purse, silly. You'll be amazed at all the stuff you got. So take stock, write it down, shove the list under your mattress, and if you find yourself unhappy with the contents of your bag, spend the night filling it up with cuter stuff.

Here's some ideas:
1. peppermint candies✱
2. tape measure
3. bubble gum
4. miniradio
5. sticker book
6. more pens

peppermint candies sparkle!

What do the contents of your bag say about you? Are you a neat freak or a slob? Do you have sticky, gooey candies in the bottom like Clea? Or opened eye shadow in your bag like Keva (baby blue glitter everywhere!)? Are you a simple chick, just the essentials? Or a pack rat, collecting everything but the kitchen sink in your bag? (Um, Keva and Clea.) Compare your list with your friend's list and declare someone the big-booty-bag queen (she'd be the one with the most stuff).

✱for the next time you play seven minutes in heaven with that cute date.

Enter the Future Files. APRIL 12

Wish you were here

Let's try a voice other than Darth Vader's, just this once. Affect a chichi French accent. Or a Caribbean island twang. And say it along with us: Future Files. Your latest addition to your ever-growing collection of magazine clippings and furious-future-focusing files is TRAVEL PLANS. So grab yet another colored folder or record album jacket or shoe box or paper bag, whatever, and scribble all over it:

wish you were here

Now, places you want to visit are tremendously different from places where you wish to eventually live. When you travel you can try out a gazillion different locales, staying a day...or twenty. If you find something inside you tugging as you glimpse a black sand beach, cut it out. Throw it in your WISH YOU WERE HERE Future File. Received any good postcards lately? If so, toss them in your WISH YOU WERE HERE Future File, too.

In Keva's Travel Plans Future Files:

Puerto Rico
London
Bora Bora (where is that, exactly?)
Tokyo

In Clea's Travel Plans Future Files:

Ireland
a tour of the South (as in the USA)
Indonesia
la la land
Japan

APRIL 13

Clea: I suppose they could sue me for saying this but I think that fake sugar in the blue packets is the devil. Real sugar, now that is the *%$@!

Keva: My friend Jeff, well, he's from the South and he and his friend Ronnie actually put that fake sugar in water. Oh, but only when they are in California. What's up with that?

Clea: That is the most disgusting thing I ever heard. My boyfriend, he puts fake sugar in a lot of things, but never water. I think it tastes too-too sweet with a chemical burn aftertaste.

Keva: So boys use fake sugar, girls use real sugar. Is there something wrong with that?

Clea: Um, I guess not. But don't you think it's sad that these boys don't know the joys of real sugar, the way the teeny tiny grains feel in your mouth? One of my favorite things is cereal, any cereal really that isn't too sweet, with sugar on it, because when the sugar gets all wet from the milk, it almost melts but not quite. Yum, I must go eat some cereal.

Keva: I'm on the new Sugar Busters diet. I'm chubby today.

Clea: No, no, no. Dieting is not so good. I mean, you are active, that is what counts. And you know you are not chubby. You are, however, buxom.

Keva: Buxom. Heck, yeah. OK, I was only on that diet for like three hours anyway.

Clea: Oh, well then, OK. Diets are only good if they last less than 5.2 hours. Or if they are anti-junk food, body-cleansing diets, then they are OK, too. But not for too-too long.

Discussion Questions:

Do you think fake sugar is bad? Do you think sugar is bad? If you're from the South, do you put fake sugar in your water? Do you know anyone, besides Jeff and his friend Ronnie, who do this? Do you agree with the wild thesis that girls like real sugar and boys like fake sugar? Us neither. When Keva says she is chubby is she A) exaggerating, B) telling the truth, or C) full of poo? (I will give you a hint, it's not B.)

Start a fan club.

So you really liked Francesca Lia Block's Weetzie Bat books. Or you don't think enough people are listening to '80s punk chick Blondie. Perhaps you read Sylvia Plath's "Bell Jar" in Lit and cannot get over how amazing she was. Or maybe, just maybe, you and your friends think the new biology teacher rocks! All you need to start a fan club is you. You can be the club. Or you can find like-minded individuals to join.

Hold a meeting. Elect a prez or forsake the whole hierarchy thing and declare all members equal. **Take notes** or "minutes" as they are called in official fan clubs.

Decide what your first action as a fan club shall be: **Make a website. Write a letter** to the object of your fanaticism. **Create a zine** dedicated to that object with articles about he/she/it. (See July 14–16.) **Make stickers!** (See January 21.) Write an ode to your object. (See January 3.) **Write a haiku.** (See December 10.) **Make tee shirts** declaring your fan club to be the numero uno. Or **create buttons** that honor your object de respect. **Make a shrine** out of a shoe box (or just a shoe, if you like) with trinkets and pictures that remind you of the person (or thing) that you are dedicating your club to.

IMAGINE YOU'RE A SPICE GIRL.

Monogramming: it ain't just for grandmas anymore.

We like the idea of monogramming because it forever stamps your name on something. Long after you've given up on that sweater and it's gone off to the Salvation Army, someone else can pick it up and wonder, "Who was KM and why did she give away this bitchin' sweater?"

And then there is the simple fact that you can monogram so many things. Your purse, your sheets and pillows, your jeans, your towels, your backpack, your tee shirts, your scarves—you name it. And naming it is indeed the name of the game.

What you'll need: A relatively thick needle and some relatively thick thread, lots of different colors, natch. Embroidery needles and threads work best if you've got 'em. Sewing transfer paper from the sewing shop really makes monogramming easy. You can pick a letter-style out of a book and trace it right onto your fabric with the transfer paper. But you can draw it freehand with a fancy-schmancy wash-out pen (also from the sewing store) or even a #2 pencil. And, of course, you'll need something to monogram.

Now, there are all sorts of fancy ways to do this, but we're talking basics here, so let's do just a basic stitch. Thread your needle, knot the thread. Basic, right? Then come in from behind the material you're monogramming and pull the needle through the material to the front. Make your stitches very close to one another, following along your template. All the stitches should be about the same size.

When you're all done with a letter, simply knot the end of the thread and snip off the excess. Now go and monogram everything you own. **Everything.**

MARVELOUS • MUSHY

got some fruit that is a little mushier than you like to eat? don't throw it away, give body shop a run for its money and make a fruit smoothie body scrub for your sensuously supple skin.

Here is what you need: 3/4 cup sunflower seeds (not in their shells!) 2 tablespoons sunflower oil & 1/2 cup mashed fruit: berries, melons, apples, pears or peaches.

MASK • NIGHT!!

dump the sunflower seeds in the blender and grind. blend in the oil. skin and/or peel and/or pit any of the fruit as necessary. slowly stir in the fruit and whirl until it's all smooth. if it's too watery, add a little flour to thicken. pour it into a plastic container.

now this is an all-over body scrub, so get in the shower or bath and take your washcloth or loofah and dip it into your body smoothie and scrub in a gentle circular motion for at least 10 minutes. rinse with warm water and "ta da," welcome to healthier, happier, pre-summery skin.

this is potentially a very big mess. be sure to clean it up right away with comet and an old rag or else face the wrath of clogged pipes and crusty tubs.

*If you are allergic to any of these fruits, by all means, DO NOT, we repeat do not, do this spa treatment. Give yourself another clay mask (see February 7) and forget about it.

PASSOVER

Passover is a Jewish holiday that celebrates the fleeing of the Jews from the evil pharaoh. The story goes that Moses parted the Red Sea and allowed the Jews to get away while flooding the pharaoh's men. You can rent the "Prince of Egypt" or "The Ten Commandments" to get the big picture.

The cool thing about Passover is it's flooded with symbolism. Legend says that the Jews had to leave their houses so fast that they didn't have time to bake bread. But they had the raw dough. They took this with them into the desert and it was so hot that the sun baked it really quickly into hard, thin crackers. Hence the whole tradition of matzos, which are eaten in place of bread during the Passover Seder (the big yummy dinner). In fact, no foods containing yeast are eaten at the Seder. There are even special dinner plates and silverware just for these big dinners. And five foods are always eaten, symbolic of the history of this story:

BITTER HERBS. In this case horseradish, which symbolizes the bitter struggle of the slaves.

EGG. Another symbol of spring.

PARSLEY. Dipped in salt water, a symbol of springtime and tears.

HAROSETH. A chunky pastelike mixture of chopped walnuts, wine, cinnamon and apples. It represents the mortar the Jewish slaves used to assemble the pharaoh's bricks while they were building those pesky pyramids.

SHANK BONE. A representative of the sacrificial lamb. Seders often include turkeys for this reason because they got a big ol' shank bone.

Give up something for Lent. It's fun. We swear. Oops.

Lent is serious and religiously monumental if you are Catholic, but it can also be fun. 'Cause sometimes we should give up some stuff that maybe we indulge in and maybe take for granted.

Give up soda . . . . do wheatgrass shots.
Give up negativism . . . . be supro-positive.
Give up anger . . . . .be more patient.
Give up nail biting....get acrylics with palm trees.
Give up gloom..... enjoy the beauty that is all around.
Give up gossiping.......... control your tongue.
Give up hair gel.......... go au naturel.

A bit of background:

Lent is a period of approximately forty days celebrated by the Church each year before Easter. All Catholics between the ages of 18 and 58 are supposed to abstain from eating meat on Ash Wednesday and on all the Fridays of Lent, as well as fast on Ash Wednesday and Good Friday. So there.

see, we told you it was fun.

Fourteen Things (We Think) Every Girl Should Know...

We've been thinking. There are a lot of skills, many of which we cannot teach here, that we believe you all should know. As girls, as women, as rock stars. So here's our basic list. If you don't know how to do any of the following, we suggest looking it up, asking an aunt or, heck, writing us a letter.

Throw a football. READ A STOCK TICKER.

Make a grilled cheese sandwich.

Effectively use the lawn mower. MAKE A BED ARMY-STYLE.

Know the lyrics to at least one Beastie Boys song.

INSTALL A DEADBOLT. Ask for directions.

BALANCE A CHECKBOOK. CORRECTLY.

Know who your state senator is. And know what he/she stands for.

Poach an egg. Play three chords on the guitar.

MAKE A THREE-POINT SHOT, AT LEAST ONCE. Change a tire.

EVEN IF EASTER

ISN'T FOR YOU, THE WHOLE EGG THING IS, NONETHELESS, REALLY FUN. BRIGHTLY COLORED EGGS ARE JUST PLAIN CHEERY. AND YOU DON'T NEED TO SPEND THE MONEY ON THOSE LITTLE KITS EITHER. YOU CAN MAKE GORGEOUS EGGS WITH REGULAR HOUSEHOLD KITCHEN GUNK. THE BASIC RECIPE GOES AS FOLLOWS:

Grab a big pot. Place 8 eggs inside. Add 2 tablespoons of white vinegar and then add enough water to cover the eggs. Add a natural dye (from the list below) and bring to a boil. Then turn down the heat & simmer for about 20 minutes. Rinse in warm water. Oh, and before cooking the eggs you can wrap rubber bands around them to create a hippie-esque tie-dyed effect.

BABY SWEET LIGHT PINK	12-ounce package of cranberries
HOT, DARK PINK	4 cups chopped beets
RACY BOLD GOLD	3 tablespoons turmeric
OUR FAVORITE ORANGE	Yellow onion skins from 6 onions
LOVELY PALE GREEN	1 bunch spinach leaves, chopped
GO GO LAVENDER	4 cups frozen blueberries

ONE MORE THING. IF YOU WANT YOUR EGGS DARKER, LEAVE THEM IN THE DYE OVERNIGHT IN THE FRIDGE.

Happy Easter.

It's time for an egg hunt. Call it an Easter Egg Hunt or a Passover Egg Hunt or even an "It's-Sunday-All-Right!" Egg Hunt.

Lauren made a good bunny, didn't you, Lauren??

Happy Easter

It's the funnest holiday thing ever. Especially perfect if there's little kids in your neighborhood. Here's what you do: Get a few friends together. Pool your money. Make flyers. Be sure to state where, when, what to bring. Everyone must bring a basket and wear their Sunday best. Distribute the invites to your neighbors the Monday before the day you're gonna do it.

If you have a yard, great, do it there. If your yard sucks, go to the nearest park. Or get creative. Indoor Easter Egg Hunt? Sure, why not. Make tons of colorful eggs ○see April 21 entry○, assembly○line style with your girlfriends. Get into it. Place all eggs back into cartons, clean up, then count your eggs and write down the number in a safe place. This is also the time to decide if you want to give away prizes. They can be fake, ya know, like a "trip to Paris" or they can be little toys like jacks or yo-yos or maybe redeemable gift certificates for services or treats. Brainstorm first, second and third prizes.

About two hours before the hunt is to begin, go hide the eggs. Make sure someone stands watch to be sure no one is sneaking peeks. When starting time is upon you, count down and yell real loudly, "Ready, set, go!" and watch all the kids run around. Be sure to choose a cutoff time. When it's over make everyone run up to you with their baskets and proceed to count. Whoever has the most eggs wins!

○For the crafty overachiever: Get a friend or relative to dress up like a bunny and show up at the hunt out of nowhere, hopping around on all fours. Tell parents to bring their cameras and kiddies can get pictures with the Easter/Passover/It's-Sunday-All-Right! bunny!

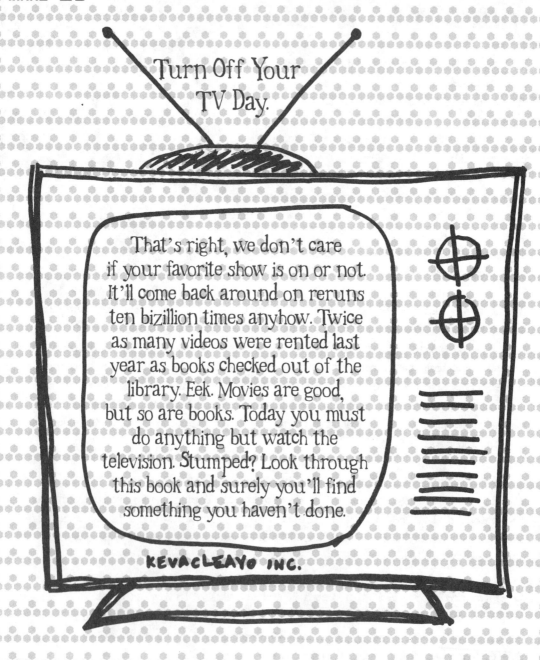

Turn Off Your
TV Day.

That's right, we don't care
if your favorite show is on or not.
It'll come back around on reruns
ten bizillion times anyhow. Twice
as many videos were rented last
year as books checked out of the
library. Eek. Movies are good,
but so are books. Today you must
do anything but watch the
television. Stumped? Look through
this book and surely you'll find
something you haven't done.

KEVACLEAYO INC.

Sometimes it is good to reflect on the hardships of your life and others' because it makes you remember the important things. It helps put things into perspective. (Like do I really care that my hair has this weird cowlick, I mean I care, but in the big picture, it simply isn't that important. And it might be gone by tomorrow.)
So, we deem today National Get a Hold of Your Life and...

Garner a New Perspective Day.

So, stop and smell a few flowers. Look at your Future Files and marvel at how much stuff you've collected (and if you haven't, get crackin'). Look at your baby pictures. Ask your mom to tell you a story about when you were little. One you haven't heard before. Think about your biggest hang-up and why it isn't all that important in the big scheme of things. Create a new adult habit. (No, not smoking.) Like read a word out of the dictionary every day and use it in a sentence with your friends. Or dab a little perfume on the backs of your knees. (Yes, adults do this all the time.) Sure they do.

la la la la la live for today

IT'S ARBOR DAY*

In honor of Arbor Day, you could plant a tree. That's pretty easy, right? Or you could make a garden gift for your mom or your teacher or your best friend or your little sister or like whomever you feel good about this week and who might appreciate such a fabulously thoughtful gift.

IT'S AN EGGSHELL GARDEN.

YOU'LL NEED

Some seeds—
you could try herbs and veggies or sunflowers or even grass. A couple of different ones would be best. A dozen eggs and the carton they rode in on. Some coffee stirrers or toothpicks or small thin twigs. And some paper and a couple of drops of glue to make tags to declare which plant is which.

DIRECTIONS

Crack eggs close to the pointy top as possible. Empty the eggs into a bowl and save for a family size omelet. Pick off just enough eggshell to make a spoon size opening. Gently rinse them out and put them back in their carton to dry. Do this for all the eggs. (Some will break—it's OK, just go with it.)

Grab some moist dirt from your yard and delicately spoon in enough to fill the eggshells halfway. Drop the seeds in, cover with a tad more dirt. Follow the instructions on the seed packs to find out how much to water them.

Now make tags by attaching a piece of paper with the name of the plant variety on it with a touch of glue to a coffee stirrer or toothpick or small twig. Stick in the eggshell, as close to the shell wall as possible to make way for the new plantling. Put on a windowsill so they get a bit of sunshine. You can give this wonderful gift now or wait till you get some leaves popping up.

You should see li'l leaves shortly. Direct the new owner of this garden to replant the delicate plants when they get about three inches tall. (They can just crack the eggshell all over and place it directly in the ground.)

P.S. Happy birthday Aimee!

*Or it's really close

FENCING

In case you don't know, fencing is the sport of swordplay. Why you should start fencing right NOW!

<u>Because</u> colleges like Brown, Brandeis, Harvard, MIT, Stanford and Yale all have respected fencing teams and many give fencing scholarships!

<u>Because</u> it's an Olympic sport!

BECAUSE
WELL, HAVE YOU SEEN "THE MASK OF ZORRO"? "THE THREE MUSKETEERS"? "THE MAN IN THE IRON MASK"? "ROMEO AND JULIET"? "SHAKESPEARE IN LOVE"? "THE PRINCESS BRIDE"? "BRAVEHEART"? FENCING IS ALL OVER THE MOVIES AND IT'S SEXY AND SMART AND SPORTY ALL AT THE SAME TIME.

<u>Because</u> you get to use cool phrases like "En garde!" "Riposte!" and "Touché!"

<u>Because</u> it's truly amazing exercise for your butt, thighs, arms and heart! BECAUSE IT MIGHT JUST BE THE COOLEST-LOOKING SPORT EVER!

<u>Because</u> there are not one but three swords to choose from: the foil, saber or épée!

<u>BECAUSE</u> YOU GET TO WEAR A COOL METAL MESH MASK AND METAL BOOB CUPS TO PROTECT YOURSELF. (AND THE BOOB CUPS MAKE GREAT CANDY DISHES WHEN YOU'RE NOT FENCING!)

<u>Because</u> Super Clea fences! (It is one of the things that makes her so darn super!)

Self-Portrait Exercise Number Two:
The Photographic Self-Expression.

Use a Polaroid or a 35mm regular camera to take your own photo.
Sure, you could take one by holding your arms straight out and shooting,
but you could also take photos of your various parts:

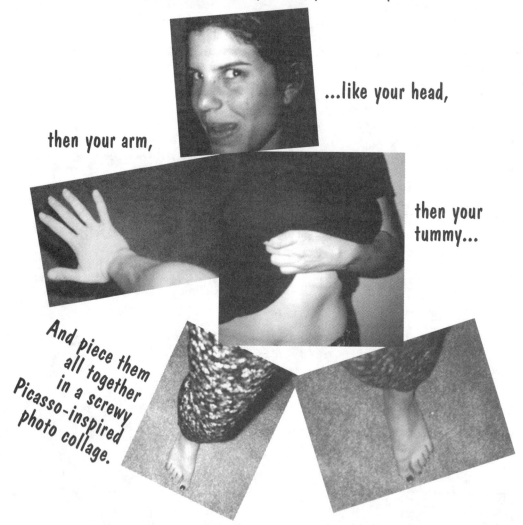

...like your head,

then your arm,

then your
tummy...

And piece them
all together
in a screwy
Picasso-inspired
photo collage.

*See David Hockney's Polaroid works for inspiration.

EVERYONE MUST HAVE THEIR OWN SPECIAL CHALICE...

Keva's lipstick Print *

Keva is....

dangling faux Pearls

lucky penny

loads of glitter

nail stickers

beads from old sweater

* MAC Rocker

AKA, a goblet or cup.

It's the very best if made by someone else, so make your friend one and hint to her to make you one. It should be in the style of a goddess dedication.

First, a bit of smashing history. The chalice is associated with the female superforces in the universe, for instance: fertility, beauty, the earth, love and emotions, instinct and the mind. Pretty hot stuff, huh? Well, it gets better. You see, they say that the chalice is a receptacle of spirituality, and once held upright it is ready to receive. Held inverted (upside down) it is a symbol for realization. Neat, huh?

Now find the appropriate glass to start with. It should be bigger than the average one so it stands out in crowds. Plastic is A-OK. Get your craft basket. Spell out a name in glitter. Attach faux diamonds and pearls. Spray-paint gold or silver. However you design it, it should be regal. Give to your friend with a note (something like this, but wing it):

"This here goblet is from now on your goblet of love and worship.
Carry it and drink from it all drinks drunk from now on."

ok just for a day we want to be serious

Imagine you're a bright, smart young woman trying to get a job, but you don't have lots of money. But you need a nice outfit for the interview to get the job. But if you don't have a job, you likely don't have the money to afford a nice outfit for the interview. This is a classic Catch-22.

Dress for Success is a nonprofit organization that provides worktype nice clothes for women who are entering the workplace and don't have lots of money to spend on the stuff that makes you look like you're ready for action. See, women come into the Dress for Success locations around the country and they go through the racks and racks of clothes to find an interview suit or ensemble that fits them. Once they get a job, they can return and get another outfit, all for free. The organization depends upon ordinary folks to contribute their used bizness type clothes for women of all shapes and sizes.

So here's what you do. Find out where the closest Dress for Success (or similar organization) is. They have a website (www.dressforsuccess.org) you can go on and see all the locations. There are tons. Or search online for similar organizations in your neck of the woods. Contact them. And then help 'em out. It will take all of a few hours of your time and make you feel all warm and fuzzy inside. Even if you don't have clothes of this nature to donate, we bet a bunch of your mom's friends and neighbors do. So hit the street. Draw up a flyer, explaining what Dress for Success does and stating your mission: to collect used business and work-appropriate clothes for donation. Give a day and a time you'll pick up the stuff. And then drop these flyers off at the various houses in your neighborhood.

Remember to actually go back on that specific day and time and pick up the clothes. Package them up and send them off to Dress for Success. (They'll give you a receipt for tax purposes and if you have a job, this will mean a bigger tax refund for you in the end. Not that that is a good reason to do this, but it doesn't hurt.) Collecting clothes for women going back to work is just plain rad. Plus, this will be a super fun way to get to know your neighbors.

DRESS for success!!!

HOW COOL ARE YOU?
HOW STOKED ARE THEY?

Grab a favorite photo, old or new, or even take a new one if you've got a Polaroid handy. Stamp it, write a short cute little note and send it to someone you haven't talked to in a least six months.

Just imagine how you would feel getting a postcard from an ol' pal. It would probably make you feel darn good that someone just thought about you enough to do that.

Ideas for cool postcards: A photo that you've written on and stamped. A magazine collage glued to cardboard. A seven-inch record that you slap a stamp on, writing all over the label. (The U.S. Postal Service WILL deliver it!) An ode (see January 3) that you wrote all fancy style on beautiful card stock. A small piece of thin wood panelling that you've written a note on in Magic Marker.

P.S. KEVA ONCE MAILED AN AVOCADO. YEP, AN AVOCADO. THROUGH THE UNITED STATES POSTAL SERVICE. SHE DID. REALLY.

photo by the fabulous miki v.

MAY

"Maypole is on the schedule."

"May is a nice name."
"May-be i'll have tacos."

"May i go to the beach?"

Celebrate MayDay!

As far as we can tell there are a bizillion traditions that
go along with May Day, all depending on where you live in the world, what
your politics are, how old you are and how free you are with your imagination.
In England, we read that many a people used to don big ears and tall
conelike hats and walk around telling people they were, um, elves. Whatever.

You could grab your giant fake ears and a cone hat or you could go
the Hawaiian way. There, it seems, May Day is Lei Day. On this day, school
children and adults alike make their own leis and wear them to school or
work and they have contests determining whose lei is the most lucky,
luscious and/or ludicrous. In other parts of the world, many people take
this day to listen to subversive folk music. Hey, it's a tradition.
We suggest listening to Ani DiFranco. We bet she'd have no problem
joining in on that elf thing, either.

An old May Day tradition involves dancing around the Maypole. Now,
this tradition sounds quite fun in fact. Find a pole, any pole (the street
sign works), and proceed to dance around it joyously. There is one more tradition
that takes little effort but will be oh so worthy. Clip some flowers from your
garden or buy some at the corner stand. If you have extra baskets lying around,
by all means, put the flowers in a basket. Or wrap them in wrapping paper
cones. Or stick them in old jars. And then secretly tiptoe over to a
neighbors' house and leave them on their doorstep. You can ring and
run, if you like. Watch from behind a bush as they open their door and
see their beautiful surprise. And don't tell who left them.
Let them think it was the May Day elf.

Help! i can't draw
a Maypole!

This is Clea's own jalopy, a '67 Jeepster!

Maybe you don't drive. Perhaps you do. But chances are you are dreamy for some shiny new car. We would like to take this opportunity to tell you about the joys of junky cars. Or, rather, old funky cars.

THE FOLLOWING ARE VERY GOOD REASONS WHY JAUNTY JALOPIES ARE THE BEST:

1. Never need to wash it (it would look the same anyhow).

2. You can enter the car "Dukes of Hazzard"–style without hurting the vehicle.

3. Step on the car. Stand on it. Sit on it. You won't really hurt it.

4. You can "customize" such a car: glue trinkets/baubles to the dashboard, let your art student pal paint a mural on the side, add welcome mats to the floors.

5. Ripped seats? One word: duct tape. (Okay, that was two words.)

6. Repairs are cheaper on old cars. It's a fact.

7. Drink spillage is not a problem.

8. Trash? No problem, toss it in the backseat.

9. Junkyards are a fun place to look for accessories.

10. Those little smelly trees simply look better in old cars. (They look out of place in new ones.)

11. They're unique, one of a kind, and no one will have the same car as you.

12. And they are CHEAP—that way you can buy more clothes!

GROW! NOW!

EVER WONDER why your hair seems to never grow past, say, your shoulders or your collarbone or your midback? It's different for all of us, but don't think just because you WANT to grow your hair down to the floor, that you actually CAN.

Keva: That is so mean.
Clea: No, it's not. It's science.

Or at least I thought it probably was, so I called a doc who specializes in hair growth. Hey, they have doctors for everything these days. Apparently every region of your body has a particular growth phase and then a "resting" phase. The hair on most folks' heads has a growing cycle between two and six years. Then it takes a breather. Usually for about two to three months. If your hair just doesn't seem to grow past your shoulders, you probably have a short growing cycle…and there is nothing you can do about it.

Keva: You are so so so mean.
Clea: No, no, no, it's just physical, natural science.

In contrast, your eyelashes grow for just seven weeks or so. Then they rest for a long time, several months even. Then when the resting cycle is over and the new growing cycle has begun, the new hairs push out the old hairs. Which leads us to the shower. After you take one, you probably leave behind a few long head hairs. More hair, some times, than others. These are your hairs that have endured the metaphorical rough school year, relaxed all metaphorically summer long and now are being moved out by some younger, bouncier freshmen hairs. You can tell the old hairs by that little white root at the end that the doctor called a "club." You can safely shed dozens and dozens (even a hundred or more) a day. It's healthy.

Keva: Healthy, maybe, but mean.
Clea: No, not mean, it's natural life, exciting and interesting and, well, it's science.

¡PIÑATAS!

TO MAKE A HUGE TENNIS-
BALL PIÑATA GATHER UP
THE FOLLOWING ITEMS:

1 round balloon
blown up
to about 11"

*

Newspaper strips
(Tear the newspapers—
don't cut and don't ask
why, it's just better.)

*

Flour-and-water paste
(one part flour to two
parts water)

*

Rubber cement

*

Tissue paper, yellow
like 10 sheets, each
about 20" x 30"

*

Small paintbrush

*

Masking tape

*

Scissors

*

Pencil or crayon

*

Light hemp rope

*

CANDY & TOYS!!!

The piñata, traditionally Mexican although originally from Italy, is the one party object that works for all holidays and events. So when in doubt, have a piñata! Olé! You make it, you fill it with candygoods, you hang it from a tree and you blindfold your pals. Then they get to swing at it with a baseball bat or broom. ARRIBA! ARRIBA!

How to make your own PIÑATA!

Wet paper strips in paste (best to mix paste in old throwaway plastic container of sorts) and cover the balloon. Apply four layers of newspaper. But don't do more than four layers or NO ONE will be able to break la piñata!

Let balloon dry. Take a pin and deflate the balloon. Take your rope and circle the piñata form and secure with masking tape. Be sure to make a loop at the top. Cut the hole for the candy and stuff the sweet stuff in! Make sure it's big 'nuff!

Paint on more paste and then layer on the yellow tissue paper. Use a black marker to draw on the tennis ball lines and voila, hang your piñata!

* Alert, alert, this can get messy, so be sure to do this outside or cover the dining room table with old sheets. The paste sticks and dries and if you don't cover the table, you'll find yourself scraping paste off with your fingernails during family dinners.

Oh, see tomorrow for the piñata party.

Today is CINCO DE MAYO, which translates to the Fifth of May. Get it? Cinco de Mayo is the perfect day to have a piñata party. But first a bit of history...

In the mid 1800s the French occupied much of Mexico, but after the big battle of Puebla, where the Mexicans defeated the French, the Mexicans felt pretty good about themselves. It was sort of a turning point where they declared no more foreign occupation. **It's a very proud day.**

Cinco de Mayo, for some inexplicable reason, has become a bigger holiday in the United States with the Chicano population than in Mexico. There is often dancing and mariachi bands and parades to honor this sort of Mexican Independence Day (although the official Mexican Independence Day is in September). And occasionally there are piñatas. So grab your tennis ball and let's go.

tres flores

old jar

Pick a spot outside that has some room around it. Suspend the piñata by the rope at a height just above arms' reach (um, the arms' reach of the people who will be playing). The rope must be strung through the piñata's loop so it spins. The contestant is blindfolded (the best part) and then given a broomstick. The piñata is given a push. When it sways back and forth it's harder to hit. The player gets three tries. If you're tough, turn the contestant around in a circle three times to heighten the dis-orientation-ness.

After three tries the next person comes to bat and so on until some lucky dog breaks the piñata and the mad scramble for the candies begins!

Cinco de Mayo

May 6

IMAGINE YOU'VE WON
THE LOTTERY.

Because sometimes we get so caught up in the idea that everything cool costs good money (like Miu Miu purses and tickets to Hole), we came up with a list of cool cheap stuff to make any girl happy for less than $5.

Or even for free.

CALL 800 NUMBERS TO GET BROCHURES AND CATALOGS SENT TO YOUR FRIENDS' HOUSES. Like, a Cheese of the Month & Club brochure, the catalog for Sears, Neiman Marcus, Dean & Deluca or dEliA's. Just dream shopping is OK and one of Keva's favorite pastimes. *CLOTHESPINS ARE JUST SO NEAT. And they're cheap. Use them everywhere. Run a clothesline in your room and just hang stuff from it. Pictures and articles and your homework. *REAL ESTATE OFFICES HAVE COOL CALENDARS. So do Mexican taco shops. Just ask. *GLITTER AND GLUE ARE FABULOUS THINGS THAT COST LITTLE DOUGH. And they add sparkle and shine to everything. *MAGAZINES FROM THE THRIFT STORE. So they are a little old; they probably cost only a quarter. *FREE SAMPLES FROM BASKIN-ROBBINS. Keep the little pink spoon. *TELL THE WAITRESS (MUST BE AT A BIG CHAIN LIKE DENNY'S), THAT IT'S YOUR FRIEND'S B-DAY and after your lunch they might come out with birthday cake and sing to you. *NUTTER BUTTERS. The best cookies on earth. And cheap! *RED LIGHTBULBS add so much ambiance for such little cash. Make your room look like a Mexican restaurant with little effort. *XMAS LIGHTS FOR ALL YEAR ROUND. *JELL-O (so many flavors, so little time). *SATURDAY SHOPPING at the ultra-big grocery store where they have the ladies that set up the tables and make free samples of stuff like Vienna sausages with BBQ sauce. *ALWAYS HAVE JUICE ICE CUBES ON HAND. There's nothing better than grape juice frozen in ice cube trays. Especially as the weather turns warmer.

Adopted pets are cool.

Sometimes, when you are feeling down and icky, the only thing that can cheer you up is your dog or kitty. So sweet and soft and right there by your side. So cute and cuddly and quiet and not asking any dumb questions. So true, so real, so ready to please...and, and, what? You don't have a dog? You don't have a kitty? Oh, dear girl, now is the time to <u>adopt</u> a <u>pet!</u>

Did you know that each year thousands of unadopted cats and dogs at the animal shelters are euthanized (that means put to sleep)? Apparently not enough people adopt pets at shelters or get pups through rescue organizations. We think that sucks. (As you probably agree.)

So we are here to say today is the day to save a pet. Today is the day to love, and you know what? That little pup or big fat pug or little skinny cat are out there waiting and hoping that someone like you will come and take them home because they can't wait to love just YOU!

But before you head off to the pound or get online to look up rescue organizations, we think you should take a minute and honestly answer these questions. Can you have a pet? Will you take care of it? Is there room in your home? Do you have a yard? Can you afford the cost of the food and vet bills? If you answered "yes" to these questions then you are ready to adopt, but don't forget that it takes work. If you feel that you are ready, talk to your folks or roomies about it.

IN CASE YOU NEED TO SELL MOM OR DAD
A BIT MORE, HERE ARE SOME TIPS:

A pet will build your sense of security and self-esteem. (It's a proven fact.) A pet is a source of unconditional love. (We can never get enough of that.) A pet will help you act responsibly toward others. (Parents will LOVE that.) A pet is a valuable source of companionship. (Three cheers for cats...and dogs, too!) And lastly, if you cannot afford or care for a pet but you still got the love, we've got a tip. Those very organizations that find dogs and cats need volunteers to walk and cuddle the animals. You can be a borrowed mommy for some lucky cats and dogs. It's all the perks with no additional costs to you.

WOMEN WHO HAVE NFLUENCED MY LIFE, Part 2, by Keva Marie.

At Seventeen, i, keva marie,

was going thru my button phase. i had sewn buttons all over my black '80s style dance bustier and the lapels of my thrift store black tux jacket. it was a little eccentric, but i was proud.

it was around that time that i went with my dear girlfriend tricia to visit her aunt nancy kay in venice, california. tricia told me all about her aunt: how she was an artist, how she lived in a loft, how she made money by selling her art and how she was friends with all kinds of other artists. i was ecstatic. it was our first out of town girl trip together and i wore all my prized button-covered items.

tricia drove. we sang along to adam ant in the car. we got to venice around lunchtime, parked, found her door and rang the buzzer. she let us in, and up the narrow stairs we hiked. at the top, there she was, aunt nancy, with her long straight blond hair, her paint-stained big white shirt and black leggings, her bare feet and her two afghans clinging to her legs. once i crossed the threshold of that doorway, i think my life changed forever.

after the hugs and introductions, aunt nancy showed tricia and me around her loft. her place was in an old 1940 brick building and she had the whole top story. the office, the guest room, the white walls, the cement floors, the big long, tall dirty windows, the itty-bitty kitchen decorated with masks from all over the world, the bedroom with art on every inch of the walls and finally the studio.

ah, the bliss i felt when she led us down the long white hall into her studio. my eyes raced over the room. tables with paints sprawled all about, stacks of canvases, buckets of brushes and pens and pencils, piles of multicolored construction paper and every tool you can imagine. oh, and books, so many books. books on thai architecture, books on paul klee, andy warhol and even madonna. more books than i've ever seen in someone's house before.

i was overloaded. overjoyed. i had a flash. a moment of clarity: people do live art. women do make art for a living. it is possible to live in the blissful creation of your own devices. i decided right there and then that when i finally had my own home i would revel in its beauty. i would live in it to the fullest and one day, one day when i was able to do it, i would work at home and make art. but in the meantime, i continued to sew buttons on everything.

May 10

"books to sink my teeth into"

you've surely been clipping away like mad, collecting articles and pictures that remind you of where you want to live and visit, clothes you want to wear, jobs you want to have.

Because that's what the FUTURE FILES are all about. So perhaps reading magazines is all you want to do in your off hours, away from school. But maybe, baby, occasionally you are reading one of those magazines and it reviews a book that sounds deliciously devilish, or your friend mentions a good read. And you think, mmm, that sounds good. But then you forget about it. Hence the Future File: "BOOKS TO SINK MY TEETH INTO." Grab a folder, record jacket, you know the drill. Label it. And start cutting. And if a book or author's name just comes to you by way of mental telepathy, jot it down on a scrap o' paper. Scraps are allowed in the Future Files, too.

KEVA'S & CLEA'S BOOKS 'TO SINK OUR 'TEETHS' INTO FUTURE FILE:

"The Dog Who Loved Too Much" by Nicholas Dodman
"Hip Hop America" by Nelson George
everything and anything by Lynda Barry
Fearless series by Francine Pascal

"StarGirl" by Jerry Spinelli
"The Big Book of Urban Legends"
"The Saskiad" by Brian Hall
"Sexual Astrology" by Martine

the Joy of Knitting!
by Keva's nana

Here is that pesky EVIL EYE again!!

Whenever I, the all-mighty Superclea, get frustrated with someone's snottiness or sarcasm, I give them the 'evil eye'. It seems harmless enough but makes me feel sneaky-evil-cool.

One day Keva finally asked, "What exactly is this 'evil eye' you so willfully dole out?"

"It's evil, it's, um, well I sort of arch my eyebrow and, um, stare for that extra second and, um — I dunno!?"

Not much of an answer. So I looked it up, with the help of Keva, of course.

As far as we can tell, it goes back as far as time itself. The evil eye shows up in the literature and the history of so many cultures, from the Turks to the Chileans to the Romanians. Pretty much across the board, across the world and across time, the evil eye has meant a look inspired by maliciousness. What's more interesting is that the evil eye has been accused of causing everything from hangnails to hurricanes. So scared of the evil eye, many cultures have devised ANTI–evil eye. Many have withstood the test of time. For instance, did you know that the locket was not originally designed to hold a striking picture of an adorable loved one but rather to hold a tiny scrap of paper with the ANTI–evil eye prayer written upon it? And thick, dark eye makeup in India was worn not only to shield a woman's eyes from the dreaded evil eye but also to ensure that she wouldn't accidentally cast the evil eye on a friend or neighbor. And animal charms, now thought of strictly as "good luck" throughout South America, were initially instituted as acceptable jewelry to counteract the evil effects of the evil eye.

Clea: See, so my evil eye thing is actually an age-old custom and I am just holding up centuries and centuries of tradition.

Keva: Um, yeah.

Clea: Yeah, I didn't believe it either.

HEADDRESS: what one wears on one's head when one has dressed it up.

A headdress doesn't have to be a diamond tiara (but it can be, right?). Headdresses, no matter what the cost, will make you feel as if you're wearing a crown. Like a glorious princess. It's a head thing. Here are just a few of the fabulous headdresses you can create:

VISOR HEADDRESS.

It's hot and you're going to the beach. But first, grab some cardboard, scissors, a magazine, tape or glue, a stapler and two spare ribbons or shoelaces. Quick! Now cut a half moon shape out of the cardboard. Measure against forehead to make sure it seems to fit well. Make end tippy parts a bit longer than on the moon though. Now scan your mag and tear out some pictures you like. Glue them all over the visor. Staple the ribbons or shoelaces securely to both ends and tie behind head. Now you got your own designer visor just for the beach and it doesn't matter if it gets sandy, wet or blows away!

BIRTHDAY HEADDRESS.

Cut out the shape of tiara from cardboard. Paint red or your fave color. Attach string or ribbon and staple to sides. Glitter-a-fy. Attach huge feather to back, and voila.

INDIAN PRINCESS HEADDRESS. (SEE MARCH 9)

Buy leather shoelaces or cord from the bead shop. Grab some beads, too. Big beads. String them on the leather cord. Tie a feather or two on. Tie on your head. Not too tight, or you will invariably suffer from massive bead headaches.

The Sunflower, by your pal Keva.

May 13

The sunflower, the beautiful, gorgeous, happy sunflower, is not just one flower, but a cluster of over 2,000 tiny baby sunflower-flowers growing together as one big fabulous one. Ahem! Not only is Kansas the Sunflower State, but Mississippi has a Sunflower County and wait, sunflowers even grow in Italy! But the sunflower is native to North America. You see, the Indians ate the sunflowers and pressed the seeds to make hair oil. Hey, you already know that sunflower seeds are good eats. But did you know sunflowers are at least 3,000 years old?

Clea: Um, that's really old.

Keva: It's true. Those guys, who dig with tools, they found seeds in ancient clay that they say were 3,000 years old.

Clea: You mean archaeologists?

Keva: uh huh, those guys.

But what I like best about sunflowers is that they grow so easily and so tall and when you grow a lot of them you can hide in between the sunflowers and no one can see you. (Which is the best kind of hiding place.) Grow some sunflowers today—just toss a few sunflower seeds (they fall helplessly from sisterly tall sunflowers) into the dark fertile soil and ponder all this history stuff.

MOM

it's mother's day, silly. be nice.

Your mom was once a kid. A young girl. A teenager. And all that jazz. Do you know anything about that part or time of her life? Have you ever asked?

Well, today we think you should interview your mom.

Ask your mom (sweetly) if she has a half hour to give you today. Make a date. Look over our questions and then come up with a few of your own. Meet your mom this time as a woman friend or even as a stranger.

¡YO MAMA!

clea's mom, jo ann

Get comfy and get down to some interviewing. If it isn't possible to interview your mom, do not hesitate to ask another older like-a-mom woman who you would like to know more about. As for the questions, think about things that you don't normally associate with Mom. Like kissing. And school. And take it from there. Here are some suggestions:

What is her maiden name? What kind of relationship did she have with her mother? Her father? What was the best advice her mom ever gave her? What did she do for fun? Who was the first person she ever kissed? Did she ever date other people besides your dad? How did they meet? What kind of music did she listen to, books did she read and movies did she like? Who was her best friend? What was her friend like? What did they do? Where is her friend now? What was her favorite part of school? Her least favorite? What was she scared of as a young woman? Is her life like she thought it would be? What did she want to be when she was a little girl? Who does she take after more, her mom or her dad? Does she think life was easier then or now for a girl? Why?

Now come up with a few of your own questions...

keva's mom, karen

• M • O • M •

The calendar says it's Armed Forces Day.
You could explore a future in the Army, Navy,
Air Force or Marines. But that isn't our suggestion. In fact,
our suggestion is to don army green as a fashion statement and to

MAKE LOVE NOT WAR!

Let's say it again in French!
Faites l'amour, pas de guerre!!

Well, not literally. Hee, hee, hee. We're not advising anyone to do anything even remotely sexual in nature. We just think today should be about spreading the peace gospel. Reminding your friends and teachers and parents and strangers that fighting is not good. War is not good. Killing is not good. But loving people and loving the earth is good. Period.

Get into the whole groovy peace hippie vibe today and go with it. Randomly hand out daisies, reminding people to stop and smell the flowers. Listen to uplifting music wherein everyone gets along. Burn candles and think peaceful, loving thoughts, even about those girls in school you don't like. Talk to someone you usually don't talk to. It doesn't have to be for very long, but connect with someone momentarily. You're one step closer to everyone getting along.

If you have a brother who owns little green army men, ask if you can play with him. Make little itty-bitty peace necklaces for all of them. Put them in a circle and pretend they're singing "Kumbaya." Snip off

TIPPING

by Keva la Diva
(Or that's what they called me at Carlos Annie's Café, anyway.)

WHO DO YOU TIP?
WHEN TO TIP?
HOW MUCH TO TIP?
ARE YOU CONFUSED?

I sure was but now I'm not.
I did some research.
I also was a waitress.
It helped. I also once dumped a guy because he always tipped like poo. Shame on him.

CLEA: HIM WHO?
KEVA: UM, I FORGET.

So here you go, on your way to a more informed life.

*If you're dating someone who can't tip, feel free to copy this page and give it to him, courtesy of us.

So, here's the deal. If there is one thing to know about tipping, it's this: If someone helps you out, they deserve a bit of appreciation. And yes, that includes pouring you those delish iced lattes you are so very addicted to. What that means is 15-20% extra on top of the price of the meal, the haircut, the nail job, the what have you, comes out of your mits and goes into the hands of the glorious guy or gal who did you right.

So from this day forth, please have greater respect for that soul who spends their nights and days working to bring you joy. To bring you exactly what you ordered exactly to YOU. I once lived off my tips. So did my GO-GO (my grandpa) and one day, maybe even as soon as this summer, you may have to as well. Be fair. Be nice. Don't underestimate the power of the karmic rule. And most important, don't forget to tip.

Now for the math lesson. Say the total was $15.90. Well, 10% of that is $1.59—easy to figure cuz you just move the decimal one to the left. So knowing that 10% = $1.59 (say $1.60—you round up to make the math easier), you double it to get 20%. If you wanna leave 15%, just add half of the 10%. (5%, duh) to the 10%. Voila. Tipping made easy.

P.S. You can thank us later when you suddenly get better at math.

$$\begin{array}{r} \$15.90 \\ \times\ .10 \\ \hline 1.590 = \\ \$1.60 \end{array}$$

20%   2 × 1.60 = 3.20

15%   1.5 × 1.60 =
(1.60 + .80 = 2.40!)
                    ↑ 1/2 of

YUM. FAIRY TOAST.

Today we introduce you to one of life's finer secrets.
Fairy toast. It's Australian, although we hear the Dutch
have something like it, too. It's breakfast, it's lunch, it's
not really dinner, but it is the best snack ever.

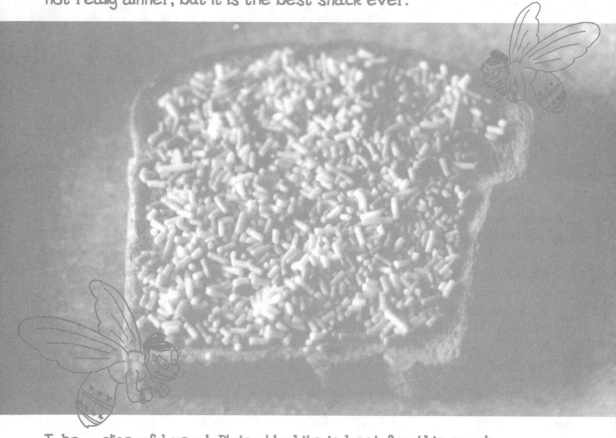

Take a slice of bread. Plain old white is best for this snack.
Toast it. Lightly. Spread a bit o' butter on it. And then cover it
in colorful "jimmies" or sprinkles like you put on sundaes. And
then stick it back in the toaster oven for just a second so it
heats up a bit more but not so much that the delicious sugar
topping burns. Wait a moment for it to cool and then eat. Yum.

Girls and glasses and what folks think of the girls who wear them.

We took a citywide survey and found that most boys have a hankering for girls who wear glasses. They say it has something to do with the girl looking smartlike (which we also found that boys love) and then imagining the wild girl hiding behind those specs.

Apparently that makes them ga-ga. Keva is convinced that when she wore her glasses to one of her first dates with her beau Tim, it was the icing on the cake and he was sunk after that day. Tim didn't care that Keva had to wear glasses that night because she drove and Keva has the kinda glasses you need when you drive at night. To Tim it wasn't about safety, it was about the look and the feel, and apparently it drove him nuts (well, OK, it was about both). Now he is as devoted as they come.

The moral of the story—glasses are sexy and if you have to wear them you should be proud. The boys will see that you are in fact smart and that drives boys nuts, although when they are young and dumb it kinda scares them so don't fret because eventually they figure it out. So, girl, strut your stuff and wear those glasses. Let them be an expression of who you are. Or even a sneak peek at the other side of you. Like your personality is quiet but your frames are bright and vivid red.

And if you don't like your current frames, don't forget that you can put prescription lenses in most vintage frames or even sunglass frames. That's what Keva did. And it seems to be working.

IMAGINE...
you are FAMOUS

keva!

clea

May 19

→ name in lights!

OR THAT SOMEONE WANTS TO DO A FEATURE STORY ON YOU, THE WONDROUS YOU. (JUST GO ALONG WITH US HERE.) MAYBE BECAUSE YOUR BAND IS PLAYING AT THE LOCAL CAFE. OR MAYBE IT'S BECAUSE YOU'RE JUST SO DARNED NEAT-O. ANYWAY, THIS COULD HAPPEN TOMORROW, SO WHY NOT MAKE A PRESS RELEASE ALL ABOUT YOUR BAD SELF TODAY.

Grab a piece of paper and write your name at the top. Start listing your finest moments. Write 'em all seriouslike because it is, after all, a press release.

THINGS TO MAKE NOTE OF:

SCHOOL ACHIEVEMENTS.
Such as a particularly good grade in a class or on a paper. By day are you known as a fast talker? The best dressed? A total joker?

YOUR INTERESTS.
Do you love music? Boys? Your dog Josephine? Do you love the intrepid, virile works of Shakespeare?

PERSONALITY TRAITS.
Are you reckless? Opinionated? Obsessive? Incredibly slobbish? What do people say about your personality?

ACTIONS.
What have you done lately that is oh so worthy? Redesigned your room? Finished a terrific book? Walked in a walkathon that benefited a women's shelter?

TYPE IT UP ALL NEAT AND WHEN YOU'RE ALL DONE, READ IT AGAIN: DO YOU LIKE THE SOUND OF YOU? ARE YOU ALL THE THINGS YOU WANT TO BE? BECAUSE YOU SHOULD BE. AND NOW IS THE TIME (WELL, ALL TIME IS THE TIME, BUT WE DIGRESS...) TO START NEW THINGS AT SCHOOL, DISCOVER UNCHARTERED INTERESTS, TO BEGIN AGAIN. WHEN YOU ARE SATISFIED THAT THIS LITTLE EXERCISE HAS FORMALIZED YOUR PERSONALITY AND GIVEN YOU NEW DIRECTIONS AS WELL, PLACE IT IN AN ENVELOPE MARKED "ME" AND STASH IT IN YOUR DESK DRAWER FOR FUTURE CONTEMPLATION. OR FOR WHEN THAT JOURNALIST COMES KNOCKING ON YOUR DOOR.

P.S. We wouldn't mind at all if you mailed us a copy of your press release. In fact, we'd love it.

Popcorn is one of nature's best, most well conceived foods.

And then those microwavable folks had to go and mess with it, making microwavable popcorn, which smells something akin to the devil bathing in a tub of lard.

You hate it.
But you can't help but remember how quick and effortless microwavable popcorn is. Well, fear your microwave no more. This is what you do:

Grab a brown paper lunch bag or even a paper grocery bag. No words on it. No ink on it. Put 1 cup popcorn kernels inside. Fold top over three times. Stick in microwave. Hit 7 minutes (it will not take this long). Stand nearby but not too near by (we still don't totally trust microwaves) and wait for popping sound to start and then slow down. When it slows, stop microwave and carefully, we mean CAREFULLY, open bag (it's full o' hot steamy steam). Pour popcorn into a bowl, add salt and any other seasonings (Chili powder? Garlic salt? Yeast? Real BUTTER!) and devour in front of TV.

P.S. Keva's mom tried it in a brown paper shoe box because she didn't have any paper bags. It worked and then she used the box as a bowl!

Make some popcorn and then pick an actor or a topic and get thee to a video store pronto. Seek the help of your friendly video store clerk. Buy the biggest box of Milk Duds you can find. And host a movie day with your random theme du jour.

Especially good for sick, sad and brokenhearted days.

MoViE DaY
* with Shannen Doherty
¥ star of stage & screen!! *

We spent the afternoon watching Shannen Doherty movies. Why, you ask? Because Shannen has the distinction of being one of those child-teen actresses who reinvents herself on a regular basis. Plus, Clea owns the Shannen Doherty doll, so it was an easy choice. And because Shannen's been very, very bad ("90210") and pretty darn good ("Charmed"). There are a couple of decent Shannen flicks, a couple of trashy but fun ones and, of course, one of the best movies ever, "Heathers." Other movies we watched during our Shannenfest — "Night Shift": Shannen's character is called Bluebird. Blink, and you miss her. In fact, she's the very last actor listed in the credits. "Girls Just Want to Have Fun": Very cheesy, very worth renting. Once again, Shannen's part is negligible, but still so worth it. "Naked Gun 33 1/3": Shannen plays herself in an uncredited role. This was in the middle of her bad reputation phase. "Mall Rats": Finally she has a starring role. She plays Rene, a smart and sassy ex-girlfriend to ex-skateboarder Jason Lee.

Keva: Why shannen?
Clea: Why not.!

All hail Shannen!

Here is Shannen on the side of a bus.

You guessed it babe, it's Victoria Day

Victoria Day is a holiday in Canada that celebrates Queen Victoria. She inherited the throne in 1837 at 18. She married her cousin, as royalty has been prone to do. ("Eww" is all we have to say.) But nobody can say she was not devoted. They had nine kids. She was a popular queen in her early years. But she was queen during the Potato Famine of 1845 and she continued to permit the export of grain and cattle from Ireland to England while over a million Irish peasants starved to death. That was lame. The whole Victorian era is named for her. After her hubby's death she became obsessively depressed and developed a fear of leaving her home (this is called agoraphobia). She died in 1901 after 64 years of rule. These books get you with the romance and the action and the intrigue, but they also deliver on beautiful fun-to-read-out-loud (makes you sound like a princess) prose.

Take this day to celebrate Victorian literature and art and to discover the innovations of the time. We're talking roughly 1830 to 1900.

Yo. OK, some more history coming your way. This stuff is cool, promise.

♀THE BRONTË♀ ·SISTERS·

Anne

Emily

charlotte

The Victorian era saw some of the first women writers achieve notoriety for their works. From one household came the likes of three sisters, all writers: Anne, Charlotte and Emily. We're talking Brontë, baby.

Anne Brontë is the least known of the sisters. Her books are righteous little tales of humiliation and consequences. A little boring, but not bad.

Emily Brontë, best known for her famous "Wuthering Heights," wrote very uncharacteristically for the era. See, traditionally Vic Lit spoke of the hardships of life, of family and home and the surroundings, but Emily's book delved far more into these truly fantastic characters and their inner workings, their overly intense feelings for one another and, well, this book rocks.

But it was Charlotte Brontë, who made her living as a writer and who broke the most barriers. She listened to what the trends were at the time. People wanted action! Romance! Intrigue! And she delivered (read "Jane Eyre," a genius book), but all the while, she sent home the message that women need to be independent, smart creatures and not solely dependent upon a man's love.

Other Victorian writers include Elizabeth Barrett Browning, Tennyson and Dickens.

We talk country talk.
For your listening pleasure.

Clea: Real country music is great. Polyester plastic Disneyland country music is scary.

Keva: Um, explain please.

Clea: Like, Hank Williams = good
Garth Brooks = bad
Dolly Parton = good and bad
New alt-country like Wilco = good
Vince Gill = bad
Rockabilly = good

Keva: What about Dwight Yoakam? (AKA country HOTTIE.)

Clea: Dwight Yoakam = good, very good.

Keva: He was so hot in "Red Rock West." Did you see that? Ah, so hot and those tight jeans. What else has he been in?

Clea: He was in that "Sling Blade" movie. He played the bad guy that John Ritter had problems with. Can you think of anyone else who can pull off tight, tight jeans like that and look so very good?

Keva: No. Well me. I can.

Clea: That's true, you wear tight denim well. Not me, though. Well, not true, I can wear anything I darn well please.

Keva: Do they make cowboy boots with platforms?

Clea: Oh, what a fabu idea! What color are your boots?

Keva: Red of course. All viva cowgirls wear red boots. Red boots and spurs!

Clea thought the picture of her for this page wasn't so good, so she put Georgia the dog in her place.

DISCUSSION QUESTIONS → DO YOU LISTEN TO COUNTRY MUSIC? THE DISNEYLAND KIND, THE SWINGING OLD KIND OR THE OTHER ALTERNATIVE KIND? IN YOUR OPINION, IS DWIGHT YOAKAM A HOTTIE OR NOT? DISCUSS. HOW DO YOU FEEL ABOUT COWBOYS? DO THINK THE GOOD ONES ARE ALL GONE?

Things that make you go, "Awwwww...!!!"

♥ xo ♥ xo ♥ o ♥ xo ♥ xo ♥ xo ♥ xo ♥ xo ♥ xo ♥ xo

When you were a kid did you have a blanket or a stuffed woobie that never left your side? It gave you comfort and security and satisfaction in an odd, little-girl-wants-her-teddy way. What we wanna know is, why can't we have that feeling as adults? Just because it isn't appropriate to bring your bee-bah to school or work doesn't mean we cannot find that special soft and familiar something that brings us joy and keep it with us, always.

CLEA'S UGLY BUT SOFT-SOFT SWEAT SHIRT

Story time. This one is from Clea:

"I have this hot pink sweatshirt that I have had for like 12 years. It's worn out so thin and so soft and I love it. My boyfriend hates it. He can't think of anything more '80s, more obnoxious, than a stretched-out, hot pink sweatshirt. But if I put it on, I feel instantaneously happier, more comfortable, more relaxed and all around more joyful. So I wear it. Despite his protest. In fact, if it's summertime and it's too hot to wear a sweatshirt (even a ridiculously thin one as this), I sleep with it. All curled up, like my baby blanket from years gone by."

So why did we just tell this story? Because you know you have pieces of clothing that are ratty or unstylish but oh so comfortable and we don't want you to throw them out because they are unfashionable or embarrassing. These are your comfy clothes. They are for wearing around the house when you feel sick or depressed. They are for balling up blankie style and sleeping with when you are extra tired. And if they are thin, they are for wearing under your clothes on those days when you need a little extra oomph of support and power. (Speech days, for instance.) They are pure comfort. They are security. They are familiar. They are your friend.

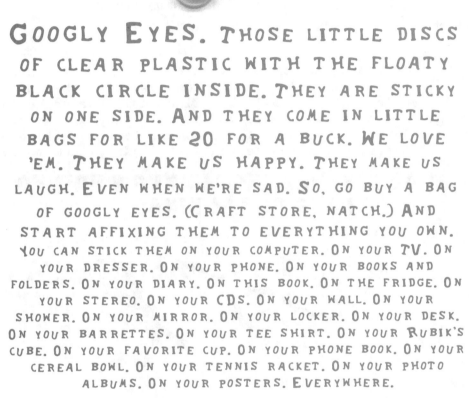

GOOGLY EYES. THOSE LITTLE DISCS OF CLEAR PLASTIC WITH THE FLOATY BLACK CIRCLE INSIDE. THEY ARE STICKY ON ONE SIDE. AND THEY COME IN LITTLE BAGS FOR LIKE 20 FOR A BUCK. WE LOVE 'EM. THEY MAKE US HAPPY. THEY MAKE US LAUGH. EVEN WHEN WE'RE SAD. SO, GO BUY A BAG OF GOOGLY EYES. (CRAFT STORE, NATCH.) AND START AFFIXING THEM TO EVERYTHING YOU OWN. YOU CAN STICK THEM ON YOUR COMPUTER. ON YOUR TV. ON YOUR DRESSER. ON YOUR PHONE. ON YOUR BOOKS AND FOLDERS. ON YOUR DIARY. ON THIS BOOK. ON THE FRIDGE. ON YOUR STEREO. ON YOUR CDS. ON YOUR WALL. ON YOUR SHOWER. ON YOUR MIRROR. ON YOUR LOCKER. ON YOUR DESK. ON YOUR BARRETTES. ON YOUR TEE SHIRT. ON YOUR RUBIK'S CUBE. ON YOUR FAVORITE CUP. ON YOUR PHONE BOOK. ON YOUR CEREAL BOWL. ON YOUR TENNIS RACKET. ON YOUR PHOTO ALBUMS. ON YOUR POSTERS. EVERYWHERE.

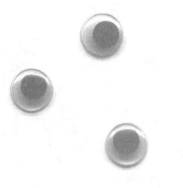

May 26 Knots

Knots

You're walking the apartment building ledge of the rat who stole the sacred jewels of Timbuktu. You need to jump down to the balcony below to make your surprise entrance. You tie a slip knot and lower yourself down, then screech like a banshee as you pummel him to the ground...

...You're scouring the woods for the secret totems of Saskatchewan. The evil Bruno has hidden them and plans to come back for them later but you're on his trail. You find them, buried behind the giant frog's lair, only to discover they are awkward and larger than you imagined. No problem. You tie a square knot around the bundle and easily carry them to safety.

EVERY GOOD SPY GIRL SHOULD KNOW HOW TO TIE KNOTS OF ALL KINDS.

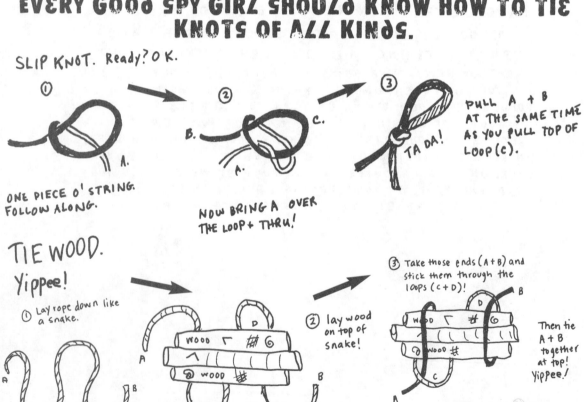

SLIP KNOT. Ready? O.K.

① ONE PIECE O' STRING. FOLLOW ALONG.

② NOW BRING A OVER THE LOOP + THRU!

③ TA DA!

PULL A + B AT THE SAME TIME AS YOU PULL TOP OF LOOP (C).

TIE WOOD. Yippee!

① Lay rope down like a snake.

② lay wood on top of snake!

③ Take those ends (A + B) and stick them through the loops (C + D)!

Then tie A + B together at top! Yippee!

THERE ARE SOME THINGS THAT HAVE A MILLION USES.

For instance, did you know that most Mormons don't drink soda but many do use it to clean toilets? And did you know that a few squirts of window cleaner on a sheet of newspaper cleans windows better than paper towels?

We think that's cool, impress-your-friends-with knowledge. Plus, like we always say, you never know when you may get in a jam. So today we wanted to enlighten you to the amazing alternative uses of one of those standard household items that you will never again think of as boring: VINEGAR! Today you learn six fancy uses for vinegar—tomorrow, anything is possible!

1. Do you have dry hair? Mix one cup apple cider vinegar and two cups water. Shampoo hair. Rinse out with the vinegar mixture. This cheapie beauty magic will add highlights to brown hair and remove soap film and oils. Who knew?

2. Do you have unsightly warts? Just mix one part apple cider vinegar to one part glycerin in your favorite lotion. Apply daily and say bye-bye to your little warts.

3. Do you have an ugly hacking cough? Get rid of that hack! Mix 1/2 cup apple cider vinegar, 1/2 cup water, one teaspoon cayenne pepper, and four teaspoons honey. Drink up a teaspoon whenever you feel the need to hack.

4. Do you got the hiccups? Mix one teaspoon apple cider vinegar into one cup warm water, and drink. Slowly and quietly.

5. Do you got an itch? Douse a cotton ball with vinegar and dab mosquito and other bug bites. It's soothing.

6. Did you get sunburned? (Bad girl, next time wear sunscreen.') If you apply vinegar all over the red hot area it will relieve some of the discomfort.

7. Do you love your hot pink tank top? Prevent it from fading by soaking it in white vinegar for ten minutes before you wash it.

OK, that was seven, but who cares, they were all good. 'And a word about the aforementioned sunburn: Once, when Keva fell asleep before she applied her sunscreen on the beach in Cabo San Lucas, she got so burned that not only was the rest of her vacation spent in the hotel room under sheets, but she had really bad tan lines for two years. Two years! Watch out.

May 28

BANK HOLIDAY
ye will spend no moola today.

This is a very simple day.
It's what they call a bank holiday in England. Stores shut down, the banks shut down. It gives everyone a rest from the commercialism that is rampant today. So what does that mean to you? It means no commerce. Do not spend money today. Do not go shopping today. Do not go to the movies today. Do not go out to eat today. In fact, take a moment to think about how much money you do spend. And what on? Today you get a respite from mad consumerism. Take special note of all the free things in your life. The smell of your neighbor's flowers. The smell of boys' necks. The smell of your dog after she rolled around in the freshly mowed grass. Ahhh. And always remember, reading is free.

Not really a holiday but we can celebrate it nonetheless

pictures of us spending quality time at the bank

teepee*tutu

Make a teepee in the backyard, Lightfoot-Moongirl. Did you pick a name for yourself on Indian Princess day? If not, do so now. Very important.

Grab some supplies:

Blankets, at least two, rope and a bunch of two-inch binder clips from the office supply store. Metal clamps from Home Depot work, too. Now, if you're saying to yourself right about now, "Why would I want to make a Teepee Tutu—I'm too old for that?" then all we have to say is pshaw.

Small hiding places make getting away from the madness that is your life all that much more fun. Or heck, just make it for your friend's birthday.

Steps: 1. Tie the rope around a branch of a tree. 2. Take the metal binder clips and secure the two blankets (or more!) together. 3. Then clamp the blankets' top part to the rope so the blankets hang down teepee style. 4. Gather a few rocks and place them on the bottom of your teepee to keep it secure.

Now put cute stuff inside. Pillows. Blankies. A flashlight for reading and a couple of books. Do a rain dance every hour on the hour. Crawl inside. Pray to the Indian moon god for great friends, brilliant futures and cute lovers. And ayy ay ya!

KEVA: HEY, CLEA, I MADE YOU A TEEPEE FOR YOUR BIRTHDAY!

CLEA: UM, OK. THANKS.

We speak SPANISH
(well, sort of...)

You already know Spanish can be a beautiful and exciting language, don't you? But have you tried using it to flirt with cute Spaniards? Have you used it to communicate with your friends in front of nosy, Spanish-ignorant people? Well, have you?? What follows is your first lesson, and even if you speak Spanish already, the following will be rather informative. Olé!

keva chattin' up some Spanish

clea going at it

Stay away from him, he's bad news.
Estancia lejos de él, él es malas noticias.

You know I can talk like a frog.
Usted sabe que puedo hablar como una rana.

Ribet ribet.
Ribet del ribet.

Let's go shopping for sequins.
Vayamos a hacer compras para el sequins.

Personally I think he's a lot dumber than he looks.
Personalmente pienso que él es mucho más mudo que él mira.

I can communicate with my cat.
Puedo comunicarme con mi gato.

this bike needs what?

why, a basket silly :-

It's Spring now.

Hopefully you have a bike. If you don't, get one—scour the papers, ask for one for your B-day or next holiday, get a used one at Salvation Army, but get one quick. It's spring and bikes are fun. Spring and bikes are like Mike and Ikes. They go togetta. People in Italy ride bikes all the time.

OK, but we're not done yet because here we have a little something extra for ya. A little something extra special. That's right. We like to call it the "ultimate bike basket."

Now go out and get yourself a cheap, ordinary, run-of-the-mill bike basket. Get some sheet moss at the local plant nursery or hardware store or big Wal-mart type store that has a garden department. Line the basket with the sheet moss; this acts as a liner of sorts. Next you'll be needing some dirt. You could buy potting soil, or just dig a hole where the ground looks moist and dark and fertile. Fill up your basket. Plant some flowers...go for something sturdy like asters, daisies or marigolds. Remember to water your "bike basket" often and be sure to take it out for a spin like a few times a week to, you know, get some fresh air.

now get on your bike and ride

IT'S
JUNE!
HOORAY!

keva stops to smell the roses.

go ahead, you know what to do...

Start A BOOK CLUB!

(Like Oprah but better)

School is out. (Or nearly so.) And you might think, whew, a respite from all that reading. But the problem wasn't the reading, it was the books you had to read. Probably lots of dead white male authors. It's time to explore the oft-alive (occasionally dead) chick writers (although it certainly doesn't have to be limited to that).

By starting a book club (yet another excuse for a get-together) you can get the experience of reading (alone) and then talking about it (with friends). Which makes reading that much more enjoyable.

So you gather together a few like-minded friends. And pick a book. Everyone picks it up. (Library or bookstore.)

You give a time span during which the book shall be read. Make a date for the first club meeting. Make it far enough in advance that everyone can be done reading by then.

And you congregate. In a partylike atmosphere. With food. In fact, the food could be somehow thematically tied to the book. Like you read "Bridget Jones's Diary" (it's British) and you serve tea and crumpets at your meeting.

Discuss why you liked the book, who the most likable characters were, if the author was sending you, as readers, some sort of message and why. Who would play the main character in a movie? What character would you want to play? And on and on and on.

Then at the end of the meeting, you pick another book to read. And you start all over again.

* for good readin' try these!

gener-
ation
X

SMACK

THE
SECRET
HISTORY

anything by
Francesca
Lia
Block

June 2 TOP ROCK!

Every gal should know how to top rock. Why? It's the classic noninvolved dance move. It's breaking. And nothing is more cool than break dancing. Honest. You stand on the sides and sort of look like you know what you're doing, even if you don't. Plus, it's fun. And cool. Don't let anyone tell you otherwise. Get a couple of friends together and practice your moves, and you've got yourself a break dancin' team.

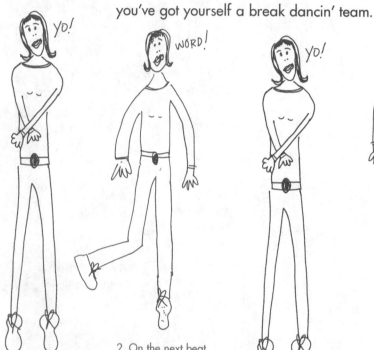

1. From a standing position, take a short hop forward on beat with the music to where both feet are even and slightly apart, while at the same time cross your arms in front of you.

2. On the next beat jump forward on your right leg with your left leg bent behind you and your arms pulled straight back. Your body should be turned slightly to the left.

3. On the next beat return to the first position, facing forward, feet apart and even, and your arms crossed in front of you.

4. On the next beat jump forward on the left foot with your right leg back and bent, your arms pulled back straight and your body turned slightly to the right.

**Rent "Breakin', the Movie" and "Breakin' II: Electric Boogaloo."

These steps are repeated until you, the breaker, are ready to go to the floor with a headspin or some other fancy footwork. Oh, but take any barrettes out of your hair before you try any headspins. You'll thank us.

THE OTHER... KEVAMARIE
by Keva Marie

There are times, in a slow brain moment, in a moment that's not filled with all the other things, that I get a chance to think of broader things. Bigger things. Life things. Stuff other than what logo I like or what shoes go with what dress. Those are the moments when I contemplate the world as I know it, the people I have met in all my years, the feelings I have about evolution, reproduction, world politics and so forth.

And it was during one of those moments that I found myself wondering if somewhere out there in the world there was someone else just like me. I even went so far as to think about other planets (maybe it was because the night before I had watched "Roswell," but maybe not). Regardless, I pondered the thought, I mulled it over, I fantasized. I thought about me in another lifetime, me as in someone with my name having the same-name experiences. And then one day not too long after my "period of deep reflection," it happened. I got an email from a girl named **Keva Marie.**

"Keva, this may sound weird, but my name is also Keva Marie. I was curious if you could tell me how you got your name. Mine is respelled from Chiva, it's Romanian and is a family name centuries old. Hope you'll answer me back. Thanks — Keva Marie — In MN"

So you can imagine how I must have felt. I thought about it for a minute, I said "weird" out loud for like five minutes and Clea thought I was being strange but, heck, what's a girl to do? I decided to bombard her with a battalion of questions and then compile my data into easy to read paragraphs, naturally. And let me tell you, the effect was truly amazing. So I invite all of you to find the other you. And when you do, let us know.

P.S. "Keva" in Greek means Friday. "Keva" in Romanian slang means Aphrodite—you know, the goddess of love.
P.P.S. By the way, "the other Keva Marie" found me on the Internet.

June 4 STOCKS

this is keva's artistic interpretation of a stock ticker, below.

WTSLA 28¼(+¾) NKE 14½(−½) BEBE 82¼(+

This is a very blatant lesson. It's about money. And stocks. But don't let the fact that this is a learning experience deter you because this could be fun, too. We think you should chart a stock for a while. We know, this is not school, but if you pick a company that sells stuff you use or a company that you could see yourself working for in the future rather than chart some faceless company you know nothing about, this will be fun. **Darn it.**

Stocks are shares in a company. When you invest in a company's stock or buy its shares, you own part of a company. Imagine saying you were a partner in dEliA's. It's traded on the stock market. Every publicly owned company is there. If the company makes money, your stock will increase in value. But there are serious pros and cons to stock investments.

Here are the cons: Stock prices go up and down, up and down and up and down... They are never guaranteed. Which means you can lose money. A lot of money.

Here are the pros: Stocks in general have a long historical track record of outperforming other investments, such as bank deposits, money-market funds, bonds and real estate. Also, a stockholder has voting rights. That means you may have a say in the direction the company goes. And you receive quarterly reports informing you of the financial health of the company. (Sort of like report cards.)

That's the basics. Tune in tomorrow when we explain HOW to track a stock in the newspaper. Oh, does it get more exciting than this? You're hoping, huh?

MMM... STOCKS

M-m-m-ore on stocks! Yippee! Hooray! Let's do a stock dance!!

So, you're sold, you say? On stocks, that is.

How do you do this? Well, if you were actually going to buy stock, normally you would research the companies (you can do this very easily online) and then you would find a broker. A stockbroker can give you guidance; a discount broker will just do the buying, period. Since you don't have actual money to invest at this moment (or maybe you do...), you just want to chart the stock's progress and see how much money you could have made (or lost) over a period of time. **Hey, it's good practice.**

FIRST, pick a company.

Decide how much imaginary stock you're going to buy. And then keep track of the growth and loss every week (or you could be obsessive and check every day) for a few months. This way, as we see it, you'll be prepared like a good Girl Scout when you got your own money to waste, oops, we mean invest.

To track how your imaginary stocks are doing, you have to look at stock listings. Stock listings are published in just about every newspaper. The listings are hard to read: lots of little itty-bitty numbers. But they are organized. They include the following information, in this order: 52-week high and low (shows how the stock has fluctuated recently), company name, symbol (their stock ticker, a few letters long), dividend (the cash amount that the company will pay you each year for each stock), percent yield (how much of the price of the stock you will be paid in dividends each year), PE ratio (the relationship between the price of a company's stock and the annual earnings of a company), volume (the amount of stocks that were traded the day before), high, low, close (the highest and lowest prices and closing price of the stock the day before) and net change (the change in the stock price from the day before).

Some publicly owned companies you could chart:

Steve Madden (SHOO)
Nike (NKE)

Abercrombie & Fitch (ANF)
Urban Outfitters (URBN)

The Gap
(GPS)

Wet Seal (WTSLA)
BeBe (BEBE)

WTSLA 28¼ (+¾) NKE 14½ (−½) BEBE 82¼

June 6

DEE-LISH ☆ DOGGY DONUTS

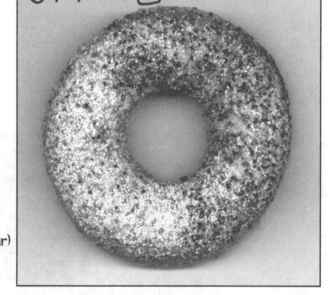

You need:

3 cups whole wheat flour

1 teaspoon garlic salt

1/4 cup bacon fat or meat

drippings or lard

(If you're stumped, ask Mom,

she should know.)

1 cup shredded cheese

(any normal cheese, like cheddar)

1 egg, beaten

1 cup milk

Preheat oven to 400 degrees. And grease some cookie sheets. Mix together flour, garlic salt, bacon fat (or drippings or lard), cheese and egg. Slowly add enough milk to form a dough. Put some flour on the counter or your cutting board. Dump the dough on the flour and knead. Then roll out the dough till it's one inch thick. Take a glass and cut out circles like it's a cookie cutter (or use a cookie cutter in any shape). If you're using a glass and want Doggy Donuts, poke a hole with your finger in the center. Place on cookie sheets. Bake for 12 minutes or until they are golden. Cool and store them in an airtight container. Feed to your dog when he or she has been extra good. (Or give to friends with dogs.)

SNAX

Of Famous people ... like our friends!

Everybody has favorite snax...

It's like having a favorite color. It's sorta a personality thing. Here are some favorite snax of our best pals. Try them, if you dare. You may be surprised. Remember, Elvis loved peanut butter and banana. And gosh, they are sooo darned good! Get yourself signature snax today so if you ever come to visit us we can have it ready for ya!

Our pal **Lisa B.**: Avocado and cottage cheese with a little bit of pepper. Why? We'll let her tell you about it. "Because you'd never expect it but the two textures go so well together." She says it tastes just like avocado-flavored ice cream.

Keva's illustrator friend **Amy Davis**: Nuggy nug. "Nuggy nug?" we asked. Yes, Nuggy nug. Apparently that is flour tortillas and maple syrup and butter all fried up in the pan. Sounds pretty yummy.

Sara Schwartz (an illustrator friend, too): Cheesecake toast. "I take a piece of hot toast, spread cream cheese on it thickly, then I sprinkle a little confectioner's or raw sugar on top! Mmm, it satisfies that craving for Sara Lee's. So, do I get a prize?"

Now make sure to request your favorite snax on your birthday and alternating Tuesdays.

*This is Clea's nasty, dirty dish towel in the background.

June 8

Welcome to the FUTURE FILES

Today's file involves scissors, magazines, a folder or record jacket and your crafty self. (OK, they all do, but...) Picture yourself reading a magazine or perusing the Internet. You come across an interview with someone or a profile of a unique individual. You think to yourself: "Ahh, I would like to sit down and have dinner with this person. I bet she would make sparkling conversation, make me laugh, and entertain and inform me. She is just plain cool."

Today's FUTURE FILE is dedicated to COOL PEOPLE. Simple enough, right?

Maybe it's the look in his eye in the photograph. Perhaps it's something she said. Or just an air about him. You want to remember this person. Cut out the article or photo or print it off the Internet. Or simply jot stuff down on a tidbit of paper. And before you drop the article, photo or tidbit into the FUTURE FILE, think to yourself..."Where would I have dinner with this person? What would he/she have? What would I have? What would we talk about? What questions would I ask?" Scribble these things in the margins of the article, on the back of the pic or in the corner of that tidbit of paper. Now place it in your file. Job well done.

inside Kera's COOL PEOPLE future file:

Madonna
Clare Crespo
Laura Begley
Lisa Ling
Shepard
Betsey Johnson

inside Clea's COOL PEOPLE future file:

Francesca Lia Block
Steve Buscemi (actor guy)
Jeanie M. (the gal who makes art out of dead mice)
David Bowie

No, this is not a negative thing. No, no. We're talking about demystifying something that people fear. And they shouldn't. Fear it, that is.

Everyone has it. You may get it. That head cheerleader at school. The Victoria's Secret model. Yes. Yes. Yes, they all have some of it. Some more than others but yes, they sure do. What are we talking about? Well, we're speaking of the mystifying, commonly misunderstood, often feared body "thing" we know as cellulite.

Ok, here's the deal: The French word for "cell" butted up with the suffix "-ite," (which literally means disease, but don't get stuck there) makes up the buzz word we commonly refer to as "cellulite." Which, girls, is not a disorder of fatty tissues, as commonly misdiagnosed in the past.

Cellulite actually has to do with the connective tissue in the body. Which leads us to the most likely cause: the oh so glorious female hormone estrogen. So, basically the very thing that makes us sexy and full breasted and, well, womanly, is the very reason we get cellulite.

So girls, fear not. The important thing here is to LOVE your bodies, your life, your freckles, the way you have a wiggle when you walk...and in a moment of doubt, take a look around. Take a good look at other women's bodies and notice there is no one perfecto shape. And, yes, even the lingerie model has got some of the real stuff.

June 10

SELF PARKING

Imagine you've been abducted by aliens.

Portuguese

otherwise known as (the) language of love...

Portuguese is a fascinating language.

It sounds a little like Spanish, with some French thrown in for good measure and then the occasional guttural throaty, phlegm-covered vowel or three. It is the language of Portugal and Brazil, two countries not located anywhere near each other. It is also fantabulously fun to speak. Loosen your throat muscles with a few mimi mimi mimis and then just go for it.

Keva pretends to be portuguese...

Clea, slightly embarrassed figures "what the heck" and goes for it!

Stop in the name of love!
Pare no nome do amor!

Your dog is cute...and so are you.
Seu cão é cute e assim que é você.

Would you like a Tic Tac?
Você gostam de um Tac Tic?

They make your breath minty fresh.
Fazem a sua respiração minty fresco.

Which is very important if you have future plans to kiss.
Qual é muito importante se você tiver as plantas futuras a beijar.

You spin me round round baby round round.
Você gira-me arredonda-se em volta do círculo redondo do bebê.

June 12
The joys of Tennis

And there are so many.
But here are just a few...

Short skirts, terry cloth wrist bands, **socks with little balls on the back,** ponytails, **boys in short shorts,** you get to say "love" and stuff, **the balls are neon green,** finding rackets at thrift stores becomes a new hobby, **tennis courts are everywhere (trust me, once you start lookin', you'll see),** did we say short skirts? (also a cool thing to find at the thrift store—they come in such cute colors), **polo shirts look great (find icky pink and yellow ones in the boys section at that same house de thrift and look so cool),** the balls make cool sounds, **you have to wear tennies and it's actually exercise, but fun.**

tennis is for Lovers

Now get yourself to a tennis court right quick.
And happy birthday to Keva's dad!

MACROBIOTIC DAY

Let's be macrobiotic for a day.

To be macrobiotic is to study prolonged life via special diet. It's about bringing your body closer to nature. It's based on whole grains and keeping harmony with the seasons. So you can be one with the little ferns and carrots and feel the wind in your body like the wind in the trees. It's about yin and yang and Bill and Jane. (Who's Jane? Um, nobody, we was just rhyming.)

Let's Make Sesame-Coated Rice Balls.

4 cups brown rice (prepared)
2 plums, cut into bite-size pieces
1/2 cup roasted sesame seeds

Wet your hands a bit. Take a cup of prepared rice and roll it into a ball. With your thumb, push a bit of a hole in the center of the ball and squash plum pieces into it and then close up the hole. Roll ball around in a buncha sesame seeds and eat. Yummy. Eat a bunch of these. Steam some veggies to go along with your sesame balls, but no overcooking. Veggies should be crunchy, no mush allowed.

Spend 15 minutes "reflecting."

Drink lots of water all day long.

No eating before bedtime.

No candy or caffeine.

Use pure soap and natural beauty products (skip hair spray today).

Don't use any positive-ion-producing appliances (which is all of them.)

Go to sleep at 9 p.m. Seriously.

And wake up extra early to do some stretching.

*We think you just might feel fresher and more alive!

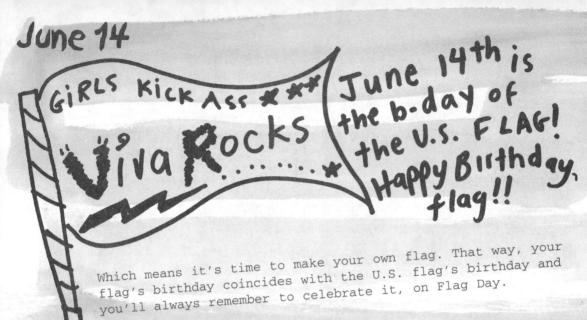

June 14

GIRLS KICK ASS ✱ ✱✱

"Viva Rocks ....✱

June 14th is the b-day of the U.S. FLAG! Happy Birthday, flag!!

Which means it's time to make your own flag. That way, your flag's birthday coincides with the U.S. flag's birthday and you'll always remember to celebrate it, on Flag Day.

Wanna big flag?
An old sheet will work.
More manageable size flag?
Nab a pillowcase.

Now get out the fabric paint or markers. Grab that needle and thread and those deliciously sparkly sequins.
And design your flag.

It should feature stuff about you. Your superhero name. Your favorite colors. Kissed two people? Add two stars! Mastered three skateboard tricks? Add three stripes! Dig the picture if you can.

When you're all done, fly that flag. It is Flag Day, after all! Be your own color guard (the gals and guys who raise and lower the U.S. flag). Where should you fly your flag? Your front porch. Off the big tree in the backyard. Or simply in your room, over your bed. And remember to fly it on all important holidays such as your birthday, Inauguration Day, Mother's Day, Independence Day, the third Tuesday of every month and the anniversary of "Grease," the movie.

Oh, and happy birthday, Grandma Ruthie.

Every town has got one...

It may be big like a mansion or small like a trailer. It may be at a college or even in a traveling bus, but all across America, you will find little kids sitting semicircle on the carpet as a Mister Rogers look-alike reads aloud to them the tales of "Green Eggs and Ham."

In any town on the map, you will find a cute old man in a cute old man's sweater sitting quietly at the table reading a Steinbeck novel. If you are lucky, you may also see some hipster kids pouring over the oh so very hard to come by 1970s issue of a "McCall's" magazine.

And if you are really really lucky, there may even be a cute bohemian boy with dark-rimmed glasses checking out the 30-year-old copy of "Gone With the Wind." To be a member only takes a few checks, a few dots and dashes. And the best thing is (unless of course you lose one of their precious items) once you're in, you're in. For life. That's right, for life. Welcome to the library, one of the greatest inventions of all time.

This is Eric. He works at the library.

And, hey, why not go today?

June 16

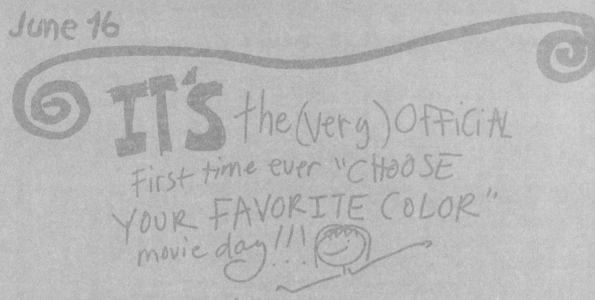

IT'S the (very) OFFICIAL

First time ever "CHOOSE YOUR FAVORITE COLOR" movie day!!!...

You could just rack your brain for movies with colors in the title. Or you could get yourself online (our favorite movie site is http://imdb.com/ otherwise known as the Internet Movie Database) and do a search for that color and marvel at all the movies that have been made with your favorite color in the title. Once you've got your list, grab your video rental card and a few best friends and get thee to a video store near you. For example, we choose blue because blue is cool.

So what's your favorite color?

"The Hunt for RED October"?

"The GREEN Mile"?

"The BLACK Hole"?

Or "PURPLE Rain"?

Mickey Blue Eyes

THE BLUES BROTHERS

deep blue Sea

BLUE LAGOON

My Blue Heaven

" i *love* blue faux fur. "

June 17

Clea: Look, I hate rodents, I mean, I am petrified of mice, rats, beavers, you name it. And a mink is just a rodent. But I still can't get into wearing it. It makes me feel beastly and not in a good way. They kill those little buggers in such an inhumane manner. Plus, fake fur is so very, very wondrous and extra soft and extra furry.

Keva: Well, maybe if Tim bought me a beautiful bright blue fake fur puffy coat I would feel like Cyndi Lauper and that's just as good, if not better.

Clea: Yes, better. Minks aren't blue. And yet it's such a fitting color for the fake variety.

Keva: I asked Tim if he would buy me one and he asked, "Um, what's our relationship in this fantasy?"

Clea: My boy would buy me a blue fake one in a heartbeat because maybe then I would stop wearing my ratty green corduroy jacket that I love but he hates. Do you own a piece of clothing that Tim does not like? He prolly likes everything of yours, huh?

Keva: If he didn't, he would never say. I would hit him. (Just kidding, beating up anyone is bad. Very bad.)

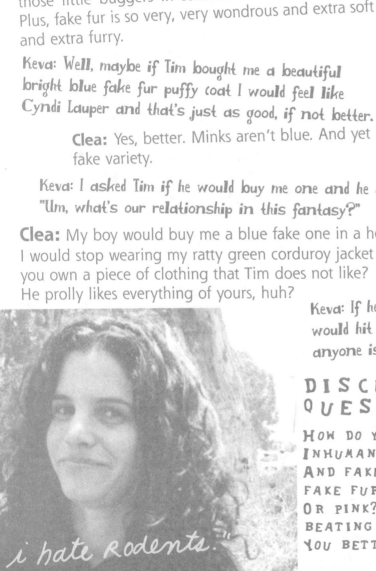

" i hate Rodents. "

DISCUSSION QUESTIONS:

How do you feel about fur? Inhumane? Or great fashion? And fake fur? Do you think fake fur is meant to be blue? Or pink? Do you agree that beating up anyone is bad? You better.

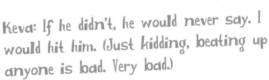

June 18

dear daddy
How i Love Thee...

Did you buy him a tie? Socks? Dads love socks. But they love photos of their little girls even more. **Make Dad a photo book.** (And if Dad ain't around these days, make it for your mom.) You could pick up a little scrapbook type blank book from the craft store. You could also cover the cover (ha!) with Astro Turf (from de hardware store). Especially good if Dad likes golf.

Hey, it's DAD'S DAY!

Happy Dad's day ♡ Me

Or you could make your own book. Take construction paper and punch a couple of holes in it.

You could make a cover from a thrift store record. Even better if you find a band Dad likes. Like Santana. Or War. Or Herb Alpert. Then take a few pictures of you (and siblings, if you got 'em) and glue them on the pages.

You could add a few words, too. Like, a poem. Or the words to a favorite (meaningful) song. Or just "I love you." Dad will cherish it forever and ever. Mom will be extra nice to you for at least two days. Trust us.

THE FIRST DAY & OF SUMMER

go clea go!!

Stuff like flip-flops.
And something terry cloth
and yellow.
And a beach chair.
And a beach ball.
Oh, and a new Lip Smacker
in a new flavor.
And sunscreen. Lots of sunscreen.
And lemonade. Make sure you
know how to make lemonade.
Or a fashionable sun scarf
(see tomorrow for details).
A bathing suit.

A beach bag.
An inner tube
(for pool, beach or river).
Sparklers. A big floppy hat.
Or a cool straw cowboy one.
Pinky lip gloss. Beach Boys CD.
Bandannas, Frisbees,
"Wahine" magazines,
beads for your hair,
beads to tie to the
strings of your bikini.
Paint your toenails all different
colors in honor of today.

first of all you need stuff:

And go to the freezer.
Empty out a tray of ice cubes.
Fill with juice and freeze.
When the cubes are
half frozen, stick a
toothpick in each.
Eat 'em the next hot day.
If you haven't done so already,
pack up all your worries and
all your winter clothes.
Label. (Ha!)
And stick under bed.
Far, far away.

Clip a
flower.
Put it in
your room,
next to your
bed in a jar.

If you don't have a pool
or a community pool or a
friend with a pool, go to the
drugstore and buy one
of those kiddy pools.
They are around ten dollars.
Put in your backyard and fill
with water. Place beach chair
in the pool. Sit and read your
book club book, sipping
lemonade with juice ice cubes,
and admire your multicolored
toenails. Ahhh, summer.

June 20

HOW TO MAKE A FASHIONABLE SUMMER HEAD SCARF.

YOU NEED:

Fabric. Might we suggest polka dots. Or anything yellow. Cloth ribbon. Needle. Thread.

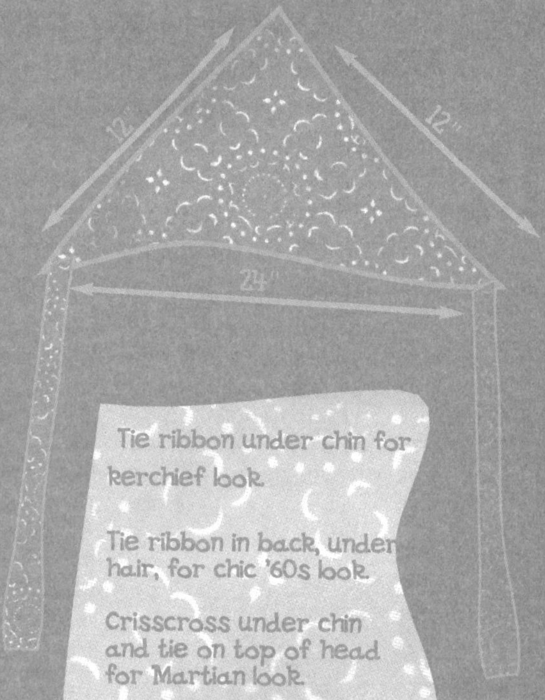

12" 12"

24"

THEE HEAD SCARF.

Cut the fabric into a triangle. If you have the time, sew a small hem around all edges. This will take a little longer but your scarf will last longer. Now cut two 12" lengths of cloth ribbon. Sew one piece on two neighboring corners like the picture. Place on head.

Tie ribbon under chin for kerchief look.

Tie ribbon in back, under hair, for chic '60s look.

Crisscross under chin and tie on top of head for Martian look.

Loosely tie in back and let strings hang down your bare back for playful wood nymph look.

Or wear around your waist for apron housewife look.

It's oh so versatile.

IT'S SUMMER NOW!!

(but you knew that, didn't you?)

It's time for baths. Long, languid baths. And this month's spa night is dedicated to baths.

THE SOFTENING MAGIC BATH BAG

YOU WILL NEED:

An old but clean foot from a stocking.

1/2 cup oatmeal

1/2 cup sunflower seeds

(shelled, please)

a little piece of string or yarn

Grind the seeds in the food processor or blender. Grind the oatmeal the same way. Mix together. Put in the foot of the stocking. Tie shut with the string. Now fill the tub. Take this little magic pouch with you. While you bathe, rub the pouch all over your body. It softens and moisturizes your skin. Let it just float in the bathtub when you are not rubbing.

MAGICAL MILK

Just dump 1/2 cup dry powdered whole milk under the running faucet of your bath. Also add 1 tablespoon good quality vegetable oil (it softens the skin!). And for a sweeter smelling bath, add 6 or 8 drops of an essential oil such as chamomile or jasmine or lavender. (You can get them from health food stores and places like the Body Shop.) Swish your hand around in the tub to mix it up and then soak.

June 22

GOT CHALK?

GOT CHALK?
YOU'RE
EMPOWERED.
YOU'RE ARMED.
YOU'RE READY
FOR THE WORLD.

We urge you to try this new revolutionary method of getting your opinions out to the world. About what? The president's actions in Bosnia. The world's inability to recognize Alaska as its own country. The depleting, deadly treatment of the beloved Brazilian rainforest. This is what we call a Hear Me Roar Action. It's virtually free. It can be a solo activity or you can get the whole gang involved.
It doesn't hurt the trees or the forests or the ozone and is more powerful than those silly mass emails.

CHALK

Grab a big piece, it don't matter
what color, and hit the streets.
(Look for cars—we don't need you getting run over.)
And then write out your message.

WRITE IT BIG. WRITE IT LONG.
WRITE IT LIKE YOU MEAN IT.

BOOKMARKS ROCK

Make your book club members little bookmarks.

That way they can keep track of how far along they are without bending corners (bad for books).

Or make one for yourself, for this book!

You can make a little collage with photos and clippings and then photocopy it, even laminate it. Once sealed in plastic, you can punch a hole in the top and feed a ribbon or yarn bow through the hole.

THE KEVA AND CLEA SECRET SPEAK CODE

"Lfwb, tfdsfu dpogfttjpo ujnf, Xibu bsf zpv nptu tdbsfe pg?"

"J ibuf vtjoh qvcmjd sftusppnt. Boe zpv, Dmfb?"

"J dboopu tjoh lbsbplf. Uibu jt npsujgzjoh!"

"Nf, upp, nf, upp!"

Decode our secret message above using the handy-dandy deciphering chart at the right. Then write your own super secret conversations using our Secret Speak Code. Trust us when we say no one will figure it out despite it's simplicity. Tell secrets, share spy tips, write lovey-dovey letters. ZJQQFF! (That's Yippee!)

Unravel the Secret Code
with the Secret Ledger

A=Z	H=G	O=N	V=U
B=A	I=H	P=O	W=V
C=B	J=I	Q=P	X=W
D=C	K=J	R=Q	Y=X
E=D	L=K	S=R	Z=Y
F=E	M=L	T=S	
G=F	N=M	U=T	

Light Switches

Tired of your room looking like a messy version of the same room you had when you were nine? Sign yourself up for the Sally Jessy Bedroom Makeover Show. Or forget that and just follow our advice. Over the next week we'll help you redo your room. Nice of us, huh? We're full of suggestions. You can take some of 'em, leave some of them, tell us we suck. But do something about that floral bedspread, please. Today's project is all about light switches. You can cover the switch plates with almost anything. Fake fur. Winona Ryder's face from the cover of "TV Guide." The same fabric as your new bedspread. A page from your diary. Velvet. Lace. Suede.

The beauty is, it's such a little surface to cover, you need just a tiny scrap, so it could be some ridiculously expensive material. Or it could just be a cool picture from your Future Files. First things first, turn off the light. Grab a screwdriver and unscrew the (usually) two screws from the plate. Remove plate. Don't lose those two little screws. And don't touch any wires.

Cut your fabric or paper a half inch larger around than the size of the plate. Stretch over plate and with an X-Acto knife make a tiny X in the center of the fabric, over the switch hole.

Spray adhesive works best but you can use regular glue. Glue the fabric down, folding it around the plate edges and taking special care with the corners. And then poke your little fabric triangles, made from the X in the center, through the hole and glue them down. Poke holes through where the screws will go. Now align it up right-like with your light switch and put a screw in the newly poked hole. Twist. Repeat with other screw. Turn on. Turn off. Admire new light switch.

June 26

EVERY GIRL NEEDS A MAGIC SHELF.

If you're like us, you probably have a few books.

> Clea: Don't you mean a <u>TON</u> of books?
>
> Keva: Well, yes, I sure do!

You maybe even have a bookshelf. It's probably even in your room. (If you have answered yes to all these, you get five points.) First of all, get thee into your room near your books. Glance over your collection. Spy your science books from last year. Spy the Nancy Drew collection from fifth grade. Spy little things like marbles and doll parts you have most likely also stuck somewhere in your room.

Well, we think it's time to add some organization to those shelves, break them down if you will. Divide and conquer. And a word on bookshelves. "Get" if you don't have one. (See January 14th's page on piggy banks and start today.) Paint them hot pink. Add some glitter. Or just sand and stain with a rad deep redwood stain. Whatever floats your boat, get a bookshelf today.

Now back to the magic plan:

Put school books together.
Fiction goes in one spot.
Yearbooks in another.
Magazines on bottom shelf and, yes, stacked is OK.
Craft books, spell books, cooking books, this book, they all go together, too.

Now for the best part. Pick a tiny spot on the top shelf. Call it the magic shelf. Put all your secret stuff up there. The key to your old house. Your diary. A love letter (or three). Your piggy bank. This is your secret stuff. Your favorite stuff, your best stuff. Arrange nicely and then when you're all done, sit back and enjoy. And reread your favorite book.

Magic Shelf

MY PRECIOUS JEWELRY

Your room must be organized. OK, it mustn't, but it could be beneficial and fun. Like this little project. You're going to go through your jewelry and organize it. Hair stuff, too, like barrettes and ponytail thingys. Unless you have one of those jewelry boxes with the dancing ballerina, we suggest you do this:

Get a piece of velvet. Like a 12" X 12" square (bigger if you have lots of earrings and stuff). Put a tack in each of the upper corners and pin to the wall. (You can do this inside your closet if you don't want it to show, but it will look astonishingly pretty when you are done.) Don't tack the bottom, so you can easily get behind the velvet square.

Now nab some ribbon. Cut a long piece of ribbon, like at least a foot, and pin under one of those tacks. This is where you will keep all your barrettes and bobby pins—they just slide right onto the ribbon and stay like magic.

As for the velvet square, just stick your earrings right into the velvet. If they are those hook kinds they will stay like magic (again). And if they are post kinds you need to attach the backs of the earring posts behind the velvet curtain. See, now your earrings are all displayed and you won't be losing the little back things in the corner of the dark jewelry box no more.

**Velvet can fray, so either sew the edges or cut them with pinking shears (the zigzag scissors) or just go with the groovy fringe look.

bear with us, the photo looked poopy

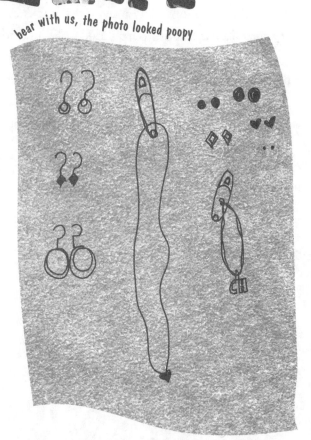

Now for necklaces. Grab a few safety pins and just pin those necklaces right on to the velvet. The same can be done with bracelets. Yippee, it's getting full now. Go, go, go. Find all the jewelry you can and pin it up. Ask Mom for any leftover jewelry she isn't using. But keep adding to this fabulously organized jewelry hanging curtain thing, oh yeah.

FENG SHUIIIIIII!!!

Feng shui AKA "harmony in your living space" AKA that yin and yang thing for your furniture. We've all heard of it and maybe made jokes about it but maybe we don't really know what it means. And maybe the books and stuff are too, well, in depth to really sink your glitter and dark purple decorating hands into, so we kinda broke it down for ya:

#1 Feng shui is at least 5,000 years old.

#2 For thousands of years people in the Far East have used feng shui to improve their home and family lives and live in harmony with the earth. It's supposed to enhance your life in all sorts of ways.

#3 It literally translates to "wind and water."

#4 Feng shui expounds that all matter (i.e., stuff) has vibrations, a sort of "invisible energy." This energy is called "chi."

#5 Chi can be tapped into by placing furniture in certain locations and combining energy producing colors and objects in a room to produce positive results.

By the way, this is Clea's fabulous fireplace.

#6 When you do this you are doing the art of feng shui.

Get it? Got it? Good! Now let's do some rearranging. And promise to write us if you start getting all straight As or get really good at DJing like overnight after you follow these steps.

Make a butterfly mobile.
Or a dragonfly mobile.

Mobiles are cheery objects. Like a big smelly flower next to your bed, they remind you life is good. Plus, mobiles are darn fun—we already established that a few months back. You'll need to take a little trip over to the craft store today. And get yourself...an embroidery hoop...embroidery thread (pretty colors)...maybe some cool paper if you see any you like...Oh, and you'll need a bunch of clothespins (wood, plastic, it really doesn't matter).

First, make your butterflies or dragonflies. That's what the clothespins are for. And the paper is for the wings. You can cut a shape like this:

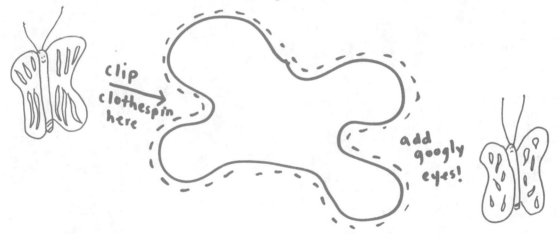

clip clothespin here

add googly eyes!

...and just stick it in the teeth of your clothespin. Instant flying creature.

Cut different lengths of embroidery thread. Loop a thread through the hole in the clothespin and then up around the embroidery hoop. Double around the hoop and knot. Keep doing this with your various flying creatures and embroidery thread all around the embroidery hoop. Then attach four pieces of thread—same length—to the hoop and pull up. Tie together in one big knot. Hang a hook screw in your ceiling— near a window is good. And hang up the mobile. Quick and painless, wasn't it?

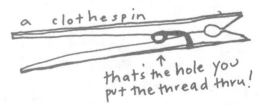

a clothespin

that's the hole you put the thread thru!

And how about that room? Does it have a fresh face? This completes our bedroom makeover exercise. Thank you for reading.

June 30

Box Ball

A sport even we can play. (We're klutzes, in case you didn't know.) We truly relish the idea of such nontraditional athletic endeavors because even we sport dorks can play. So grab a few friends, four total, including you, jocks and nonjocks alike. Get yourself a tennis ball. Borrow it from the dog if you must. We're gonna play BOX BALL.

YOU NEED A PIECE OF CHALK. AND A FLAT AREA. NOW DRAW A BIG SQUARE, LIKE FIVE FEET ON ALL FOUR SIDES.

DIVIDE IT INTO FOUR EQUAL BOXES.

DRAW A CIRCLE OFF TO THE SIDE, AWAY FROM THE BOX, BIG ENOUGH FOR TWO TO STAND IN, AND CALL THAT THE BATHROOM. NOW EACH OF YOU SHOULD STAND IN A BOX. DESIGNATE ONE AS THE STARTING BOX. YOU'LL ROTATE INTO THIS BOX AS WE GO ALONG. MAKE ONE OF THE BOXES THE QUEEN BOX. WHOEVER IS IN THE QUEEN BOX SERVES ON EACH PLAY. SERVING: BOUNCE THE BALL IN YOUR OWN BOX, AND THEN USING YOUR HAND ONLY, HIT IT INTO ANOTHER PLAYER'S BOX. THIS MUST BE DONE UNDERHAND BECAUSE IF YOU WHACKED IT OVERHAND IT WOULD JUST HIT YOU IN THE NOSE.

NOW YOU'RE PLAYING: WHEN THE BALL COMES TO YOUR SQUARE, ALLOW IT TO BOUNCE, THEN HIT IT TO ANOTHER PLAYER. (NOW, YOU CAN SHOOT IT OVERHAND AFTER THE SERVE, BUT PLEASE, IT'S GONNA BOMP YOU IN THE NOSE.)

NOW, WHEN A PLAYER IS OUT, THEY MUST GO AND STAND IN THE BATHROOM. AND EVERYONE MUST ROTATE ONE SQUARE. WHOEVER IS IN THE QUEEN BOX NOW WILL SERVE.

A PLAYER IS OUT WHEN...
...THE TENNIS BALL BOUNCES IN HIS/HER BOX MORE THAN ONCE...THE TENNIS BALL BOUNCES IN HIS/HER OWN BOX FROM HIS/HER OWN HAND (ONLY THE SERVER CAN DO THAT ON THE SERVE) ...HE/SHE HITS THE BALL OUT OF BOUNDS, OR OUT OF THE FOUR BOXES, WITHOUT THE BALL BOUNCING IN SOMEONE'S BOX...HE/SHE DOESN'T LET THE TENNIS BALL BOUNCE IN THEIR BOX FIRST BEFORE HITTING IT.

PLAY UNTIL ANOTHER PERSON IS OUT. THAT PERSON MUST GO AND STAND IN THE BATHROOM, TOO. AND WHEN THE SECOND TO THE LAST PERSON IS OUT, EVERYONE RETURNS TO THEIR SQUARES AND YOU START OVER. THE WINNER OF THE LAST ROUND GETS TO BE IN THE STARTING BOX AND THE FIRST PERSON WHO WAS OUT SHOULD BE IN THE QUEEN BOX. WE CELEBRATE LOSING IN BOX BALL. YIPPEE.

yippee, it's July

Happy
birthday, Clea. And happy
birthday to Canada's Federal Government. Both were born
on this day, July 1, AKA Canada Day (although they were born in
different years). It's a good day to celebrate all things that are Canadian
(and also all things Clea, even though she herself is not, in fact, Canadian).
Such fantastic Canadian things include bacon! And the beaver (it's their
national animal and Canada's largest rodent) and maple leaves. In honor you
could watch "Dawson's Creek." See, Joshua Jackson is Canadian (and cute!).
Another cute Canadian is Mike Myers. Get the Austin Powers movies or "So I Married an
Axe Murderer." Or you could forget that whole Canadian thing and just celebrate Clea.
Walk around severely opinionated today as an ode. Make your hair as big as it can get.
Clea would want it that way. And make sure you sing out loud at really
inopportune moments, like while you're in line at the movies. Wear
orange and pink together and if people look at you in any
way, shape or form that is slightly derogatory, just flash
them the biggest grin you can muster up and say,
"Howdy."

"Ode to Clea," by Keva. Super duper Clea. She loves the music of weird people. She dances and prances. And signs to all the songs. She's cute. She's smart. She looks really good in orange. She's Clea. She made me eat my first Chick-O-Sticks. And always talks about Tater Tots. That's Clea. She's got a dog. And a funny, funny boyfriend. Her hair is all curly, and, well, she's Clea.

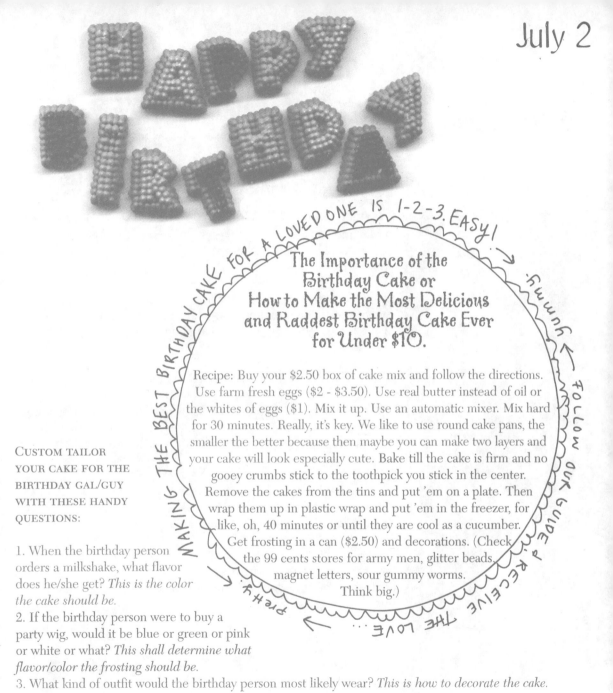

HAPPY BIRTHDAY

The Importance of the Birthday Cake or How to Make the Most Delicious and Raddest Birthday Cake Ever for Under $10.

Recipe: Buy your $2.50 box of cake mix and follow the directions. Use farm fresh eggs ($2 - $3.50). Use real butter instead of oil or the whites of eggs ($1). Mix it up. Use an automatic mixer. Mix hard for 30 minutes. Really, it's key. We like to use round cake pans, the smaller the better because then maybe you can make two layers and your cake will look especially cute. Bake till the cake is firm and no gooey crumbs stick to the toothpick you stick in the center. Remove the cakes from the tins and put 'em on a plate. Then wrap them up in plastic wrap and put 'em in the freezer, for like, oh, 40 minutes or until they are cool as a cucumber. Get frosting in a can ($2.50) and decorations. (Check the 99 cents stores for army men, glitter beads, magnet letters, sour gummy worms. Think big.)

Making the best birthday cake for a loved one is 1-2-3. Easy! → yummy ← follow our guide & receive the love... pretty →

CUSTOM TAILOR YOUR CAKE FOR THE BIRTHDAY GAL/GUY WITH THESE HANDY QUESTIONS:

1. When the birthday person orders a milkshake, what flavor does he/she get? *This is the color the cake should be.*

2. If the birthday person were to buy a party wig, would it be blue or green or pink or white or what? *This shall determine what flavor/color the frosting should be.*

3. What kind of outfit would the birthday person most likely wear? *This is how to decorate the cake.*

Follow these three rules and you will surely produce the most spectacular and, most important, personal birthday cake that birthday person has ever received. Which is, after all, the point.

1 2 3 4 5 6 7 (8) 9 0

CRAZY EIGHTS IS CRAZY COOL. WHAT NUMBER? 8! WHAT NUMBER? 8! 8! 8! (IT'S THE CRAZIEST OF NUMBERS.)

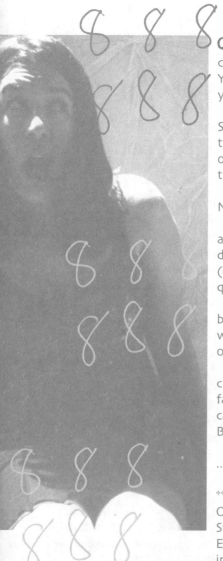

CRAZY EIGHTS IS SO CRAZY COOL. It's the best card game to play with your aunt. Or your sister on a rainy day. You need two people (or more). The object is to get rid of all your cards.

Someone deals five cards to each player (or seven if it's just the two of you). The remaining cards get put facedown in the center of the table. Turn over the top card and place it faceup next to the stack.

Now you take turns. At each turn you have several choices:

a. If the top card of the face-up pile is not an eight, you may put down any card that matches the rank or suit of the card on top (e.g., if the top card was the queen of hearts, you could play any queen or any heart).

b. If you have an eight you can put it down on any card (it's wild). If you do this, you have to pick a suit (hearts, clubs, spades or diamonds) and deem that card one of those.

c. If you can't play a matching suit, matching number or matching face card and you don't have any eights, you need to draw a card from the face-down pile until you get a card that plays. Bummer, because...

...the first player who gets rid of all her cards wins!

**Crazy Eights is also known as Switch, Swedish Rummy, Last One and Rockaway. In Germany it is called Mau-Mau. In Switzerland it is Tschausepp. (Say that three times fast.) In England it's called Black Jack even though that's a betting game in America. Hmm. We like Crazy Eights best.

4TH of JULY

Hey, we always remember the date of this holiday, eh?

WOO HOO. FOURTH OF JULY.

The very best excuse all year long to eat hot dogs. And light sparklers. And fly your own flag. There are a couple of key things that must be accomplished on July the Fourth. You must eat something red, white and blue. You must consume hot dogs (if you are a vegetarian, veggie dogs count). You must don some odd hat, preferably something inspired by the Statue of Liberty. The rest is optional.

You can plant your own watermelon seeds right from your own slice. Instead of spitting the seeds at your brother, save 'em. Find a sunny space in your yard. Dig down about one inch. Put some seeds in the ground. Cover. Water right away and then once a week after that. Wait (very patiently) for watermelon to grow.

Decorate your bike. Weave colorful red, white and blue crepe paper streamers through your spokes. And let some fly from your handlebars.

Hot dogs. Oh so yummy.

If your family is BBQing, by all means, go this route. Hot dogs are especially, 'special-ly good when you make a slice down one side, smear with peanut butter and then wrap in bacon.°° Cook on grill till bacon is crisp and peanut butter is melted. Oh. °°Fakin' bacon and veggie hot dogs may be substituted and in fact are very good this way.

Keva: Um, that hot dog thing sounds kinda nasty.

July 5

Be a fairy
child for a day.

Find a field of wild daisies. (Or a florist with cheap ones.) And weave yourself a crown of daisies. (Dandelions work, too.) Pick at least 25 daisies with stems. Cut the stems so that they are about three and a half inches long. With a knife carefully cut a small (quarter inch) slit through each stem, two inches below the base of the flower. (Dandelion stems are soft enough to do this with your fingernail.) Pick up two flowers. Stick one stem through the hole in the other stem. Pick up another flower. Stick that stem through the last flower's stem. And so on and so on. Until it's long enough to wrap around your head.

mmm! smells good!

STICK The
flower stem
in the Xhole.

→ ↕ CUT

When it's long enough, twist the last stem around the very first stem that started your chain. If the stems are poking out, tuck them into the chain, it will make your crown more secure. Wear your daisy crown. Feel like the fairy child you are. This is a great activity on a day you're not feeling so good, because you simply cannot be unhappy while wearing a daisy crown. Footloose and fancy free are you.

BUG MAGIC POTION

Hey, if you think we're gonna tell you that this magic potion is gonna get rid of those bugs that bite, you're right. It will make all these pesky critters get the heck away from your hot bod.

Think we're talking about boys? Nope...

Mosquitoes!

OK, here's what you need:

A cool empty bottle, preferably clear.
Or it can be blue and glass.
Or it can be an old jam jar.
It can have a spritzer pump or not.
Whatever floats your boat, baby.

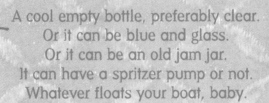

Get some unscented body oil from the health food store. Pour into your bottle. Get essential oil of eucalyptus. Add a few drops. Get essential oil of pennyroyal (try the health food store). Add a few drops of this one, too.

Shake, shake, shake.

Now every evening when the bugs usually come out to play, spritz yourself a few times. (Try your ankles and wrists, but not your face.) It's magic.

BUTTONS

So, you're in the thrift store and you're shuffling through the racks and racks of shirts and you find this fabulous black button-down, almost-silky shirt and you throw it on over your tee and it fits! Hallelujah. And you begin to button it and you realize that the buttons are on the right, much unlike all your shirts at home, which have the buttons on the left. And you think, no problem, but um, why?

Well, that fabulous almost-silky black shirt is a men's shirt. Men's shirts button on the right. Women's shirts, on the other hand, button on the left. Why the wacky discrimination? Why do they need to be different? What screwed up historical event has caused the garment industry to go haywire?

Well, we will tell you. It was indeed a screwed up historical event. During the Victorian period, buttons were very expensive and only worn by the very rich. And the very rich, well-to-do ladies were dressed by their servants. Since most people are, right-handed, the buttons went on the servants' right, or the ladies' left. But gentlemen of this time did not dress with the help of a servant, they in fact dressed themselves. So their buttons were placed on their right.

Even though many women not of the upper class made their own clothes and dressed themselves, they still chose to place the buttons on the left, copying the styles of the rich.

This tradition has stood the test of time, through the Depression, through the Women's Movement, through it all. Not that it really makes a difference. By the time a girl is old enough to know that her buttons are on the left and a boy's are on the right, she's become far more adept at buttoning to the left anyhow. But it is odd, isn't it? Know that every time you don a boy's shirt you're making a statement against the patriarchal and classist society of yesteryear. Well...um, sort of.

A Beginner's Guide to the Spooky Art of Palmistry

Since the late 1800s (and probably even earlier) there have been a group of people who call themselves scientists and study palmistry as a "true science." They call it "chiromancy." Whatever. We like to think of it more as a party game, especially if you're in PJs with a whole bunch of your girlfriends and there is plenty of Fire-flavored Cheetos and Pepsi. So that said, the following is NOT a science, but it is fun, especially when you concentrate on how this relates to your LOVE LIFE. Now follow along, turning the palm of your own hand, whichever one you write with, toward you.

The line marked 3 is your LOVEY LINE. Now, if there is a three-way fork at the end of this line, this is a sign of a happy marriage.

Number 6 doesn't have a good name as far as we can tell so we will call it the GEORGE line after Clea's dog. (The line has nothing to do with dogs, we just like the name.) The GEORGE line should start somewhere between your thumb and LIFE line and swing into and cross the LIFE line. Where it hits is said to predict approximately when you will get married. Clea does not even have that line. For reals. Nada. Not one. Always a bridesmaid... (Which is fine by her.)

Number 4 is your HEAD line. The stronger, thicker, longer and steadier that line is, the smarter, more in control you are. (Sure.)

OK, **numero 5** is the LIFE line. This is supposed to indicate your health and physical strength during the duration of your life. You're looking for a wide, strong, long line—they say it means a healthier you.

The small lines **numbered 1 & 2** represent LOVE RELATIONSHIPS. Several lines means you'll have several short-term relationships. Deep ones signify marriage. If you have LOTS of deep ones, prepare to be married over and over again. Usually if the deep line is close to the LOVEY line then you will marry earlier in life.

HABITAT FOR HUMANITY BUILDS HOUSES

Hey, an igloo is a house, too.

Do you ever think about how your parents bought the home you live in? Or maybe how they come up with the rent money each month? For many people, due to circumstances out of their control, it's too expensive to buy or rent a house in today's world. Do you ever think about what happens then?

See, homeownership is a pretty great thing. It's like this milestone in life for many, many people. And yet for a whole lot of people, it's totally unattainable. Well, not exactly totally.

See, there is this organization called Habitat for Humanity. There are others that do the same kind of work, but Habitat has been around the longest and has probably built the most homes. They do have a religious connection, but they welcome the help from people of all backgrounds and, more important, they dole out the help to people of all backgrounds.

So what do they do and why are we telling you about this? Habitat for Humanity gathers volunteers, often for a week or a weekend, and they build houses. Yep, whole houses. They don't make a profit on the houses. The loans are no-interest. The mortgage payments (the owners' monthly payments to buy the house) are put right back into more houses. And the people who will live in the house also help build it—they call that "sweat equity." We like the sound of that.

Habitat builds all over the world, including right here at home in the U.S. The cost of a house varies from as little as $700 in some developing countries to an average of $42,500 in the United States. Habitat also has offices all over the world, an awesome 1,900 total in 64 countries, including all 50 states of the United States, the District of Columbia, Guam and Puerto Rico. To date they've built over 80,000 safe, affordable houses. Hello, 80,000!

Habitat even has chapters on college campuses and youth programs at community centers. If you're over five years of age (and gosh, we're betting you are), Habitat can put you to work.

We're telling you about Habitat because there are organizations out there that help you contribute to the demise of almost every one of this world's ills. And maybe this particular problem is one you feel "at home" with but don't know how to lend a hand. And Habitat needs people to do just that, lend a hand. A strong, earthy, physical hand. Because houses are built with the physical labor of one's hands. Plus, hammering and sawing and painting can be terribly rewarding pursuits. In other words, they're fun.

You just played back-to-back soccer games. Or built a house. (Ha!) Or rode your bike what must have been like 20 miles. Or maybe you just helped your pal move her bed to the other side of her room. But here's the thing: you're sore. Your muscles, they ache, ache, ache. What should you do?

BATHE IN THE I-WORKED-MY-BUTT-OFF BATH SOAK.

There are a lot of ingredients in this one. If you can't find them all, do not fret, just get what you can and go with it. (Remember, the oil is usually available at the health food store, the spices from your 'rent's rack.)

You'll need:
A piece of an old stocking (but a clean one)
1/2 cup Epsom salts
1/2 cup baking soda
1 tablespoon sage
1 tablespoon marjoram
1 tablespoon chamomile
1 tablespoon pine needles
2 teaspoons peppermint
10 drops essential oil (any scent)
string

Put all the ingredients in the stocking and tie shut. Now tie your little bag of fun under the faucet so that the running water flows through it. Fill the bath. Get in it. Relax. Grab the stocking sack and rub into your aching muscles. Relax some more. Listen to soothing music. Relax. And feel your muscles loosen and ache, well, less.

P.S. Keva used this after Jeff became her personal trainer.

FAKE SCARS

We were going to wait and do these fake scars closer to Halloween but then we decided this is great year-round fun. You can create a little mystery about yourself with a well-placed oozing wound. And you can craft some intricate and involved story about how you acquired said scar. Make it juicy. If you can pull off this story, we assure you you're destined for a tremendous career in the TV and film industry. (And if all you can pull off is creating the scar, maybe you're destined for a career in TV and movies after all, just not in front of the camera. Maybe as a gory fake makeup artist. You can win an Oscar doing that stuff.)

You'll need a hot glue gun (and some glue), a little wax paper and something called Liquid Latex. You can usually get it at drugstores. It's cheap and comes with a little brush in the cap. You'll also need a little makeup to disguise the seams. Cream makeup that you get at costume shops (and the drugstore in October) is great because it's thick and comes in white and black plus colors (blue is good for bruises!). But you can absolutely use normal foundation mixed with a little black eye shadow. If you want a gaping wound, you'll also need fake blood.

1. MAKE A LINE ACROSS THE WAX PAPER WITH YOUR GLUE GUN AND LET COOL. THE GLUE IS THE BASIS OF THE SCAR, SO MAKE THE LINE AS LONG AS YOU WANT THE SCAR.

2. ONCE IT'S DRY, CUT AROUND THE GLUE SCAR, MAKING SURE TO LEAVE SOME WAX PAPER AROUND SCAR. DON'T PEEL IT OFF THE PAPER. THE PAPER IS HOW YOU'RE GOING TO ATTACH IT TO YOUR FACE, NECK OR LEG.

3. BRUSH A LITTLE OF THE LIQUID LATEX ON THE BACK OF THE WAX PAPER AND APPLY TO YOUR BODY. IT SHOULD STICK PRETTY WELL. (BUT NOT SO WELL THAT YOU CAN'T REMOVE IT BEFORE THAT BIG DATE WITH BILLY.)

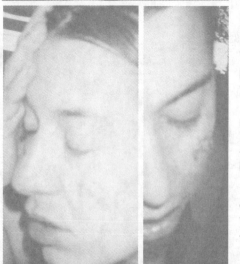

4. DAB MAKEUP AROUND THE BASE OF THE "SCAR," COVERING THE WAX PAPER. IF YOU WANT IT TO OOZE, ADD THE BLOOD AFTER THE MAKEUP. VOILA! SICK AND TWISTED FUN!

*No animals or people were harmed for this essay. In fact, Keva actually had fun

FRANK-BEAN BAKE

July 12

Future Files.

Today's Assignment:

Food!

Because who doesn't love food?

And because what better way to impress your friends and family and exercise your love of food than whipping up some delectable smelling, aesthetically pleasing and otherwise choice meals.

So break out the magazine. The scissors. The (dun dun dun)...Future Files. Add another file or record jacket or paper bag to the pile and entitle it "FOOD." Or "RECIPES." Or "Yummy Yummy in My Tummy."

From now on, keep your eyes peeled for terrific looking recipes that you can create for your book club meetings, movie nights, various parties throughout the year, school lunches and future bake sales.

You could even create subfiles within your one big FOOD file. Categorize the recipes into groups like "Family Dinners," "SNAX," "Dee-zertz" and "Vegan Friendly."

If you happen to catch an episode of Jacques Pépin (Clea wants Jacques wit ze fabu accente to be her papi, no offense to her own talented, loving father), scribble down those recipes that sound delish, too. Stash them in the file. Amen.

July 13

Spin the SPINNER and call the shot.
TWISTER ties you up in a knot.

That's Twister! (That's from the official song.)

Twister puts players in your face in a freaky, silly, daring group yoga exercise. ❁Say that ten times fast.

Plus, it's very Brady Bunch. Lay down the sheet and spin the spinner. On each spin, a player has to move a hand or foot.

Then you got to freeze. Argh! The more spins, the fewer circles, the weirder it gets.

Man oh man, think about how and why they invented this thing. It's totally fabu. Far out. Groovy, man.

Forget playing truth or dare to get giggly with that cutie. Have a Twister party! Get tangled up and try to make everyone else fall down.

Alternative uses for your Twister, um, "board" for lack of a better word:

Make it a tablecloth, a shower curtain, fabulous wall decor or even a room divider!

Cut holes inside the circles and paste pics (it's a frame) or cut-n-paste and line the inside of your drawers!

Over the next three days we're gonna make one fantabulous zine. As in maga-zine. A zine is better than anything you've ever seen before because YOU made it. And you made it about anything you wanted to make it about. Your butt, your friend's butt, ice cream, cement trucks, the Donnas or LeeLee Sobieski. That's right, whatever you want. We're gonna make us a zine about Keva's sister, Aimee. Otherwise known as Aimee Wins! Here we go! Pick your theme. Write down everything you want to say about your theme in a notebook (preferably one just for the zine).

*hi, my name is aimee. i like cheese!

Here's what we wrote

SHE'S KEVA'S SISTER.
SHE ROCKS.
SHE HAS THIS SUPER WEIRDO PSYCHIC CONNECTION
TO THE NUMBER 43. SHE SEES IT EVERYWHERE ALL
THE TIME AND WHEN YOU HANG OUT WITH HER, EVERY
COUPLE MINUTES SHE CALLS OUT "LOOK, 43," AND
EVENTUALLY YOU START TO SEE THEM, TOO!
SHE'S GOT THE SMALLEST FEET EVER
AND HER TOES AND HANDS ARE REALLY CUTE.
HER FEET STINK (A LOT).
UM, SHE THINKS THAT CHEESE
IS LIKE THE BEST THING EVER.
SHE MAKES KEVA GIGGLE
AND SOMETIMES KEVA'S VERY SERIOUS.

OK 'nuff said. Now you make your list. Carry your notebook around with you for the rest of the day, adding things as they come to you. If you're crafting this zine about something you care about, it will come to you.

July 15

43 It's GATHER STUFF DAY.

With your zine notebook in hand, reread your list. Look for things and photos and notes that remind you of your list. Got a photo from that time you saw Ben Folds Five? Cool, grab it and stick it in your notebook. Proceed until you are done with the list. Now, they all don't have to be photos, they can be bits of scrap or flowers or some buttons or whatever gets ya going.

Now, decide on the stories you want to write up. Think big—there can be quizzes and they can be fun. Use a pen, the typewriter, your iMac (like us, yippee!) to write the stories.

IN THE "AIMEE WINS" ZINE

10 things Keva loves about Aimee Wins

10 things you never knew about Aimee Wins

Aimee at age 6

Aimee's handwriting

Ode to Aimee (see January 3, for how to write an ode)

Collage of Aimee's friends

Copy of one of Aimee's report cards (ha!)

...OFFICIAL ZINE WEEK

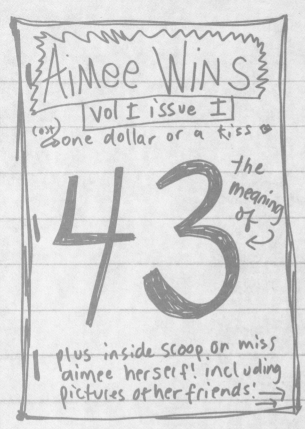

Aimee Wins

Vol I issue I

(cost) one dollar or a kiss

'43 the meaning of

plus inside scoop on miss aimee herself! including pictures of her friends!

IT S LAYOUT TIME:

...AKA time to be the art director. Figure out what size you want your zine to be, then gather supplies. Paper, glue, scissors, tape. Take all of your gathered items and tape and glue away. Now hit the copy palace of your choice. Always good to make friends with the folks who work the counter. They can really gouge you, but if you are nice to them maybe they will give you a break, cut you a deal, let you in on a slice of their pie. Tell them you want it double-sided and make sure it all fits on the page just fine. Then go for it.

As for distribution, you can start by handwriting notes on the inside and mailing them off to your pals. Drop some in the girls dressing room of your favorite clothing store or ask the chick working there if they will put them on the counter for free. "Aimee Wins" was for free, but if you think other people would want to read your zine, get bold, charge $1. But free is always best. Dropping them in cute places is cool, too. Under the door of your crush's house. On your teacher's desk. Mail one to Grandma and freak her out. Anything goes. If you get a really good response, start working on issue #2.

This is when you can start getting cheeky: sell ad space, charge money, mail to other zine pals across America. Post it online as a homepage with Excite or another web portal. Yep. Your zine can be everywhere.

...OFFICIAL ZINE WEEK

IMAGINE

...you discovered
you could have
a secret power
of your choosing.
What would it be?
Why?

wallpaper cards

This little craft combines the letter and the envelope into one. You can make invitations this way or just send pen pal letters or use this formula to make your future holiday cards (or cards just to say 'hi').

You'll Need:

Two pieces of wallpaper (or improvise with paperlike material the thickness of wallpaper). One should be cut 6" wide x 8" long and the other 5 1/2" wide x 7" long
A piece of card stock, cut 5 1/2" wide x 7" long.
About 8 or 10" of ribbon
A piece of writing paper
5 1/2" wide x 10 1/2" long
A handy-dandy glue stick
A small photo

Fold the wallpaper pieces in half so that they are 6" x 4" and 5 1/2" x 3 1/2" respectively. Do the same with the card stock. Center the card stock on the inner side of the large piece of wallpaper. Glue down.
Now cut your ribbon in half. You should now have two pieces of ribbon. Glue one end of one piece to the top end of the card stock (not the creased end) and the other piece to the other bottom end. Now take your smaller piece of wallpaper and glue over the card stock and ribbon ends, sealing the ribbon to the wallpaper "card."

Now fold the writing paper in thirds. Put a thin line of glue on the top edge of your writing paper and glue down right underneath the crease of your wallpaper card. Write your letter on that page. Fold up. Glue down your small photo above the crease on the inside of the card, just about an inch above where you glued the writing paper in. And then tie ribbon, closing your card up securely. Now mail it or hand deliver it or stash it someplace secret for later usage.

IT'S THE MIDDLE OF SUMMER!

You're outdoors lots. You're feeling good—hopefully there is no school. Really, all you need in your life is a new sexy cute next-door neighbor and a bottle full of sweet-smelling bubbles. We haven't quite mastered the whole Cutie Next Door Spell yet so here is a recipe for making come-hither, free-wheeling, happy-inducing smelly, nelly bubbles.

Get yourself: 2/3 cup clear dishwashing soap (it is widely believed that Joy and Dawn work better than other brands). 1 gallon water. 2-3 tablespoons glycerin (available at drug-stores). (Or you could use white corn syrup in place the glycerin. It works and is cheaper, but your bubbles will be less colorful and less sturdy. You can buy corn syrup at any ol' grocery store.) A dozen drops or so of lavender or gardenia or rose essential oil (You can find that at Body Shop type places or health food stores.)

Mix all the ingredients together in a bucket or really big bowl. It works even better if it sits overnight. Look for things that will create bubbles. Like the plastic rings that hold a six-pack of soda pop together. (But even your hands will work.) Dip into your solution and blow. Six sweet-smelling, relaxing, rejuvenating bubble-bubble toil-n-troubles in one fell swoop.

Oh well, holidays in Japan are just so lovable. Marine Day is a pretty new holiday in Japan. It's also called Ocean Day. It marks the beginning of summer holidays in Japan, plus it sort of pays tribute to both the ocean creatures and advancements in boating. (See what we mean? The holidays in this neck of the woods are simply rad.) So refrain from eating any seafood today in honor. No tuna sandwiches either. Doodle only colorful fish while you talk on the telephone. **Make fish faces in the mirror at least seven times today. Heck, make fish faces at strangers on the street.** It will make you laugh, we promise. Visit the aquarium if your city has one.

Oh, and one more thing. This month is also host to the Tanabata Festival in Japan. Legend says that two constellations meet during this month, making it the perfect time to make a wish. You're supposed to write down your wish on a colored piece of paper (called Tanzuku in Japan). Then you tie your wish to bamboo branches. (Or some random tree.) Pray to the stars in the sky. And your wish shall come true.

We love Japanese holidays.

July 21

Hey, We are regular old Girl Scouts.

remember this...

Leaves of three, turn and flee
(or leave them be or don't tread on me!)

...or you can say it in French...

Feuilles trois ~ Partez du bois!

We are speaking of poison ivy!!

POISON IVY and its friends aren't really poisonous—just allergy inducing. And more people are allergic to poison ivy than any other thing. If you've experienced it once and didn't break out and therefore think you are immune, you are wrong, bucko.

See, the first time you encounter poison ivy it often does nothing but stimulate your immune system. But then the next time you're around it, whoa, you might break out by just brushing against it ever so lightly. And some people who are immune for years might one day find themselves with one of the worst cases of poison ivy ever. That's sort of the plant's own peculiar type of drama—it's very mysterious.

You need to know about poison ivy if you venture into woods or fields, if you hike or picnic or take strolls in wooded areas with your love. Because take it from Clea, it sucks. She was hiking with four other friends. She got it the worst—fever, blistering, oozing sores all over her body. She still has ugly gray scars. It lasted for two weeks. It was humiliating.

A few key things
to remember about
the poisonous
threesome that is
ivy, oak and sumac...

IVY: Leaves are red and the berries are very pale or white in fall. There are always three leaves, with the center one being the largest. (Course, strawberries also have three leaves and they aren't poisonous, but better to be safe than sorry.)

OAK: Poison oak also has three leaves but they look more oaklike (duh). That saying about three leaves is catchy and all but only partially true. Poison oak leaves cluster in groups of three, five, seven or nine. Ugh.

SUMAC: Poison sumac has a row of six to ten leaflets. One leaflet is at the end of the stem. The others are in two rows opposite to each other.

Poison ivy, oak and sumac tend to grow on boundaries like the side of the road or along fences and near streams. But really, it can grow most anywhere from Canada on down to southern Mexico. You're simply not safe anywhere! (Except maybe in France.)

If you do think you came in contact with any of these three, wash yourself quick and well with soap and water. This may or may not work, but it is so worth the try. Apply rubbing alcohol with cotton balls to the parts of your skin that came in contact. Do not touch your shoes or clothes—they could recontaminate you later. And we recommend seeing a doctor right away if your rash is inflamed in any way.

P.S. You can also get poison ivy from your dog if he or she rubbed up against it and then you petted him or her. So keep your doggy away from this stuff, too.

July 22

tots all-around!

TOTS & POPS
(TATER AND OTTER, SILLY!)

OTTER POPS

cherry otter pops

yum!

We have this friend Gary who liked to throw parties but was a little unsure about his party skills so he always made sure to theme the party—that way, he presumed, there was always something to talk about. His "Trolls and Tambourines" party was fun but noisy. His "Where the Wild Things Are" shindig was just too confusing. But his "Tater Tot/Otter Pop" soiree was a hit. (Otter Pops, like Fla-Vor Ice, are really cheap Popsicles.)

← STICK FANCY TOOTHPICKS IN THEM

New flavors:

Lazy lime

rockin rubarb

mint madness

angry avocado

Sure, it's partially because Clea loves Tater Tots so much. But it was more than that. It was the middle of the summer. It was hot. And the only refreshments he offered his guests were two of life's finer foods... (say it with us, out loud) "OTTER POP! TATER TOT!" No one was dressed in any silly costumes. But there was plenty to talk about. Gary had every flavor of Otter Pops available on the market today. His freezer was packed with the pops.

And Gary offered four dipping sauces with the toothpick-skewered little plunkets of potato. There was ketchup with a dash of horseradish, bottled BBQ sauce, plus a homemade cranberry sauce and a spicy peanut dip. Gary wandered the party with his tray in hand offering everyone an hors d'oeuvre. It was a popular refrain..."Otter Pop? Tater Tot?" Everyone had a good time. No one went hungry. It was a smash hit. Try your hand at the concept for your next party. It's better than Trolls and Tambourines. Trust us.

Otter Pops

they melt fast!

← more tots!

SEXSTUFF

OK, so a few words and tips on the topic of sex. And that is whether you're having it or not having it or wanting it or grossed out by it or whatever. So, the main point is that sex is something you should talk about, it is not something to keep under wraps.

We mean, we all got questions, right? And we all got a right to ask those questions and we're not talking just about questions for Mom (yikes) or Mrs. Johnson (um, hello?). We're talking about questions to ask that boy (if you're even thinking you're gonna do it and we hope that you thought long and hard, but we're sure you did).

We know. It is a bit uncomfy. But if you can't bring yourself to even talk about it, then you probably should not be doing it. We know it's reeeeeeally hard to ask those frightening questions that you just can't get out of your mouth, but we're here to say that no matter how funny or weird it may sound to you, just the simple act of asking makes you a self-assured rock mama.
Sorta like this! "So, um, have you, um, ever been HIV tested?"
And hopefully the answer is yes but if it's no, aren't you glad you got the information beforehand?

But say you don't, you don't ask. You just proceed with caution, hoping not to get your heart broken and not thinking about the other scary stuff like herpes and warts and HIV and all that stuff 'cause it's scary and big and you think that kinda stuff doesn't happen to girls like you and so you move on. But in the back of your head, you are maybe always wondering, "Oh, geez, I hope it's cool," and maybe you might begin to feel separated from that person that you think you're falling in love with. Like you're not being totally honest even though you're working on building a good relationship.

As if you're not already worrying about other things, like if you like him...if he treats you right...if the way he talks to you is something extra special. All those things are big things, big diary writing things, but let's stop a minute and think: If you like someone and they like you, then ask! You have all the right in the world. Get tested, get your friends to get tested. Play smart. Act the part.

July 24

IF YOU FIND YOURSELF IN NEED of a spiritual model and Buffy the Vampire Slayer isn't working for you this week, we suggest checking out all the world's many goddesses of yore. Gods and goddesses are found in the folktales of most cultures, from China to Mesopotamia to Chile. It seems our forebears needed someone or something to explain the inexplicable. Therefore, a lot of the gods and goddesses are representatives of the curiously undefined, like death and nature and, um, reproduction. Since mythology is essentially a series of exciting, bizarre, fictional tales, the history of these goddesses is pretty darn fascinating. We'll periodically tell you about the goddesses we find so gosh darn interesting and odd.

Today's choice comes to us by way of Chinese Buddhism. You see, there is the lovely, the divine Kwan Yin, a name that translates to "she who hears the cries of the world.'" She is the goddess of mercy and compassion. Kwan Yin is most always pictured sitting cross-legged on a lotus flower, dressed in all white and holding an infant. Her horrid story begins at the hands of her father, who killed her. For some unexplained reason, she was sent to Hell. Was she bad? Why did her father kill her? We just don't know. That part has been left open-ended. What we do know is that once in Hell, Kwan Yin sat complacently, reading from the holy books aloud. The ruler of the underworld could not make the dead souls suffer as they were far too entranced with her readings to feel pain. So the disgruntled god sent her back to the world of the living. She studied hard and attained great spiritual insight and for this, Kwan Yin was rewarded with immortality by the Buddha. Kwan Yin now has her own temple at the Mount of the Wondrous Peak for devotees of Buddhism. People go there and shake rattles and set off firecrackers in her name. Kwan Yin's virtues include mercy, modesty, courage, justice and wisdom, and she offers her devotees strength, clarity and compassion. So if you are feeling the need to gain an understanding of the world around you, you might consider checking out Kwan Yin's history and powers. After all, from her hands flow the heavenly dew, which is pretty darn cool.

BADMINTON

Badminton** is an Olympic sport. Betcha didn't know that. Actually, though, **Badminton** was invented a long-arse time ago, like 2,000 years ago, way back in ancient Greece. It is named after a house that an English duke lived in so it's a very regal and trés chic sportique. Why don't we make today **Badminton** Day?

Wear old-fashioned clothes. Long skirts, even—it will be cute. Pretend you have a butler and play lazily, for today is Badminton Day.

Sing it, babies:
"Summertime and the living is easy, get a **Badminton** set and live like a bird"

Badminton is sort of like tennis but on grass and the net is higher and, well, you have these little things that you hit that are called shuttlecocks instead of balls and you can play hard without hardly sweating, unlike tennis, where it's all sweating.

Badminton is very cool. You can even play it while drinking a Coke or talking on the tele. You can have all-day **Badminton** events where everyone gets a chance to win. Visors were invented just for this game, and your team should have special ones.

You can get a badminton set for cheap and once it's up, it's there for like the whole summer. And your Slip 'N Slide will still fit underneath, so don't worry. Go get a set today.

** "Every time I spell it I spell it differently."—Keva Marie

Clea: OK, every gal I know wears thong underwear, but I can't. I just cannot get over that feeling. That squirmy, icky feeling. I like my undies full and cottony. And preferably with the days of the week on them.

Keva: But what about when you're wearing some tight bootie huggers?

Clea: Um, I don't know if I can say.

Keva: We can say whatever we want. Well...almost. Which makes me wonder about email. Do you think there are people out there whose job it is to just read your private emails?

Clea: And they wear uniforms with wraparound '80s glasses and they never leave their dark rooms. Yes, I think so.

Keva: I think my office is bugged.

Clea: I think someone goes though my desk at night and takes mini–spy photos of all my "documents."

Keva: That's cool. I think my bosses have little cameras and record me picking my nose.

Clea: And singing in your car?

Keva: I don't mind that really, but I get an icky feeling when I think of them maybe listening in on the phone when I'm talking to my mom.

Clea: I mind them watching me pick my nose AND sing in my car. Those mean spy bastards.

Keva: Maybe we should film them back? Wait...how would that work?

DISCUSSION QUESTIONS Do you wear thongs? Do they feel squirmy to you? What do you think Clea means when she says she can't tell? Do you think there are people out there whose job it is to just read your private emails? What do you think those people wear? Do you pick your nose? Sing in the car? How do you think we can film those bastards back? Who exactly are those bastards? What does the word "postmodern'" mean?

Sarongs

Sarongs are fabulous because no matter where you are, as soon as you tie one on, you will instantly feel like an island princess. And sometimes, when things ain't going as well as planned, feeling like an island princess is all the pick-me-up you need. Really, any piece of material can be an instant sarong. The standard sarong size is about seven feet by five feet, but as long as it is BIG, it's not a problem. The classic way to wear them on the islands is to wrap the fabric around your waist, rather low on your hips, and knot on one side. But you can also wear your sarong as a strapless dress, wrapped and tied just above your boobs. Or you can even wrap it around you once, but instead of tying on the side, under your arm, you can wrap the points over one shoulder, knotting there. you can wear them over your bathing suit. Over a tank top. Really, with any shirt. You can then use as a beach mat. Or a tablecloth. Or as a room divider. Sarong means freedom in some language or another. Really, it does. And that's because in wearing something so light and simple, you have a newfound sense of freedom. Try wearing one instead of a robe this summer. It will give you a mysterious, tropical mystique. Ooh la la.

our sarong song
aloha oye
eat some poi
enchant a boy
be ever so coy

in your sarong
you can play ping pong
or faye wray and king kong
can't we all get along
while wearing our sarong

P.S. Every culture that wears sarongs has a different name for them, but essentially they are the same thing. A simple piece of material to wear. Call them a pareo or sari or lavalava or sulu or lunghi or canga or pakome or boubou.

p.s.: hey, tricia! happy birthday! xok.

July 28

GOT NOTHING
TO DO TODAY?

HERE ARE A FEW SUGGESTIONS,
courtesy of keva and clea.

Play board games. Read a short story. GARDEN.
COUNT ANTS. invent something. Listen to music
and dance round + round! Collect dustballs.
teach someone younger than you something
u know. call someone you haven't talked to in
awhile. go to the library (and not to study but
to read fun magazines you don't subscribe to... OR
look up various topics like Elvis or Motorcycles
or chick painters + peruse the shelves.
GO FISHING! Sit back + imagine yourself
in an exciting situation. :) Write a song.
Write another song! Don't watch TV,
decorate it! (only ok if it's an oldie.) Make
faces. Name your faces. Try yer faces
out on random people walking down the street.

Walk Backward!
:) ok bye :)

a few words about flowers

We all know that when you give roses to someone special it means "I love you." However, during the ancient times, the art of secret messages in flower giving was much more complex and detailed. For instance, if one sent her lover a red tulip, it meant that she had great passion for that person.

But the flower lore ran deeper than that. In fact, flowers were associated with superstitions, love potions and even someone's livelihood. And this wasn't limited to the type of flower but also the color of the flower. So next time you want to send a message, check this ancient list and be all the wiser.

The pansy was one of the ingredients in a famed Celtic love potion. Sending pansies meant that you had romantic thoughts. Pansies were not only supposed to have magical love powers but the petals were thought to cure a broken heart.

Sending irises meant that the receiver would carry a piece of heaven with them. A natural good-luck charm.

Now, if you wanted someone to know that you found him presumptuous, all you had to do was send him a bouquet of snapdragons. Apparently this gesture really let the recipient have it, and with no bloodshed.

We like the idea of communicating through flowers. It seems to be just a cheerier way to conduct one's life. We would like to reinstate this practice in the modern world. Now, what flower do you think will represent the thought, "You're not as cool as you think you are"?

July 30

Do you ever think,
"Wow, I know this person (your best
friend, your sister, your mom) so very well,
they just cannot surprise me," and then in an
instant they shock you with some new side?
That's a beautiful thing. Those newly discovered
sides of people.

Clea: What is this?
Keva: It's a crochet hat. I made it.
Clea: You crochet?
Keva: Yes, I do.
Clea: I know you, but I don't know you.

That moment from our history was just reenacted for you for a reason.
See, we work day in and day out with each other. We've known each
other for years and years. And yet I didn't know that Keva crocheted.
No idea. And that's amazingly cool. How did that little nugget of
information slip by me?

But the undiscovered sides of people don't have to be just about
physical talents that they possess, like crocheting. It could be the
so sweetly surprising way your grandma quietly and powerfully holds
up after a family tragedy. Or it could be how your best friend
remembers the particular clothes you were wearing when
you guys met, but she doesn't tell you until you're like 35.

We're only telling you this because we think it's one of life's
little pleasures and we want you to be aware. And
remember not to take people for granted. People are
surprising creatures, intricate, exciting, surprising
creatures. And you never know, that pesky
little sister of yours might have
something deliciously cool up
her sleeve, you just don't
know it yet.

CLEA'S GRANDMA

COLD CREAM RULES! I use it for everything!

In days of yore, it was the beauty treatment. It was used to take off makeup, as a night moisturizer...you name it, if it had to do with beauty, women turned to cold cream.

So we're gonna make cold cream. It's really good for removing makeup. You can rub it into your hands as moisturizer. You can rub it into your feet and cover with socks before bed to keep your toes smooth. And you can use it as night moisturizer on your face. Pretty all-purpose.

You will need a small jar to keep it in. This recipe makes enough for about 15 uses. And you do need to use the stove and stuff for this, so make sure that's cool. You need

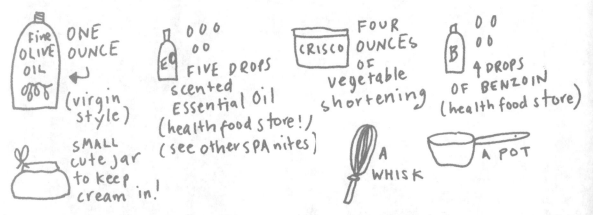

ONE OUNCE (virgin style)

FIVE DROPS scented ESSENTIAL OIL (health food store!) (see other SPA nites)

FOUR OUNCES OF vegetable shortening

4 DROPS OF BENZOIN (health food store)

SMALL cute jar to keep cream in!

A WHISK

A POT

Now melt the olive oil and shortening together over low heat. Stir. When it's all combined, take off the heat and stir in the benzoin and essential oil. Let it cool for a few minutes and then start whisking. You need to whisk for a couple of minutes, till it's really creamy. Pour into cute jar. Now you're ready to use.

As makeup remover, just put a drop on a cotton ball and sweep over your eyes and face. As foot lotion, use about a tablespoon per foot and cover with socks. Sleep peacefully and wake with silky soft feet. As moisturizer, use a teaspoon or two and spread over cleansed face. And if you don't use it up in three weeks or so, refrigerate it. It will feel really cool, too, if it is actually COLD cream. Brrrr.

August
Stay out of
the heat,
baby.

Appreciation Day

OK, so today is the day for appreciation.

You have to say it kinda like you have marbles in your mouth.

We'd tell you why but we might get in trouble, so just do it. Appreciation Day. You

must make a point of appreciating your best friend or your sis or brother today.

You could tell them why you appreciate them. Or you could write it out and give it to

them. This paper could also be the answer you give them when they look at you

funny and say, "Um what's this?" You say, "Appreciation Day."

Clea wrote this one about her pal Jessica.

My friend Jessica is the smartest gal I know.
She can talk about everything and mo'
she makes me laugh and giggle and spit
even when I am low and slow and in the pits
and she is sassy and sarcastic and full of attitude
but you know she's rarely ever rude except to stupid guys
who are mean...and that is why I think Jessica is queen

I appreciate you, Clea

I appreciate you, Keva.

Yes, they are like odes.
Don't you think you
need more of these in
your life?

Imagine you switched
places with your dog.

Maybe you made your zine dedicated to Björk but now you want to immortalize her in another way. Or maybe you need a present for your best friend (who has everything). Or perhaps you just need new decor in la bedroom.

Make Patron Saint Candles.

You know the type, the highball glass candles that often feature the Virgin Mary or a deity of some sort. Well, you can make your own. All you need is the glass candle part, some paper and a little creative juice.

Alleged male potency assistance

Saint Aristotle "Telly" Savalas
aka Police Lt. Theo Kojak
1922-1994

Pray to this bald-headed golden Greek for solace in all of life's travails, for Saint Telly overcame many obstacles: he was a runaway, an immigrant's son, bald, a failed boxer and ultimately a lollipop suckin' cop named Kojak.

Usually you can buy the candles at 99 cent stores. If they are plain, great. If they already have pictures on them, no problem, you'll just paste over. We've found that craft paste or even spray mount (an art glue that sprays on) works best.

First, choose your subject. Is it Björk (patron saint of motherhood?) or your best gal pal (patron saint of friendship?) or maybe it's Leo DiCaprio (patron saint of washed-up teen stars?) or Buffy (patron saint of chick power?).

Cut a piece of paper that will fit around your glass candle with not too much overlap. Now, on the left half paste a picture of your saint to be. On the right half write a passionate plea (like we wrote here) as to why you think this person would be the patron saint of motherhood, friendship, washed-up teen stars or chick power. Decorate the rest of the paper. And then glue onto your glass candle. Burn when you are in need of support.

It Is Poker Time

While we don't suggest you become a betting fool, poker is a fun way to pass the time with the girls. Just stick to betting cheddar goldfish or bobby pins. There is a whole poker culture that you need to get in the swing with before you play. Like you and your friends need to give each other poker names. Like Foxy LaRue or Shim Sham the Flim-Flam Man or Joey. And you need to dress the part.

Grab hats of any kind. No, wait, hats like gangster hats. Tip sideways. Wear a tight old tee, the grosser the better, or it can be plain and white but not look too new. Wear slacks, men's slacks or a long Bonnie-style skirt, and then wear some dress shoes or boots. Stash a pencil behind your ear and chew on wads of gum.

Make sure you have snax. (You could be betting with snax. Like cheddar goldfish.) Set up a card table. Play some old-time music, either swing or Frank Sinatra or Louis Prima. Maybe even put a red bulb in the table lamp by the phone. You know, to give the room some ambiance.

And then play. We recommend making a big cheat sheet of what hand beats what. Write it up poster-size. And hang it on the wall where everyone can see it.

The object of this card game is to have the best hand at the end of each round, winning the communal pot of bets. You can find the basic rules online—just go to your favorite search engine and type in "poker rules." It's pretty easy, and once you get going there are so many variations of the game that you and your friends will never be bored again.

This is a good summer tradition: Girls' Thursday Poker Nights.

Get your
PICNIC
Basket IN GEAR!

Just in case any picnics
arise. Or, heck, plan a
pleasurable picnic yourself.
It's summer.

And remember, a picnic basket doesn't necessarily have to be a basket. It could be, though. Or it could be a shoe box. Or an old potato sack. Or a lunch box from the thrift store. Or an old suitcase that's on the small side. (Oh, I like this idea best! –Keva) And here is what you should put inside (all scrounged from the neighborhood thrift stores and Mom's unused cabinets):

Cool plastic plates, metal cups, plastic silverware
(write yer name on it!), baby pocket knife, salt +
pepper packs from Mc Donald's, oh, and sugar packs,
too AND baby jams + some moist toilettes from
yer favorite BBQ joint, pretty cloth napkins (from
thrift store – don't have to MATCH – but wasH first – you
could even monogram them!), Maybe some votive
candles + matches, too (for romance) + NAPKINS
(in case yer in the woods and need to pee! ☺).

Concoct a few transportable snax. Keep it simple. Stick to the time-old tradition of bread, cheese and chocolate. Nab a new friend and take off on a picnic. Happy picnicking.

Ecstacy (X-T-C;
Clarity; Lover's Speed)

It's technically MDMA or methylenedioxymethamphetamine and you shouldn't be ingesting it even if you can say it.

But our feeling is that you are gonna make your own choices. And if you're gonna make choices, they should be informed ones. So we thought we'd take this moment to explain to you exactly what MDMA, or Ecstacy, does to your hot bod.

Chemically, MDMA is similar to the stimulant amphetamine and the hallucinogen mescaline. So what that means is that MDMA produces both stimulant and psychedelic effects. It speeds you up and freaks you out.

The, um, "high" lasts about three to six hours, but the after-effects[1] can last up to weeks. MDMA produces a significant increase in your heart rate and blood pressure. The stimulant effects of MDMA, which enable users to dance for a long, long time, also easily lead to dehydration, hypertension, and heart or kidney failure.[2]

MDMA frequently causes a significant increase in your body temperature. Hot and sweaty is all right. Except that this can cause your tiny but strong muscles to break down and can cause your kidney and cardiovascular system to fail.[3] People, young people, otherwise healthy people, have had heart attacks and strokes and seizures while on MDMA.

But maybe you're feeling daring. You're feeling lucky. MDMA is neurotoxic. That means that chronic use of MDMA was found to produce long-lasting, permanent damage to the neurons that release serotonin in your brain, which consequently will impair your thought processes. You think pot smoking wipes out your short-term memory? This stuff obliterates it.

So that's the poop on the stuff known as MDMA. We've said enough. The choices are all yours, babe.

---

[1] Confusion, depression, sleep problems, anxiety and paranoia.
[2] Um, that's B-A-D.
[3] Which, yeah, leads to death when it is severe.

Meow!!

Maybe you're a cat lover in distress.
Maybe you need guidance in letting loose,
having fun and all around being happy. Well then, we
think you should check out the Egyptian goddess Bast.

You may recognize Bast from art books or Egyptian tombs, for
she is the one with the ladylike figure and the really big cat
head. Bast is officially the goddess of joy, music and dancing and
a symbol of animal passion. She is also the goddess of life, family and
the domestic cat. See, the ancient Egyptians held cats in the highest
esteem and, if you injured or, goddess forbide, killed a cat, well, the
punishment was very severe.   Like death.

Copy this
page and
post it
over the cat
bed. Perhaps
your cat will
become filled with
a regained sense of his or
her aristocratic heritage and
stand taller, walk prouder and
get in fewer cat fights.

In Egyptian lore wild serpents would attack the Sun God and ultimately
those very serpents would be killed by Bast's great cats. You'd think the
snakes would learn after the first time, but no, this is reported as
happening over and over again. Bast's festivals, held in her honor,
have reportedly been very licentious and quite popular. Check
out her history and maybe you too will feel like partying
in the name of Bast. Maybe you'll choose to rename
your cat Bast. Or perhaps you just want to
dedicate this little book to your cat, in
the name of Bast.

The Martial Arts

Do you ever find yourself wondering if Buffy just pulled a move from her tae bo class or if she really is doing some fancy jujitsu? Maybe you always wanted to kick some booty but didn't know how, exactly, you wanted to kick it. Well, today is your lucky day, for we are going to give you a beginner's background on all the different types of martial arts. You know, just in case.

Aikido

This particular martial art allows you to defeat your enemy without hurting him or her. This may come in handy with the law. That must be why it is so often referred to as "the way of harmony." But don't worry, if you study aikido, you will still kick some ass.

Tae Kwon Do

This is a martial art that demands that the body has the agility of a professional ballet dancer. If you don't dance, don't do this one. No, we're kidding. But it's graceful and pretty.

Tai Chi Chuan

This is the one where everyone moves really really slowly, allowing your chi (life energy) to flow freely throughout the body. This makes it possible for mind, body and spirit to all work together.

Judo

This is the maybe strange, but often exciting, Japanese art where grown men roll around sort of cuddling each other without doing any physical damage. Back a long-ass time ago some guys in the Far East felt that jujitsu (another martial art) was way too violent, so they eliminated some scary stuff from it and came up with a new martial art called judo. In judo you try to "upset the enemy's balance."

Kendo

More of a hobby than a martial art. This weird study involves hitting each other with sticks while making grunting animallike sounds. This is what Keva practices.

BLOODSHOT EYEBALL CUPCAKES.

THE PERFECT DISH FOR A BAKE SALE. OR JUST BECAUSE.

Get a box of chocolate cake mix. Mix it up, quicklike. Bake in cupcake tins. After they cool, take a teaspoon and dig out a spoonful of the chocolatey goodness in the center of the cupcake. Eat. Now fill the hole and cover the cupcake top with white frosting you bought in a can. Place a single black or blue gumball in the center. Now you need one of those tubes of red piping gel. Draw in red, bloodshot lines radiating from the gum eyeball. Sell for $1 apiece.
Or devour hungrily.

August 10

You know that urge to not tell people your dreams, your wants, your desires because somehow, some way, you think that will jinx you? Well, you do know that's a bunch o' hooey, right?

TELL SOMEONE

Keva is dreaming.

See, when you don't tell a soul about some master plan you might have concocted, then you have no one to go to for moral support. No one to garner feedback from.

TELL SOMEONE

So what shall you do?

TELL SOMEONE

Clea is listening.

Sit down with one person, a person you trust. And tell that person your dreams. Tell him or her that you don't want the world to know (unless of course you do, and then by all means, spread the gospel!).

TELL SOMEONE

And maybe your confidant will have advice on how to get there. Or ideas you hadn't thought of. Just maybe he or she will have dreams to share, too. And we promise, if things don't work out quite as planned, it wasn't a jinx. It just means it wasn't your time. But maybe your time is just around the corner...

TELL SOMEONE

Do you sign your letters with X's and O's? We do. Do you ever wonder how that X came to mean a kiss? We did. So we looked it up.

Apparently it goes back to medieval times. Most people were unable to read or write back then. And yet they had all sorts of official documents that needed signatures. So the illiterate medieval folks would sign these papers with an "X" mark. However, an X is not much of a signature. So, to add a sense of commitment and a personal touch, it became customary to kiss the X after writing it.

Kissing the X became "performance law," a ritual act that bound the parties the way legal documents bind us today. Anyhow, this act of kissing the X, witnessed by the person who wrote the text, represented a solemn guarantee of the truthfulness of what was written. It was an oath to carry out whatever obligations were stated in the document.

Over time, people learned how to write and the X and the kiss became interchangeable. The X has lasted the test of time, but not as a signature, more as a final sentiment of love. And now a few Os are thrown in, for hugs.

XOXO

August 12

IT'S BEAUTIFUL OUT. YOU CAN ACTUALLY BE OUTSIDE IN
THE EVENING WITH JUST A TEE SHIRT AND SHORTS ON.
AND YET THE TELEVISION IS INDOORS. WHAT TO DO?

You'll need the following: Parents' permission, twinkly XMAS lights, extension cords, um, POPCORN (duh), telly-vision + VCR, lots of chairs for everyone you invite, rented movies (best if they're old + mushy), wind machine. (OK, scratch that last thing!)

Once you have all of the above (and we mean ALL of the above), check the weather forecast and make sure it's not gonna rain. Call some friends and invite them over. Hang the twinkle lights in the trees or in bushes or just off the back porch. Bring the TV and the VCR out (please get help, they're heavy!). Place them on a table outside. Feed the extension cords through a window and out to your backyard, then connect to the lights, TV and VCR. Set up the chairs around the TV all theater style. Feel free to use patio furniture or even lounge chairs. Have music playing (classical even?) when your guests arrive. Start popping the corn. Maybe give your little sister

a buck to blow soap bubbles from behind a
nearby tree for a little bit (it's about atmosphere). Once
everyone has arrived, plop in the movie, kick back and enjoy
the summer nights, watching flicks under the stars.
P.S. Happy Birthday, Jeff.

YOU USE YOUR FEET EVERY DAY. YOU'RE QUITE HARD ON THEM
IN FACT, TRAMPLING AROUND ALL DAY LONG, AND WHAT DO YOU GIVE
THEM IN RETURN? QUITE OFTEN TINY LITTLE SHOES WITH POINTY
TOES OR, WORSE, HEAVY, CLUNKY ONES THAT MAKE YOUR FEET ALL RED AND ACHY.
SO, LET'S DO SOMETHING TO PAY THEM BACK FOR ALL THEIR HARD WORK.

THE PAYBACK foot scrub

1/2 cup oatmeal
1/4 cup cornmeal
a couple drops of essential oil
like lemon or peppermint
1 tablespoon salt

WHIZ THAT OATMEAL IN THE BLENDER TILL IT'S GROUND UP GOOD.
MIX WITH CORNMEAL AND SALT.
THEN ADD A COUPLE DROPS OF WATER TO GET A GRITTY PASTE.
NOW ADD THE DROPS (JUST A FEW) OF OIL.
MIX AGAIN.
SIT ON THE EDGE OF YOUR TUB
AND MASSAGE THIS STUFF INTO YOUR BELOVED FEET.
SCRUB WELL, OVER THE HARD SPOTS, BETWEEN THE TOES

(IF SOMEONE OWES YOU A BIG FAVOR,
ASK THEM TO DO THIS PART FOR YOU).
NOW RINSE AND DRY.
DRY WELL.
AND THEN RUB SOME MOISTURIZER OR LOTION INTO YOUR FEET.
COVER WITH SOCKS.
AND DON'T FORGET TO WIPE OUT YOUR TUB AFTERWARD.
BECAUSE OATMEAL CAN CLOG YOUR DRAIN.

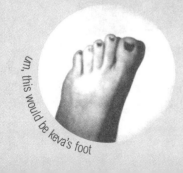

um, this would be keva's foot

August 14

future files

a. a snapshot of new orleans that we both love b. a painting from clea's house c. the famous "not" sign from keva's house accompanied by garry davis's feet

Sure, we've given you loads of tips on how to redo your room. But is it ever enough? Can you ever stop changing your room around, crafting new looks and accessories? No way, Jose.

Enter the (c'mon you know what to do: find that Darth Vader voice deep inside you and say...) FUTURE FILES.

The latest and greatest file is dedicated to DECOR. This is where you cut and stash any and all articles about crafts. And this is where you cut and stash any pictures of hotel rooms or Alyssa Milano's living room or some Arab sheik's tentlike abode. Anything and everything that is inspiring to you and your room.

A cool color?
Stick it in the file.
A weird painting?
Stick it in the file.
A pic of a '60s donut phone that you adore?

Stick it in the file.

Variety is the spice of life. It's a cliché and it's the truth. And chances are you will never want to stop mixing it up in your room, so get those ideas together in one safe place and you can pull them out at will. Scribble on the folder or record jacket or brown paper bag in big golden letters, DECOR. That's really all there is to it. But then, you already knew that.

What makes you, you? August 15

Can you shave your legs with your eyes closed and not bleed?
Can you draw a perfect horse though you don't even like horses?
Do you know all the lyrics to tons of great punk rock songs?

we don't know you, but you know you. or do you?

(Say that ten times fast.)

DOES CLEA GO "OUMM"?

DOES KEVA TAI CHI?

OK, LIST TIME:

Now, write down 12 things that rock about you.
Everything that makes you, you. Everything you are good at or feel good doing. (But they have to be truly about YOU, not about how someone else makes you feel good.) You're now gonna give yourself a superhero identity...and that list of 12 things, those are officially your superhero powers.

All right!! Now you need a name! Think: "Queen Latifa" or "Super Clea" or "Catwoman" or "Kittykittykokogirl." Write it down every chance you get. Make it your Hotmail password. Now for your superhero outfit: Is it skintight Lycra and red-white-and-blue? Is it Hawaiian and floral and loud? Is it black on top and pink on the bottom? Whenever you need your superhero powers: Cross wrists together with a bang. Repeat your name to yourself three times. Voila. Activated!

Next time you're feeling low, like when you stuttered in front of superfox Billy and he looked at you funny, call up your superhero. Let your inner superhero powers come out and fight the fight against evil and boredom. (Or stuttering...)

And when you are having a great day and everything is going your way, scribble your name across notebooks, soles of shoes, backs of test papers, the dirt in Mom's car window. Go with it.

August 16
eat like a bodybuilder day

Keva: Whoa, Clea, really, I have to do this one? Clea: Yep, it's all you.
Keva: OK, I guess I'll ask Jeff.

OK, then I called Jeff or actually I made him come over. (Hi, Jeff!)
See, he's here to help. He even brought me juice.

Keva: Um, so if I wanted to eat like a bodybuilder
for a day, where do I start?
Jeff: Ugh, arise at the crack of dawn.
Keva: At the crack of dawn? How about 6:30?
Jeff: 6:30 is OK. Now run, bike, swim, bounce up and down really fast or
speed walk in your room but DO NOT eat yet.
Keva: For how long?
Jeff: At least 30 minutes but no more than 40 minutes.

who's in the mask?

jeff's tuna sandwich

1 can tuna (white meat in water)
Mix with 4 hard-boiled egg whites
(no yolks). Mix with nonfat mayo.
Add pepper. Pile tuna on one slice of bread.
Only open face sandwiches allowed.
Make the night before and tote to school
with some protein bars for snax.

ohh la la muscles

jeff's dinner

Chicken breasts, no skin, salad,
light or fat-free dressing, veggies,
rice, no butter, no oil, no
Gummi Bears, no fun!!!

Ok, so I lasted five minutes. But think about all those people
who train for stuff and how hard it is and how much
dedication it takes, and now after your fat-free day of lunges
you may just have some more respect for where all those
muscles came from. And we don't suggest eating like this
for reals. We mean, one day is cool to stand in someone
else's shoes and all, but this is kind of hard-core
for a growing body like yours.

Boom ÷A÷ Rang

A STICK A 'B' a boom-a-rang

Whatever you call it, it's supposed to come back.

Make your own boomerangs. It's a sport. Sort of. Throwing lesson below. Now, remember, this is somewhat of an art form and you probably will suck at first. But keep trying, it will impress your friends. But remember, boomerangs can be dangerous when used improperly. These are just cardboard, but still. Don't throw them when there are kids around. And it won't work when it's windy. If it's windy, go fly a kite.

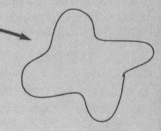

Cereal Box Big Boomerangs

Cut up a Cocoa Puffs or Special K box into three or four winged shapes. (PICTURE) Slightly bend each wing up. You can decorate them, too. To throw, pinch between your thumb and first finger and flip it out with a snap of the wrist, like throwing a dart. This boomerang should fly about five or six feet and return. Remember that the boomerang should be in an almost vertical plane when you release it, tipped sideways maybe 10 or 20 degrees, and you should throw it straight and forward (again, like a dart).

"i still suck, but i won't stop trying, i won't!" keva

Rabbit's foot ≠ good luck

bunny yum

Rabbit feet. Lucky? Not for the rabbit. When I, Clea, was a young girl, I assumed that they were fake feet, just some stuffed animallike foot. But no, those turquoise and pink and red rabbit's feet are just that: rabbit feet. Or rather, a dead rabbit's feet. It got me to wondering, do they kill rabbit just for their feet? So some lucky bastard gets to walk around with a fuzzy little charm in his or her pocket? This seems too cruel to be true. We tried to contact the makers of rabbit feet (yes, they are still produced) but to no avail. So we thought we'd check into how this animal and their beloved feet got into such a predicament.

The rabbit's foot is one of this world's oldest superstitious icons. Rabbit feet amulets have been used since before 600 BC, when the feet of the rabbit's slightly larger cousin, the hare, were made into charms throughout western and northern Europe. Why? Hares and rabbits were seen as very mysterious creatures. First off, they're born with their eyes open (unlike many other mammals), which freaked the good folks of ancient times out. Then there was their burrowing. People saw that as a connection to the underworld spirits. And like the cheetah and greyhound, the hare's rear feet land in front of its forefeet when running swiftly. That was pretty unusual for such a little animal—it impressed the primitive men. Hares also thump the ground with their hind legs as if speaking with them. A secret language all their own. And lastly, hares and rabbits are, um, prolific breeders. They have lots and lots and lots of baby rabbits.

So the creatures were seen as symbols of fertility, which, in ancient times, translated to good luck in general. After all, the more kids you had, the more workers you had to till the crops and, well, the more money you'd make. The feet of the animal were specifically used because they were sized right for a pocket, they came fuzzy and, we're told, they are easy to preserve. (Ewww.) Technically, the only lucky part of the poor little animal is the rabbit's left hind foot. Somehow, we're betting that all those colored little rabbits feet are not all back left paws. We say abolish the superstition that is rabbit feet. We say instead, sing the song when you're in need of a little luck. What song? "The Bunny Hop," silly.

PUT YOUR RIGHT FOOT FORWARD. PUT YOUR LEFT FOOT OUT. DO THE BUNNY HOP, HOP, HOP, HOP!

BOOK CLUB MEETING

Get ready. Now, you should host this first one. If you're not the host, you should be instrumental in helping set up. How many people are coming? Gather enough chairs or make sure there is room around the couch (and Mom doesn't mind your using the living room today). Snax are good. You really must have snax. You could create a theme to go along with the book or just go with a good sturdy crowd-pleaser like those cereal mix thingys. And it's good, since you are the host (or co-host), to come up with a few starter questions. Just to get the ball rolling in case your friends are there and someone says, "Now what?"

grab a notebook and write down a few:

did you like the book? why?
Could you relate to any of the characters?
was it believable? Does it matter if it wasn't? Who are your favorite characters? why? What was your favorite part? Who would you wanna play if they made this book a movie?

clea loves to read and she also is in a book club. go, clea!

Put on some nonobtrusive music. Nothing too loud. Something you can talk over. Again, maybe theme it to the book. Some possible book-music-food combinations to try out:

"Endless Love" by Scott Spencer
romantic Verdi arias
soft and fluffy meringue cookies

"Weetzie Bat" by Francesca Lia Block
Zydeco music
toast with avocado smooshed on it

"The Saskiad" by Brian Hall
songs of the humpback whales
trail mix and cornmeal pancakes

Maybe if you're Irish you know all about those rings. But maybe you don't. We're talking about the little Irish rings that feature a heart in between two hands, topped with a glorious crown, otherwise known as the Claddaugh! (Pronounced CLAW-dah.)

So what's the deal? Well, traditionally the heart is a symbol of love: the hands symbolize friendship and the crown represents loyalty. We love that symbol stuff. These rings are given between friends to indicate a closeness or between lovers to indicate a commitment. Even if you're not Irish, they make for cool symbolic jewelry. There is even a proper "way" to wear the ring.

Here goes: If you are unattached, wear it on your right hand with the heart pointing out, toward your fingernail. This says to the Claddaugh-informed that your heart is still available. If you are in a romantic relationship, wear it on either hand with the heart pointing in, toward your wrist. This tells the gentlemen you're very much taken. And worn in this way on the left hand, a Claddagh ring usually means the wearer is married. More fascinating history from the Super Clea and Keva Marie. We know, you're impressed.

*women
who have influenced me.
part two, by clea*

It's hard for me to pick one woman (besides my grandma)
because it was a group effort, influencing me to be
the person I am today. But I credit the women of rock.

That may sound cheesy, but it is true. Music was my refuge.
And I spent more time with Patti Smith, Sugar Pie Desanto,
Etta James, Joni Mitchell, Janis Martin and Rickie Lee Jones
than I did with girls my own age, back then.
If you've never heard of any of them, don't be alarmed,
I'm not 50. I just liked old music, especially by women.

As a young kid, I just made my way through
my mom's and grandma's albums.
Then later it was women like Kim Deal, Björk,
Kim Gordon and Liz Phair who influenced me.
And not just musically. But in life.

I took my attitude from Sugar Pie and the Kims.
I got inspired creatively by Patti and Björk.
I got strength from Etta and style from Janis
and wit from Rickie and sex appeal from Liz.
Individually, they created and produced insanely
fantastic music, but together, they became a schoolhouse
of the best teachers and role models a girl could ever want...

a symphony of inspiration!

TALK LIKE AN ENGLISHMAN

"Cheers darling"

Cockney Rhyming Slang is this brilliant "language" created in London. You can use the classic phrases or create your own. The trick is to come up with a phrase that rhymes with the word it stands for. Like instead of saying "bed" you'd say "Uncle Ned." Often the English say only the first word of a phrase, so to the average listener it sounds like gibberish. "I'm tired, think I'll hit uncle." But you and your friends know what it all means.

FOR INSTANCE...THESE ARE CLASSIC COCKNEY RHYMES

kiss	hit and miss	"Well, it's about time John hit and missed Katie."
hell	ding dong bell	"Oh DING DONG BELL!"
sister	skin and blister	"My skin and blister is such a witch."
sleep	bo-peep	"I was out till 4 am—time for some bo-peep."
sweethearts	jam tarts	"Meg and Steve have been jam tarts for years."
girl	twist and twirl	"I'm just a twist and twirl..."
legs	ham and eggs	"Roger's a runner; he's got good ham and eggs."
dope	bob (hope)	"That new outfit of yours is bob."
telephone	dog (and bone)	"Just give me a call tomorrow on the dog."
money	bread and honey	"Buy me this burger, I am out of bread and honey."
!&%	friar tuck	Um, you get the picture....

And here's a few we made up...

boy	Siegfried and Roy	"That Jeff is one hot lookin' Siegfried."
fox	shoe box	"That Jeff sure is a shoe."
lust	pie crust	"I pie over that Jeff dude."
tramp	summer camp	"Judy is all over Jeff—she's such a summer."

this is tim, keva's englishman

Bank Holiday

yes, this is a castle in England

Today is a bank holiday in England (yes, again). What does this mean to you? Well, nothing really. But it seems like a perfectly good day to rent the movie "Bonnie and Clyde" (see, they were bank robbers in the '30s, get it?). And Faye Dunaway, the actress who plays Bonnie, wears the most fantabulous clothes in this flick.

Bonnie was only 19 when she started running with that bad boy Clyde. She wasn't even five feet tall, wasn't even 100 pounds. She got a lot of press for smoking cigars, but she hated them. See, a friend shot a photo of Bonnie with a cigar in her mouth as a joke and it made the papers. Boy, was she ticked off. Clyde wrote the newspapers endless letters asking them to please stop calling her a "cigar mol." We kinda like the "mol" part, though. Do you have a friend who is a real mol? A mol is a sophisticated bad girl. A dolled-up babe from days gone by. You could dress the part of the mol today, don a chic '30s hat, a retro knit dress and real full red lips.

Anyhow, this story does not end happily. No, Bonnie and her gang of miscreants killed at least 12 people in their bank robbing rampage through Texas. And she was killed at the age of 23, her body riddled with bullets. Ah, a life of crime does not pay. But you already knew that.

hi clea, let's go to england! ok? ok, bye – k.

August 24

YOU WEAR WHAT?

Clea: I hate socks, but love Peds. Only problem is, I can't hang on to them longer than a week.
I think they spontaneously combust because one day they are in my sock drawer, the next they're—poof!—gone.

Keva: Well, aren't you picky about your clothing accessories. Were you terribly fussy as a little Clea as well?

Clea: Um, maybe. Don't you have weird clothing Keva-dos and -don'ts?

Keva: I was style frustrated as a kid and wanted to sew stuff (funny, huh) and then I would and it would be really weird and I'd wear it to school and everyone would sorta be like..."Um, that's, ugh, cool, Keva."

Clea: I bet it was cool. I had big boobs from the time I was like 11. It was so sad. So I wore lots of big tentlike things even though I was real tiny. I tried to cover my boobs. Ha!

Keva: I've made it my lifelong goal to flash someone (boyfriend or sister) at least once a day for the rest of my life.

Clea: Interesting. I have never seen this side of you. Who'd you flash today?

Keva: Kim at work and I fake-flashed Richard, but didn't really, I only made him think that for a minute I was going to but I would never.

Clea: Who is Richard?

Keva: Some silly guy I work with. The first time I met him I was wearing a yellow chiffon miniskirt and a hot pink tank top and a camo cowboy hat and I wanted to go dancing in Tijuana.

Clea: My cowboy hat is one of my most favorite possessions ever.

Keva: Wait till you see mine. Oh, yeah, do you know how to reshape a badly shaped cowboy hat?

Clea: Steam? The shower? Let my dog run around the yard with it in her mouth?

Keva: OK, let's do it next time we hang out, OK!?

Clea: You betcha. I'll bring my dog!

Discussion questions: Do you hate socks? How do you feel about Peds? Do you think it's possible Clea's socks spontaneously combust? Or is she just a slob and therefore loses said socks? Are you picky about your clothing accessories? How so? Were you fussy as a child? Do you ever make your own clothes? How about your boobs, large or small? Discuss. Do you think Keva should be flashing random people? Why or why not? Dancing in Tijuana...good or bad? Why? Do you have any idea how to shape a misshapen cowboy hat? If so, feel free to write us and tell us how!

Back to school time is here. Oh joy.

Well, it's an excuse to grab all your clothes and go through them and revamp some of your old things, making them new again. Here are a few things you can do. And if you want these groovy homemade looks but don't have the gear at home to use, hit the thrift palace du jour and pick up cheap stuff to cut and resew.

Old sweater?

It's icky? It's scratchy? It's riddled with holes? Cut the sleeves off and wear just the sleeves. It's called a muffetee and it's a divine boho look for the avant-garde young gal.

Thin little belt?

It's too small? It's too thin? It's just ugly? Make a bracelet. Like rocker style. Cut off four to five inches of the "hole" side and cut off just the buckle. Take your duct tape and tape the buckle to the other piece with the holes. Wrap around your wrist. Or make a little longer and wrap around your wrist twice.

Turtleneck?

It's too tight? Too bright? Too ugly? Cut off the turtle part and wear as a head band. Now, if you're feeling sew-crazy, redo the neckline of the old turtleneck, turning it into a boat neck. Stitch hem.

Anything that's boring?

Just add sequins. Or beads. Or embroidery. Or a monogram. But decorate it. Man pants? Why, add glistening, glittery beads in the shape of a flower at the bottoms.

LET'S MAKE BAGS

Yep, bags.   For school, silly.

1. Get two pieces of sturdy canvas from your neighborhood fabric store (1/4 yard each) and yes, they can be different colors or the same. And some heavy-duty thread.

2. Then tear off the strap pads from an old, ugly backpack or pick one up at a thrift store for like $1 and rip those off. Get all the materials in your hands, clomp on over to the sewing machine and plop on down.

3. Follow the below instructions for one fly bag! Cut fabric pieces into two squares, 14" x 14". Lay them down on top of each other, nice sides facing each other. Pin the sides together and then sew, sew, sew on three sides. Zigzag stiches make it strong. Then take the backpack straps and measure them around your shoulder. If one strap is long 'nuff, use that. If you need two, sew them together first, then cut to your size.

Sew here

14 x 14

4. Now sew the strap ends to the inside of the bag at the seam. (See drawing.) Zigzag a few times. Make sure your hands are steady. Now turn your bag inside out, and voila. You got bag.

5. You could add a pocket on the outside or monogram the bag with your initials or iron on a patch. This bag is perfect for PE clothes!

¡MAKE NOTEBOOKS!

forget that trip to the drugstore to get new notebooks and such for school. instead, make your own. it could actually come out cheaper and far, far cooler. you'll need to get a big pack of ruled paper, preferably with no holes but it doesn't matter. try the stationery store for bulk prices.

and you'll need to hit the thrift stores and grab a few old record albums. look for titles that speak to you. the "grease" soundtrack. some old james bond soundtrack. grover does disco. you're going to cut them up, so if the album itself is beat up, all the better.

now you need to go to the copy center place, like kinko's. you are looking for two things there: a paper cutter (industrial strength), and a guy or gal who can spiral bind things. binding usually costs only a buck or two. if it's more than that, they are ripping you off and tell them so. rip the album cover apart so you have a front and a back. now, using the paper cutter (this is cardboard, after all, and you will get a straighter line with such an instrument as opposed to, say, scissors) cut two pieces, one from the front of the album jacket, the other from the back. they should both be 8 3/4" x 11 1/4". now take your paper and your new notebook "cover" over to the spiral binding person. they will punch in those little holes and attach the spiral like magic. (the spirals often come in colors too, so ask.) it takes only a minute or two unless they are really busy. and you and your one-of-a-kind "grease" notebook are ready for school.

August 28

Bulletin Boards

We dunno if you're like us, but both of us scholarly girls can't keep track of a single thing unless we post it big and bright on our bulletin boards. So in honor of going back to school, we think you must create for yourself a brand-new bulletin board. And if you already have one, then this will be even cheaper and easier for you.

Grab a bulletin board. The kind with a wood frame. Can be gotten at Target type stores for very cheap. Look around house for random paint. Paint wood. Let dry. Meanwhile look for a scrap of material as big as your bulletin board. A scarf will work. In fact, a cool vintage scarf will be easy and fun and can be had for a buck or two at some local hall de thrift. Now you want to cut the material to the size of the bulletin board (if the scarf is smaller than the board, center the scarf): Lay it down over the board. Pull the material tight and put a pin in all four corners. Now, with some sort of chalk or pen or something, mark the size you need by following the pen along the borders. Untack the material and cut out along the lines you just marked.

Now get some glue. Good glue. Not glue-stick glue, but real glue, like wood shop glue or model airplane glue or white pastey glue. And a paintbrush would really help. Pour a little glue into a small bowl and dip paintbrush in. Brush the glue all over the cork part of the bulletin board. Spread it thin. Now take your piece of material (have the pins ready, too) and align the top corners of the material with the top corners of the cork board. Now smooth, from top to bottom, adhering the material to the board as you go. Use tacks to pin down any seams that are curling. Get it all smooth, all bubbles out. And let dry. It's pretty, huh?

Now hang it up in your room and pin your new class schedule to it and some inspirational words from us and maybe a picture of your best friend. You're now ready for school.

You write. Diary entries, poems, odes, haikus, eight-volume novels, whatever. You've got something to say, you want the world to hear.

How do you go about doing it?
AKA
How on earth did Clea and Keva get a book deal?

If you do in fact write and you do in fact want the world to know it, there are so many places and ways to get your stuff published. You just got to grow a layer of thick skin (because not everyone will be clamoring to run your stories) and get proactive. Rarely do publishers come and find you. You've got to go to them. (For more inspiration, see "Persistence Is Key," March 23.)

MAGAZINES
Many still publish reader fiction: some publish poems or little ditties. There is usually an address at the bottom of the reader stories for you to send your work into. But even if they aren't publishing reader-written works, if you think your story truly would fit in their magazine, by all means, send it. Write up a nice cover letter explaining why it is you think they should publish this story. Remind them you are their demographic (the persons whom they are trying to reach). Flatter them, but not too-too profusely. And mail.

WEBSITES
There is a website for every interest, every hobby, every demographic these days. Find the one that best suits your writing and email off a short note and a brief description of the story. If you have a great story about poodles (and Clea does!) then maybe try sending it to PETA's website (the People for Ethical Treatment of Animals) or type in "Poodles" in a search engine and see if a poodle fan page turns up. And if it doesn't, well, maybe you should just start your own website.

SCHOOL NEWSPAPERS
Do not discount the all-mighty school newspaper. If your writing is more of the factual nature, this is a great avenue, and trust us, they are ALWAYS looking for more writers.

THE LOCAL WEEKLY PAPER
If your town has one of these, this is the perfect opportunity to hone your rock journalism skills (or your environmental writing skills or your restaurant reviewing skills). Write up a short story or review and mail it off to the editor or the assistant editor with a cover letter. Offer to write about other concerts (or issues or restaurants). This is how Clea began writing.

START YOUR OWN ZINE
We've already covered this, we know (July 14 to July 16), but publishing yourself is often an easy and effective way to get your word out. This is how Keva began writing.

Lastly, people are impressed by someone who is published. It's true. So the more stories and writings and odes and poems and letters you get out there, the more doors that will open for you in the future. Check your ego at the door and put on your persistence cap (Keva's favorite item of clothing) and get crackin'. You've got a lot of writing to do.

the keva + clea all-new

LUNCH MENU

established 2001

We like peanut butter and jelly as much as the next gal, but how about trying some new and varied sandwiches and snax in your Strawberry Shortcake lunch pail this week? And if your lunch consists of the Taco Bell value menu, take a bean break and come with us down the road of righteously random mealtime menus meant for the middle of the day.

variety is the spice de life!

Banana Rama: The Sandwich

You'll need bread of some sort. Two slices. We like sourdough here. But not too-too sour. You'll need some cream cheese—the whipped kind spreads all nice 'n' stuff, but is not so necessary. And you'll need a banana or two, sliced and laid out over the cream cheese. Now here is the part that makes this sandwich sing: horseradish. We know, you're saying, "phooey." But horseradish has a mildly zingy flavor that really does go well with bananas. Just don't use very much or you'll burn those little nose hairs you can't see but you know are there. Just about a fingernail's worth is plenty. Put the other piece of bread on top, smoosh down good and wrap in wax paper or baggy for later consumption.

Triple Decker Turkey Day Sandwich

Maybe turkey is your favorite treat. Maybe Thanksgiving is your favorite holiday. Maybe you like feeling woozy-tired from all the tryptophan. Maybe you think turkeys should not be eaten but, rather, kept as pets. You'd be wrong. They are mean.

You need wheat bread—soft, mushy wheat bread. Three slices. You need some turkey. You need some stuffing. Instant stuffing would be just fine. In fact, it's quite yummy. And you'll need some cranberry sauce (although we've wondered why they don't call it cranberry jelly or cranberry glob or something else because it doesn't have the consistency of any sauce we've ever seen, but we digress). Now you put the turkey and the cranberry goo on one piece of bread, add the second piece of bread and then the stuffing. Finish with the last piece of bread, and voila, instant lunchtime Thanksgiving meal in August (or April or January or whenever). Feel free to add any leftover veggies to this sandwich, like baby peas.

Spa-a-licious Night.

More homemade treats for your face. Not only can you make this recipe for your at-home use, but you can package it up all pretty and share with a friend. Or give to your mom. Or your favorite teacher.

The Breakfast Exfoliant.
Don't let the name fool ya. You can exfoliate morning or night. This recipe just happens to feature a few borderline breakfast ingredients. You need:

2 tablespoons powdered milk
1 cup or so old-fashioned oats
1 teaspoon cornmeal

Grind your oats in a blender or food processor for a minute or so, till it's as fine as flour. Dump it in a resealable bag with the powdered milk and cornmeal. Seal 'n' shake. Or, if you want to pretty it up, put it in a small jar. Don't forget to seal 'n' shake. When you are ready to exfoliate, take 1 tablespoon of the mix and put it in a small bowl. Drip a few drops of water in, stirring, till it's the consistency of paste. Allow it to thicken for one minute. Practice your dance moves in front of the mirror. And then massage the goop into your face and neck. Breathe a deep, deep breath. Rinse. This recipe makes enough for about 10 treatments. Just take a tablespoon of mix every night and add the water.

THE MONTH
IS...!?!

september

S   S

Shoes

The Keva Cheer,
in honor of her
birthday. Ahem.

The most energy in
the world.
The most spin when
she does a twirl.
The most groovy
kind of girl.
She's Keva.

With a mom who makes
yummy cauliflower, fried.
And an attitude that
makes all the boys cry.
She doesn't even really
have to try.
            She's Keva.

Happy
Birthday
KEVA

september

0 1 SEP

FROZEN FOOD ↑

She lives in the
bitchin' sugar shack.
She doesn't take no
flickety-flack.
You never have to watch
your back.
(She's watching it
for you.)
She's Keva.
She's Keva.
She's Keva.

Have a party
in honor of
Keva's birthday.
You must wear feather
boas and tiaras.
It's just the way it
is. Everyone must dress up.
And you must have some
sort of yummy food.

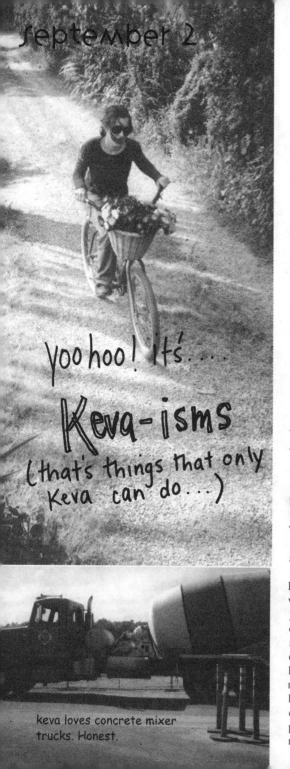

yoo hoo! it's.....

Keva-isms

(that's things that only Keva can do...)

keva loves concrete mixer trucks. Honest.

Keva has so much uniqueness abounding all around her that it's hard to know where the Keva-ness ends and the Keva-isms begin. It's just a big walking Keva-fest when she's around because no one, and let me repeat, no one, is like Miss Keva Marie. Keva-ism #43: She loves her family and must tell each and every member "I love you" at the end of every single phone conversation she has with them (and Keva loves to talk on the phone, Keva-ism #68). Even if she's just had a "fight" with her sister (not that she fights much, but...they are sisters after all), she will still end the conversation with "I love you." I love that. Keva-ism #87: My boyfriend Jeff came up with this one. He says Keva talks in slogans (like, "Girls Kick Ass!"). And clever cute sayings. And nuggets of sugary goodness. He's right. Keva-ism #101: She loves words like "Chihuahua," but not just because of the dog and not just because of the pronunciation but because of the essence of the word and the spelling. I mean look at that word: Chi-huahua. It's weird. And Keva notices that and then uses it in her conversation often. Keva-ism #123: Keva understands that it is OK to wear zebra to any occasion. And with anything. And she does. Keva-ism #175: This Keva-ism is related to #68 because it involves talking on the phone. When we drive around together, she usually drives (I think she hates my driving but she will never say so, Keva-ism #32) and she always must be talking on the phone, too. Talking on the phone and driving, driving and talking on the phone. And her mom often calls and says, "You're not driving and talking on the phone, are you?" But of course she is. Keva-ism #184: Cupcakes. Yes, cupcakes. Keva will fight any battle with them. If people just aren't friendly enough to us, we buy 'em cupcakes. And then she has me write funny sayings for the tops of the cupcakes. It works every time. Kill them with cupcakes, that's her unspoken motto. Keva-ism #199: Any person, male or female, who comes into her office or her home to fix something, like the air conditioning, or maybe to deliver the FedEX packages, they all love and remember Keva by name. Why? Because she is Keva.

Family Trees

Family trees are pretty cool. They are like a book about your whole family but in picture form. We think you should make one. But if it doesn't interest you at all, make a friend tree, connecting the ways you met various pals over the years.

This makes an excellent birthday present for your parents or your nana or for your best friend.

Whichever you make, you will need the same stuff. A pot or bucket or jar. A big branch with lots of little branches coming off, plus more little branches to attach to the tree if need be, tape, ribbon, paper and pen (maybe even photos?!) and something to anchor that branch into its pot, like dirt or marbles or dried rice or dried beans.

Start by getting that big branch in the jar, bucket or pot, and make sure it's relatively secure.

Now, on a piece of paper, start to trace back your family. Ask your parents for some help. Or Grandpa.

*Do this with duct tape. (You can cover it up with glitter.)

And if you are doing one for friends, think about how you met all your friends. Like kindergarten? Or through another friend? Next, make sure your big branch has enough little branches in the right places.

If it doesn't, just prune off excess branches & reattach them.*

Now take some paper and make a little card...

...one for every person on your tree. Glue on photos of that person or draw pictures. Write words that describe them. Add their birthday...

...punch a hole in the top and loop yarn through it.

Now start putting each person's little card ornament on the tree where it belongs. You can add little signposts, too, at the connector branches that say how these people met...

...like "second grade" between Suzy and Marie or "Married, 1972" between your mom and dad.

september 4

LABEL-DAY

Originally we thought we'd introduce Label Day on Labor Day but no, our editors nixed that idea. That's cool.

STILL, LABELS ROCK

And those label guns are the most fun. You dial in the letters of your name or goofy words that describe the contents of said box. And punch. And punch. And punch. Sure, your fingers get sore, but it's so worth it.

Even if you don't have access to a label gun, you can still pick a pack of pickled labels at the drugstore. Grab your favorite pen and start labeling.

THINGS TO LABEL

Any and all files that have not been labeled thus far.
School stuff. Label your stuff by subject. Or date.
Shoe boxes filled with photos from your vacation. And that slumber party. And that ex. Label that one, "Whatshisname."
Shoe boxes filled with shoes. Label 'em things like "clunky cloggy cherry choes" or

MY SEXIESTHEELS

Shoe boxes filled with letters. Dedicate a box to letters and cards from family members. One dedicated to pen pals. One dedicated to local gal pals. Don't forget to label your box of craft supplies if you have not done so prior to this date. Feel free to name it after us.

Offer to help Mom or your younger sib organize their stuff, too. Make sure to remind everyone...

LABELING IS FUN

Toast to bread, for without bread, there could be no toast.

We love toasts.

Not toast, as in stale, crunchy bread, although we love that, too. No, toasts, as in minispeeches or odes to friends and loved ones.

And they don't have to be just for special occasions, either. You can toast every night at the dinner table. "To Sissy's B+ on the math quiz." "To Mom's fabulous new hairdo." Make 'em up as you go along. Or consult books or websites for historical, meaningful ones.

Toasts date back to medieval times. It was common to kill your enemy back then by offering him a poisoned drink. To prove the drink was A-OK to one's suspicious guests, a host would put a small amount of the guest's drink in his own glass and both would drink at the same time.

But if the guest wasn't that suspicious, they would simply clink glasses as a show of good faith. Even though most of us today don't kill our enemies with poisoned liquids, this custom stuck. So when did this clinking of the glasses become known as a "toast"? A few hundred years ago it became common practice to drop a small chunk of toasted bread into your drink. This custom has left us, but the word "toast" remains.

So, raise a glass to those nutty medieval folks, stale bread, your good pals, Clea & Keva, and yourself.

september 6

OK. So you're back in school. The monotony has begun. You eat lunch with the same people every day, in the same spot, usually ingesting the same food. Mix it up a bit. Organize a weekly lunch party of sorts.

You could pick a New SPOT. ●
Say every Wednesday you and your friends will eat in the big oak tree in the park down the street. Yeah, up in the tree, like tree-fort style. Or you'll have a full-blown picnic, with blanket and basket on the lawn at school. Or maybe you have to eat in some lunchroom. Then pick a day, um, Thursday, when you will move to a different table and maybe even bring tablecloths and real silverware. (Candlelight is probably pushing it.)

You could eat with New people.
Invite along someone you don't normally eat with. Maybe you can have lunch with some younger kids who lunch at the same time. Or you can ask those, um, boys to join you. Entice new friends with cookies.

You could eat new & different food.
On this particular day you are not allowed to bring the same peanut butter and jelly sandwich or eat the same value meal from Taco Bell. No, you can assign things, like a pot luck. Say one friend brings the salad. And another brings the cheese plate. And yet another brings a lovely loaf of bread. And you bring the cookies. Each week it rotates so the meal is always different.

viva la differance!

Gather your friends together. From top to bottom here is Susannah, Lauren, Michelle, Lisa and Karen.

Throw a Slumber Party!

And NO, you're not too old and yes, they are super fun. Pick a day, pick a house, pick the girls, pick a theme, pick your nose, make cute invites and pass 'em out and get organized.

Things to look forward to:
Bond sessions with your girl pals.
Good snax…no, GREAT snax.
Cute PJs.
Masks. As in facials.
Photo ops. Nab that Polaroid.
Gossip. Oh, the gossip.

Themes:
Cat on a Hot Tin Roof, Southern style.
Horror Movie Freak Out.
Ladies Night, '80s Night with "The Breakfast Club," "Sixteen Candles" and lots of hot-pink PJs.

Gather all your supplies, spruce up the room you will all sleep in (make sure your little brother is sleeping at his friend's), make sure the TV and VCR are ready to go, rent the movies (hey, consult our movie days for ideas), get the snax, make sure Mom and Dad aren't having guests over and, well, you are READY! Oh, and maybe plan a breakfast, too. (Household tip: prearrange a deal with your bestest friend to help you clean up in the morning because doing it alone is no fun!)

**Ideas for Snax:
Popcorn, homemade, with real butter.
M&M's with peanuts mixed together in bowls.
Chips and dip!
Shirley Temples! (cherry juice & 7-UP)

*By the way, Susannah & Lauren are sisters!

september 8

Need something to do tonight? Well, provided it's relatively clear out (no rain, no clouds), you could...

STAR HOP.

This activity is good alone or with a friend or three. Here's what you do. Go to the backyard after dark. Bring a portable stereo and a tape or CD of something trippy and soothing. Lie down on the ground (check for dog poo first). And gaze up at the stars.

Now, the first thing you need to do is locate the Big Dipper, seven illuminatingly bright stars that form the shape of a pot, sort of. Four stars form the bowl and three stars make up the handle. Once you find it, you can start star hopping.

To find Polaris (the North Star) you need to first locate the two stars that make up the right side of the bowl (the side that doesn't touch the handle) in the Big D. Those two stars are called the pointers. Now, in your mind, connect those two stars and make an imaginary line that extends outward in the direction of the opening of the Big Dipper's bowl. The bright star your line will run right into is Polaris.

Polaris is the tip of the handle on the Little Dipper. The Little Dipper looks a lot more like a soup ladle with a curved handle. Enjoy the Little D. It's cute, ain't it?

Cassiopeia

NORTH STAR

little dipper

Big Dipper

Now imagine Polaris is the center of a clock. Draw a line out to 1 o'clock. The grouping of bright stars you will run into is called Cassiopeia or the "Queen's Chair." It looks like an extrasmall dipper to us, but whatever. It's still cool.

The story of how the constellation Cassiopeia got there rocks.

Cassiopeia was a very beautiful but vain queen, married to King Cepheus of Ethiopia. She went around boasting that she was even more lovely than the exquisite Nereids, the fifty(!) sea nymphs who were the daughters of the nice god Nereus, otherwise known as the Old Man of the Sea. (Following us so far?) Amphitrite was one of those sea nymphs and she was married to Poseidon, powerful god of the sea. She and her 49 sisters talked Poseidon into punishing Cassiopeia's pride. He did, all right: He sent this monster, Cetus, to destroy Ethiopia (harsh punishment, eh?). Well, it gets worse. Poseidon said that if King Cepheus gave his daughter, Andromeda, to the monster Cetus, it would not ravage his land. So get this, the king just gave Andromeda to the beast. But before it could take her away, this young hero dude, Perseus, came and killed Cetus. Now Poseidon was bummed. So he placed Cassiopeia in the sky to revolve around the "celestial pole forever." And because she "revolves," she is often in very undignified positions, such as, oh, upside down.

Recycle. Duh.

CANS

Plastic

Bottles + Glass

When I lived at home, every Thursday night like clockwork my dad came to me and said, "Where's your trash?" I'd hand it over and quickly get back to homework. But I knew that any moment he would yell for me, and sure enough the yell came: "Keva, you have to flatten the cardboard, and the plastic water bottles go in the plastic bin!"

For years this went on. It was awful. It was like my conscience was determined to let me down every week. But still, for the first few years of this repetitive torture I chose to be a brat and ignore and defy my father. I did nothing. I continued to chat on the phone while I heard him going through my trash and separating out my recyclables. I knew I was being a bad daughter, but I just couldn't get out of my lazy mode. I suffered from feelings of guilt and failure as a daughter and got in the habit of calling myself "the bad daughter." Which, by the way, took more energy than actually doing what my father wanted me to do. I know, lame, huh?

Then one day I took the train to Los Angeles. I spent the whole time daydreaming out the window and peeking into everyone's backyards. It was all pleasant until we got to the part of L.A. that is right near the train station. The place where they drove around in the movie "Grease," and the part where you see all the graffiti and little cardboard houses where homeless people live. It was really dirty. And there was trash everywhere. I got really depressed and irritated at how sloppily these people lived. I thought to myself, "Well, if they can't get a house and they need to live outside, then at least they can clean up," and then it was like I got a slap in the face and someone called me "BRAT!" and I realized what I had said. And that the way those people were living was no better than what I did, and if I lived on the streets I would be just like them, but I was worse, and I felt awful. Like a spoiled bratty teenage girl who was lazy and didn't care about the earth and let me tell you, it didn't sit well. I didn't like that label at all. Being "the bad daughter" was one thing, being this was quite another.

In fact, when I got home I went through my trash and pulled out all the plastic bottles and put them in Dad's "plastic" bin outside. And you know what? I felt better. And you know what else? On that Thursday night when I was on the phone with my friend and had already done the trash my dad yelled up at me and said, "Thank you!"

FUTURE FILES: SCHOOL.

MAYBE YOU'VE GOT YOUR FUTURE ALL PLANNED OUT. YOU WANT TO BE A VETERINARIAN, JUST LIKE YOUR DAD WAS A VET AND YOUR GRANDMA BEFORE HIM. OR MAYBE YOU ARE EXPLORING SEVERAL OPTIONS. (HMM, NAIL POLISH MOGUL OR RACE CAR DRIVER? TOUGH CHOICE.) AND MAYBE YOU ARE LIKE MOST PEOPLE AND HAVEN'T A GOSH-DARN CLUE. FEEL FREE TO GO BACK TO THE FUTURE FILE MARKED "JOBS" AND PERUSE IT FOR ANY AND ALL IDEAS.

BUT WHATEVER YOUR DIRECTION, IT PROBABLY INVOLVES SOME SORT OF SCHOOLING BEYOND THE HIGH VARIETY. A UNIVERSITY OR BEAUTY SCHOOL OR ART INSTITUTE OR CLOWN COLLEGE OR THE McDONALD'S McDONALDLAND HAMBURGER ACADEMY.

SO TODAY'S (SAY IT WITH US, DEEP AND THROATY) FUTURE FILE INVOLVES SCOURING MAGAZINES FOR BOTH TYPES OF SCHOOLS AND THE CITIES THAT THEY ARE BASED IN. GRAB THAT FOLDER (OR RECORD JACKET OR BAG OF SOME SORT) AND WRITE ON IT: SCHOOL. IT'S A BORING TITLE BUT THE STUFF INSIDE WILL MAKE UP FOR THAT.

YOU PROBABLY OCCASIONALLY SEE AN ARTICLE ON THIS SCHOOL OR THAT ("SAN DIEGO STATE'S A PARTY SCHOOL" OR "RHODE ISLAND SCHOOL OF DESIGN IS THE MOST NOTED ART SCHOOL," STUFF LIKE THAT). CLIP IT. SAVE IT. FILE IT. ALONG WITH OTHER ALTERNATIVE TYPES OF SCHOOLS. LIKE THAT HAMBURGER ACADEMY.

MAYBE YOU CAN EVEN DO A LITTLE RESEARCH. GET ON THE WEB AND LOOK FOR INFORMATION ON SCHOOLS THAT OFFER PROGRAMS YOU MIGHT BE INTERESTED IN. BECAUSE ONLY CERTAIN ART SCHOOLS OFFER FILM OR FURNITURE DESIGN. AND SOME COLLEGES DON'T OFFER VITICULTURE & ENOLOGY CLASSES (THE STUDY OF HOW TO MAKE WINE). AND MAYBE YOU'VE NEVER SEEN AN ARTICLE ON THE STUDIO MAKEUP ACADEMY** BUT YOU'RE CURIOUS. LOOK IT UP. PRINT THE INFO OUT. AND FILE IT.

**THAT'S WHERE YOU GET BETTER AT MAKING FAKE SCARS. SO YOU CAN WIN THAT OSCAR.

september 12

YO. MORE TALKING.

Clea: Cats are fine, but dogs, now, dogs rule my world. Literally. My dog, George, she controls my life. She sleeps next to me in my bed and if she wants more covers, I give them to her.

Keva: That's gross. Do you let her lick ice cream off your cone, too?

Clea: I would , yep, if I let her eat people food, which I don't. She talks to me, though. She sounds just like Chewbacca from Star Wars. How 'bout you, cats or dogs?

Keva: Dogs. But it makes me sad 'cause I wanna get a puppy but I don't know if I could take care of her good 'nuff.

Clea: You're being responsible. You'll get one eventually. What kind do you want? (I like mutty mutt mutts).

Keva: I want a Boston terrier. They are like big dogs that are small.

Clea: I don't know any Boston terriers personally but they seem like decent dogs. My dog snores.

Keva: Boston terriers are supposed to snore, too. I think that's cute. I drool. What about you?

Clea: Oh I drool, big-time. I have to change my pillowcases often cause they get all crusty and hard. My dog snores and drools. And she sleeps with her head on my pillow right next to mine.

Keva: Sometimes, when my dad is really tired or sick, he talks in German in his sleep.

Clea: Do you understand what he's saying?

Keva: Oh, heck no, it's super weird. We talk back to him, though.

Clea: That's cool. My dad just snores. But so loud you can hear it clear across the other side of the house. It does have a little singsong pattern to it, though. Like this, "Allalalalalalalal."

Keva: Wow, are you OK?

DISCUSSION QUESTIONS

ARE YOU A DOG OR CAT PERSON? WHY OR WHY NOT? DO YOUR PETS SNORE? TALK? SLEEP WITH YOU? HOW DOES KEVA KNOW HER DAD IS SPEAKING GERMAN? SHE HERSELF DOES NOT SPEAK GERMAN. ISN'T IT POSSIBLE HE IS SPEAKING GIBBERISH AND SHE JUST ASSUMED IT WAS GERMAN? DOES ANYBODY IN YOUR FAMILY SPEAK GERMAN?

Polaroid Day is simple, really. We love Polaroids: their instantaneousness, their squareness, their runny, dark colors. They are one of the modern world's greatest inventions. However, they are expensive. Even though you don't pay for developing, the film costs a buck a shot. So use wisely.

The following are just some things you can do with Polaroids.

Draw on them. Permanent markers work best. Draw a frame right on the photo. Leave a message. You can take a pic of yourself and write your note all around the edges. Leave it on a car or in a locker. Make a magnet. Just glue a little magnet on the back and they will stick right-like to the inner walls of your locker or on your bathroom medicine chest. Make a mobile. Create a bookmark. You can figure that one out. Build a house of cards. You know, like they made on that one "Brady Bunch" episode where their dog Tiger knocked the whole thing down and the girls blamed the boys and the boys blamed the girls. Make friendship streamers. Take a Polaroid of every one of your friends. Punch holes in upper left and right corners. String together with ribbon, or paper clips, making a long chain of pictures. Hang in room. It's a friendship streamer. Hang photos on a clothesline above your bed. Take a piece of twine and attach it to opposite corners of your room and with clothespins clip up pics of your favorite pals or your kittens, that way you can look at them as you fall peacefully asleep.

it is polaroid day!

september 14

Typewriters are cool.

Keva picked one up at the thrift for $8 and it works great. It's old. It's kinda small but that don't matter. It's just the keys, the keys and the way they type, are so cute, so neat, so special, so sleek. Type type type. Certain kinds of letters should be typed and not the computer way, but the typewriter way. It has a more meaningful feel. And if you mess up it still looks cool.

If you leave your typewriter out in your room and have people over, you'll find that one of those friends typed you a note on your typewriter when you weren't looking. Those are always the best. You see, people can't help it. They see the typewriter, they see the paper, and they are compelled to leave behind a little dis or dat. Besides, the typewriter itself is cloaked in all kinds of fabulous history. It's very romantic, in fact.

Mark Twain was one of the first people to fiddle with the first ever typewriter and he was also the first person to submit a novel in typed form to a publisher. That was way back in 1833! And the original typewriter was heavily decorated with colorful decals and gold paint, which is way cool, and it looked a lot like those old-fashioned sewing machines, which is even cooler! This is because the guy who designed the first typewriter had been transferred from the Remington sewing machine department. Gosh, we are just full of knowledge, like real knowledge.

Now who wouldn't love to get an old-fashioned typed love letter in this day of supro-technology?

Letters to type with the typewriter:
Notes to self, Screenplay, Ransom note, Love letters, To-do lists and your best poems.

Respect
Your
Elders Day

It is yet another Japanese holiday. Today is Respect Your Elders Day, which seems reasonable to us. So today, do just that.

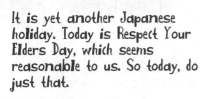

Be incredibly polite, like excruciatingly polite, to your parents and teachers.

Imagine what you will look like, act like, be like when you are the age your mom is right now. (By the way, don't ask her how old she is if you don't know—after all, it is RESPECT Your Elders Day.)

Walk 'round singing that Aretha Franklin song, "Respect!"

If you have time, make your parents breakfast. Cereal and milk counts, too.
It is, after all, the thought.

Call your grandparents. Say hi.

Offer to do the dishes after dinner. Just this once.

And maybe bake some cookies and bring them to your aging next door lady neighbor. Or bring a bouquet of flowers by her house. But don't tell her why, that might be insulting. Just tell her it's "Because."

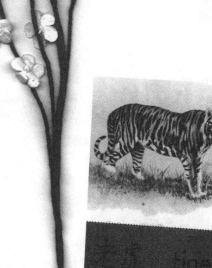

tiger

MEXICAN Independence DAY

=VIVA= LA MEXICO!!

Since we are all about hot dogs on July 4th, America's Independence Day, why not craft a Mexican-inspired hot dog recipe for this particularly special day? Why not indeed.

Mexi-Mummy Dogs
are nummy yummy

2 tubes pizza dough in refrigerator rolls
1 cup grated pepper jack cheese
Nonstick spray
4 tablespoons or more salsa
8 hot dogs
Optional toppings: onions, green peppers, olives, jalapeños

Preheat oven to 300 degrees F. Spray a cookie sheet with nonstick stuff. Cut pizza dough into eight squares. Press it kinda thin with your fingers. Add salsa to each square. Add a hot dog on top of salsa. Then the cheese and anything else. Encase the whole dog and all its stuff in the pizza dough. Pinch ends. Bake for 15 minutes. Dip in more salsa when you eat them.

CONDITION YOUR HAIR...
and then wash it.

This stuff will condition your hair. Like real conditioner. But if you have oily hair, skip it. If you have oily hair, invite a friend over with dry hair and play hairdresser. Or you could put it on just your ends.

You will need:
1/4 cup virgin olive oil (Yes, like you cook with.)

10 little drops essential oil, maybe lavender or rosemary

A shower cap

That's all you need. Now wet your hair a little. Or if you took a shower then towel dry your hair real well—it should not be drippy-wet—before going to the next step. Combine the olive oil with the essential oil and coat your hair (do this over the tub, it could get messy). Cover your head with that attractive shower cap. Run your tub water pretty hot and stick a towel under the faucet. Soak that towel in the hot, hot water. Then wrap your shower-capped head in the hot wet towel, Egyptian style.

Now sit back (even though your head is now feeling very heavy, thanks to that soaking wet towel) and read a really juicy magazine or book. Sit and relax. For 30 long minutes. Paint your toenails, maybe. After the 30 minutes are up, remove towel. Remove shower cap. Take a shower and wash your hair, maybe even twice, to remove the remaining oil. And, ta da, your hair will be shinier and more lustrous than ever.

september 18

they played croquet in alice in wonderland in fact i think it was the queen of hearts croquet is so very righteous and so british - lisa b

the sport of CROQUET

*Nab the book "**The Basic Eight,**" wherein the main character has a gruesome use for croquet mallets. Oh no!

In no other game can you wear traditional white apparel, sip tea and sit in a lawn chair between shots. And really, what could be better?

Oh, we know: drinking iced tea with fresh mint AND playing croquet! Yes! Not to mention the awesome feeling that swinging a tall wooden mallet can bring ya. Become one with brightly colored balls and narrow white wickets, and plan a posh picnic with salmon pate and sparkling water. Croquet, a centuries-old game, is the ideal social activity for your party, club outing, corporate gathering or charity fundraiser. Heck, yeah.

What to wear: Ah, the mere mention of white will brighten any day. Cotton or linen. Girls must wear dresses. Everyone must wear hats.

Ask a few key people to bring one or more of the following: Crackers, cream cheese, olives, cheese, a baguette, strawberries, sparkling bottled water and lemons & limes.

It's not BBQ day, it's F. Scott Fitzgerald at the Hamptons.

Who to invite: aunts, uncles, sisters, the friendly librarian. No more than 15, please. This is a social gathering, not a rager.

The object is to hit the little ball through the bent wire things and back again. Check out the directions that come with your set. We really do recommend that you and your friends go in on a set and plan on playing several times a year. It's classy, classic fun.

Clea has great white teeth.
She doesn't smoke.
Hmmm. Coincidence?

I might come off as the biggest dork in the history of dorks, but I, Clea Hantman, have never smoked a cigarette. Never even tried it. And many people will think that's a lie or they will think that dork thing, but it's all true.

See, my mom smoked since I was a very small girl. And we lived in Florida, in the crazy steamy heat of Florida, which meant that we lived with all the windows shut tightly and the air conditioning on. The air conditioning just re-circulated that smoke around the house, pushing it through my room, my little brother's room, the kitchen, the den and back again. Our whole house reeked of cigarette smoke. I reeked of cigarette smoke. I was a seven-year-old girl in grade school and I stunk of smoke. There was one defining day when a teacher actually asked my extrasmall seven-year-old frame if I had been smoking. I was mortified. I vowed that day never to smoke. And I have held that vow.

I even went as far as to vow never to date anyone who smoked. That particular promise I broke, once. It was for a pseudo rock star, and if you haven't noticed by now my intense desire to BE a rock star in the pages of this book, well, you haven't been paying attention. It was the biggest temptation. So I went on one date with this musician and his cigarettes, one date. At the end, he leaned in to kiss me goodnight and I was sent reeling back to my childhood years and that smell of stale smoke. And that cliché is true, it was something akin to licking an ashtray. We never went out again.

I don't judge people who do smoke. It is, after all, one of life's little choices. And I really try hard not to preach. But I do remind people of my childhood and then I hit the zinger home: my mom now has emphysema. She's young, too. She's not one of those old, wrinkled up, bent over old ladies hacking up stuff when she's not hooked to a machine. She's a young, once-beautiful woman hacking up stuff when she's not hooked to a machine. When she was younger, she smoked, but always thought she'd quit soon. But when the bumps of life came a little quicker down the highway than she thought, she kept it up till she was smoking three packs a day. You know what else?

She still smokes.

OK, maybe that was a bit preachy. As a side note, Keva doesn't smoke. She's tried it, sure, but she doesn't now. In fact, her very adorable boyfriend smoked when they started dating. She informed him that they would never be serious as long as he was a smoker (she just couldn't see herself "long-term" with one). He quit the next day. True story. Go, Tim!

WAIT . . . HELLO!

DON'T BE LIKE ANNIE.

I will start my photo album tomorrow.
I will wash my cat tomorrow.
I will start a band tomorrow.
I will stop drinking soda tomorrow.
tomorrow, tomorrow, I will love ya tomorrow...
WAIT!!?????

DO IT NOW!

If you're in the "Annie habit" of always puttin' things off till tomorrow, now is the time to cut that crud out! Annie may have been pretty cute and all (orange afro, little red dress) but come on, let's get real. We say don't be an Annie. Do it NOW!

Some things you may be putting off for many tomorrow's but could easily be done today:

Redye your towels pink 'cause they be fading...Go to the zoo just 'cause you never did...Read the Weetzie Bat books...Paint your bedroom baby bobby blue...Find missing socks and your diary from the fifth grade...Put those stacks o' photos in a photo album...Shoot some hoops with good ol' dad...Take your dog to the park & play ball till she lie down from sheer exhaustion...Donate stuff. Just stuff. Good stuff...Mail a card off to your nana...Hit the library, read silly books in dead silence.

Butterfly Wings

Make yourself butterfly wings. This could be for Halloween or just because. Just because you felt like wearing wings today. Or tomorrow. Or a week from Thursday.

You'll need: Several wire hangers, masking tape, crepe or tissue paper of all colors, the handy-dandy-what-would-we-do-without-it glue stick, two pieces of wide ribbon approx. 15" long (it may need to be longer or shorter depending upon your height), needle and thread.

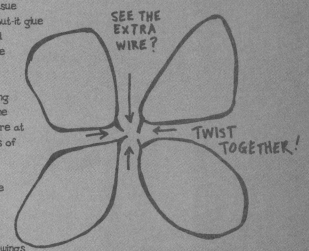

SEE THE EXTRA WIRE?

TWIST TOGETHER!

Unbend your hangers. Carefully, we don't need anyone getting hurt. Then you want to reshape them into four section of the butterfly wings like this, leaving an inch or two of straight wire at the end. If the wire is not long enough, just make two pieces of wire into one with some masking tape.

Now trace the shape of all four parts of the wings onto the crepe paper. Cut out two pieces for every section (there should be eight crepe paper pieces). But don't attach yet.

First you want to join the four wire hanger "petals" of the wings together. That's what that extra inch was for. Twist those four extra pieces into one and cover with masking tape. Now you have the frame of your wings. Take those crepe paper pieces and carefully run the glue stick all along the edges. Press the wire hanger frame onto the glue. Glue stick around the edges of the reverse piece of crepe paper. Then sandwich the hanger in the middle of the crepe paper.

Do this for all four sections. You can now add decorations to your crepe paper wings with the glue stick: cut-out shapes of crepe paper, glitter and sequins—but be careful, crepe paper rips easily.

Now for the final part. We need to make backpack type straps out of the ribbon. Basically you want to make two big loops, large enough to go around your shoulders. So measure out how much ribbon that actually is. Then just loop one ribbon around the center of the wing frame and stitch the ends together. (Or tie in a knot!) Do the same for the second ribbon. They're loose and floppy but who cares. Once on your back they won't be. Now try them on. Make adjustments. And fly away...

Ode to a red rubber ball!

THE NAME OF THE GAME IS KICK BALL.
YOU SURE DON'T HAVE TO BE SHORT OR TALL,
JUST COORDINATED ENOUGH NOT TO FALL
WHEN KICKING THAT RED RUBBER BALL.

IT'S KICKBALL MADNESS!!!

We like kickball because everyone can play. Even your most uncoordinated friends. And yet, it's exercise. And it's group camaraderie fun. And it's about a red rubber ball. We think you should start a kickball club with kickball teams. Come up with team names and mascots. Wear matching ensembles. Challenge one another on the weekends. You don't need much. Just a red rubber ball. Which everyone should own anyhow, so go get one.

As for bases, this is kickball, nothing fancy necessary. Try pizza boxes from last night's dinner. Or paper bags. Or rocks. You already know how to play, that's part of the genius of it all. It's baseball with a big red rubber ball. Set up the bases, like the bases in baseball. One team puts a few people in the outfield. Not too many or the game will be over too quickly. The first team up to kick should have a kicking order. Make it official, write it down on a clipboard. When it's your turn to kick, whack that ball into the open space and run for your life. Three outs and your team's in the outfield. The other team is up to kick. Play nine innings until your toes ache from kicking that darn red rubber ball.

AND WHEN IT'S ALL OVER, PLAY RED ROVER, RED ROVER!

YEA FOR AUTUMN

Autumn is the coolest season of all.
Hello? It has two names, Autumn and Fall.
The leaves change colors and the wind blows cool.
If you don't love autumn, you be one giant fool.

It's the first day of autumn. Yippee. Get all your fall stuff ready. Embrace the day. Here's what to do.

If the leaves are already changing color in your neighborhood, box up a bunch and mail them off to a friend who lives someplace where the leaves don't change. If you live someplace where the leaves don't change, get on the horn and call someone who does and remind them sweetly to send you a giant box of red and gold leaves.

Get out your sleeping bag. If you don't have one, then get one. If you can't get one, then fold up your comforter like it's a sleeping bag and sleep in it tonight. On the floor. Camp-out style.

Start thinking about Halloween. What will you be? How will you make your costume? What will you need? Also, dream of candy. While sleeping in your sleeping bag on the floor, have visions of sugar daddies dancing in your head.

Get out any and all sweaters. Yeah, it may not be sweater season quite yet but it is around the corner. Make sure you have enough soft and fuzzy ones. Also check for ski caps and gloves. You will want these things very soon.

Go to Chinatown (if you have one in your city) and buy Moon Cakes. They are little pastries eaten in honor of autumn. They are filled with lotus paste and weird berry jams and goopy stuff like that.

Get your hands on some apple cider. Revel in all its appleness. Bob for apples. Bake apple pie. Dip apples in caramel. Give an apple to your teacher. Take note of all the pretty varieties they have at the store. Do more reveling in appleness.

P.S. Happy birthday, Tim!

september 24

TODAY'S MOVIES WILL HELP YOU GET OVER ANY PAST, PRESENT OR FUTURE HEARTACHES BECAUSE ALL OUR FILMS ARE EITHER ABOUT BREAKING UP (OR BREAKING UP AND GETTING BACK TOGETHER) OR THEY ARE INTENDED TO MAKE ONE FEEL BETTER ABOUT SUCH A DOOMFUL EXPERIENCE.

clen is sad. very sad.

If you have any friends currently going through tumultuous, heart-wrenching scenarios, today is the day to invite them over. Make them some popcorn or brownies. Turn on the TV.

Need to feel love struck by another? Try a John Cusack movie, the most fantabulous "Say Anything." He is simply the very best boy, ever.

Looking for sheer stupidity in a break-up movie? Simple, rent "Bio Dome."

POPCORN

Depending upon what mood strikes you here is our guide.

Wanna remind yourself that guys are so very cute and simultaneously so very dumb? We suggest "Swingers" because it's got the sad, pathetic, cute, dumped boy and his smarmy, dumb but foxy friend.

Wanna forget about guys altogether? Why, rent "Thelma and Louise," of course.

Is your heart shattered into so many pieces that you think you will never believe in romance again? "The Princess Bride" never fails to reawaken your dreamy, romantic side.

keva is more sad. oh, keva.

Do you like your break-up films adult and artsy? "Next Stop Wonderland" is the perfect choice. Just-dumped beautiful woman's mom places a personal ad in the paper for her daughter. Ah, humiliation.

And finally, do you want your break-up movie with an '80s twist? There is no better than "The Wedding Singer." He gets dumped on his wedding day but in the end, all is good.

DON'T STRESS!

Forty-three (or more) things to do when you are stressed out. Buy books at the thrift store...paint toes and nails all different colors...don't clean up...make doggy clothes out of your old tee shirts...tape Xs on the back pockets of your jeans...talk to yourself even if other people can see...listen to your favorite bad music, guilt-free...read an old diary...bleach your upper lippy (see March 4)...watch silly Nickelodeon...rent an old movie with Marilyn Monroe...in fact, have a Marilyn Monroe movie extravaganza...do jumping jacks...cruise around the drugstore...get a jump rope...go online and get an instant messenger service...go to the library...drink carrot juice...squeeze lemons on your elbows...eat a tablespoon of honey...write a love letter (see February 11)...do yoga...see if you can suck your big toe...take a bath, a long, languid bath...dance around wildly and not to the beat...braid your own hair...get ice cream at 7-Eleven...watch the sunset...look for the green flash...eat mashed potatoes...get over it...measure your feet...listen to the Go-Go's...throw a hex...turn off the phone...do an all-over body lotion treatment...whistle, loudly...wear white lipstick...vacuum...then roll around on the carpet...do a mask...hoola hoop...get some chalk and make a hopscotch thingy outside...play war (see March 13)...read the dictionary...don't talk for 45 minutes...go to the movies, alone...don a tiara (see May 12)...freeze a banana for later...do a bunch of "ommms"...talk to your doggy (or kitty)...get fake glasses...wear a bandanna...make dreads...string beads onto the ends of your bikini strings...do super-powered butt squeezes...talk like a valley girl...make a list of all the things to do next time you're stressed.

Make a Handmade Book

We're gonna make a book to write your bestselling romance novel in (tomorrow's project). But you don't have to limit yourself to just romance novels. These books make great diaries, terrific sketch pads and petite notebooks for school.

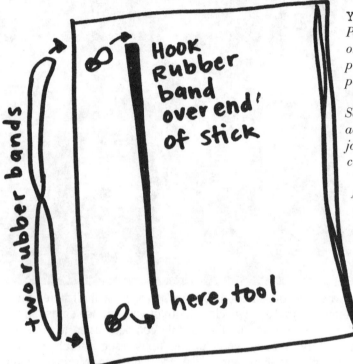

You will need:
Paper, doesn't matter what size or color. For this particular novel project, anywhere from 25 to 40 pages will do.

Some stiff paper or cardboard to act as a cover. Look to record jackets if you must. Or construction paper.

A stick or twig or chopstick, about an inch shorter than your book will be tall.

A large sized rubber band. Or two small ones knotted together.

A hole punch.

Step One. *Punch two holes in your paper, each about an inch from the ends. You will have to do a few pages at a time 'cause most hole punches don't go through big stacks o' paper. And remember to punch holes in the cover, too.*

Step Two. *Line the stick up along the vertical edge of your book, on top of the holes. Now feed one end of the rubber band from behind and through the top hole. Hook it on to the end of the stick.*

Step Three. *From behind, stick the other end of the rubber band through the bottom hole and hook onto the bottom end of the stick. Voila, your book is bound.*

Step Four. *Start thinking romance— you've got a book to write (see tomorrow for details).*

Ooh la la!

You made the book (or books) yesterday. Now you are gonna fill them out. It's time to write the most romantic bestseller of the year. With the help of your friends, of course.

On the first page write your name. This is the sign-in sheet. Now you start the story on the second page by setting up a premise. Creating characters. Give them names and describe the characters and their looks and their clothes. Then pass the book on to a friend. Tell her to sign in on the first page, read what you wrote and then write the next page of your book. Then let her pass it on to another friend who signs in, reads what came before and then writes the next passage, and so on and so. Keep passing it around to everyone you know and let them write a part. Try to fill up all the pages. If it's made it through your group of friends but it isn't finished, circle it around again. Keep going till it is filled and finished. Make sure to let everyone who helped create it read the finished product.

jeff was beautiful his eyes sparkled like little disco balls he was a fireman by day an espresso barista by night and he was all fire and coffee his love for the little chiquita named josefina was insane but unfortunately she did not return his feelings

But it wasn't because he was short or had a lisp. It was because she did not know he was alive. Monday thru Friday he saw her walking up and down the sidewalks. He marvelled at the way she carried herself, innocent yet worldy, in a way he didn't understand.

There was something about this little chiquita that drew him closer. He began to show up earlier at work, just so he could get a glimpse of her. But one morning he got to work late, too late to see Josefina, and he spotted the lovely Mary!

september 28

IF YOU NEED TO FIND THE KIND OF SPIRITUAL GUIDANCE THAT ONLY A WOMAN CAN GIVE, YOU TURN TO THE GODESSES OF THE WORLD, RIGHT? OR AT LEAST WE DO. THERE ARE GODDESSES FOR EVERY SITUATION WE CAN THINK OF.

ONE OF OUR FAVORITES, BECAUSE HER DOMAIN IS BOTH GENERAL AND OBSCURE, IS THE CELTIC GODDESS BRIGHID (OR BRIGIT). HER SPECIALTY? WHY, HEALING AND CRAFTSMANSHIP, MOST SPECIFICALLY METALWORK. YES, METALWORK. AS IN WELDING. OR JEWELRY MAKING. OR BRIDGE BUILDING. ALSO THE PATRON OF LEARNING AND POETRY, BRIGHID POSSESSES THE ONE AND ONLY BUBBLING CAULDRON OF KNOWLEDGE AND INSPIRATION. THE CELTS SO LOVED BRIGHID THAT THEY COULD NOT ABANDON HER EVEN WHEN THEY BECAME CHRISTIANS, AND SO MADE BRIGHID A CHRISTIAN SAINT. SHE SOMETIMES GOES BY THE NAME "SPHERE OF FORM." THAT'S COOL. AND BRIGHID LOVED GNOMES. IT'S TRUE. SHE'S SORT OF THE GODDESS OF GNOMES. ELVES, TOO. THOSE BLESSED WITH BRIGHID'S PATRONAGE INCLUDE THE CRAFTSPEOPLE (THAT'S YOU!), THE STUDENTS OF THE SCIENCES, THE HEALERS AND THE VISIONARIES. IF YOU KNOW OF SOMEONE WHO IS NAMED FOR THIS GREAT GODDESSS, SEEK HER OUT TODAY AND REVEL IN HER POWERS FOR SHE IS A TRUE SISTER. CELEBRATE HER BRIGHIDNESS. BEFRIEND ALL BRIGHIDS.
SEE BRIGHID. BE BRIGHID.

the SECRET life of Clothes.

by cled

One Christmas I was given a marvelous secondhand purple velvet zip-front jacket as a present. I treasured it. I wore it all winter and the next one, too. It wasn't just a jacket but a symbol of winters past. I knew someone else had endured the cold while looking stylish for years before me. But the following winter I passed it over for a wild leopard fake-fur coat with big bushy lapels and chunky buttons down the front. It was the new winter me. The purple velvet one was the old winter me. So I did what any self-respecting fashionista would do—I gave it to Goodwill.

Several winters later I was going out to eat with a new friend and she showed up wearing my old but still marvelous secondhand purple velvet zip-front jacket. I stared at it, I touched it, I tried it on—it was the very jacket I had once called my own. My new friend had had the jacket only a few months. Where had it been all those years? What was it up to? Did it get worn? Did it hang in a closet, threatened by moths? It looked no worse for wear. Like an old friend who had just reappeared in my life, the jacket left me wondering, what had it been doing all this time? Where had it been, what had it seen? What kind of secret life did my clothes live when I wasn't with them?

hey,
hand me
the soap!

ROSH HASHANAH

scrub!
scrub!
scrub!

Rosh Hashanah is a holiday that celebrates the New Year of the Jewish calendar. Well, we're all for celebrating new years because that means we get to wipe the slate clean of all wrong-doings from last year, so get that metaphorical washcloth out, it's a NEW YEAR! Of course, if you belong to the Jewish faith, this day has even more significance, but we think we should all partake in this New Year cleansing.

So, put that Prince single on (because we're gonna party) and grab your trash can. If you've been fighting with a girlfriend, throw away any and all bad notes or letters you two have exchanged. Call her and tell her it's a new year, no more fighting. That boy you've been crushing on hard who hasn't been returning your admiration? Grab anything that reminds you of him and throw it out. He's done with. You're moving on to greener (and cuter) pastures. Think about developing a new crush. Bad habits you've picked up lately? Well, you're forgiven if you toss them in that trash can right now. No more nail picking. No more nose picking. And god knows no more cigarettes if you've gone down that road. It's cleansing time. Drink a big glass of water. Chant a few "oms." It's meditation, cleansing for the soul. Breathe deep. Relax. OK, back to the trash can. Pick up real trash that's lying around your room. New years must always start with a fresh, clean room. Light a few candles. Go through old makeup. Throw it out if it's crusty and bacteria-ridden (it is if it's old). Drink more water. Say more "oms." Dance a little to Prince.

Lastly, if you haven't been living up to your potential (and frankly, who has?) pick one thing, just one thing, that you know you can do better. Is it French? Or soccer? Or helping around the house? Whatever it is, resolve right here and now to try harder, do better and all around be good at that one thing. It's your Rosh Hashanah Resolution. hallelujah

Clea looks tired, huh?

O is for October C is for cake
T is for tim O is for orange juice
B is for bread and butter
E is for everything that's fun
and R is for raviolis

October 1

Talk in Song Lyrics

Today you shall attempt to talk in song lyrics, all day.

Everything that comes out of your mouth shall be phrased in a song. It works especially well with oldies but goodies. Start your day with one of these or find your own...

"Hello, is it me you're looking for?" (Lionel Ritchie)

"Domo Arigato, Mr. Roboto" (Queen)

"Hi! My name is ... Slim Shady" (Eminem)

You'll find it's easier than you think, provided you listen to the words in songs)—otherwise, it's difficult as heck. Therefore see bottom of page for alternate plan of action.

Happy birthday, Aesop!

"Yesterday, all my troubles seemed so far away." (the Beatles) If today ain't going your way, express it in a song.

"Isn't it ironic." (Alanis whatshername) Random and sort of ironic (not).

"In your eyes, I am complete." (Peter Gabriel) Not recommended unless you know the person super-duper well.

"Don't stand so close to me." (Police) Very good on subways.

"In a big country dreams stay with you." (Big Country) So random, so funny.

"You're a heartbreaker." (Pat Benatar) This is a great random thing to say to some random boy. Make sure to snarl, too.

"All I wanna do is have some fun." (Sheryl Crow) An appropriate expression any time of the day. You can also work in "Girls just wanna, just wanna have fun." (Cyndi Lauper)

Random things to say to people when it gets awfully quiet:

If this is simply too difficult for you because you know no lyrics to songs, then try this: Phrase everything in a question. Instead of starting your morning with "Hello," try "How are you?" "Wanna have lunch with me?" "Didn't I hear you love spaghetti?" That sort of thing. And so on. Deem it "Jeopardy" day. Get your friends in the act, too.

la /a la lala/a la /a la /a la lala/a la /a la la la la la

when in need
call on alcmene
when incompleter
call on demeter

When you need a helping hand, why not call on one of the dozens of Greek goddesses. (Hey, the more help, the better.) They each have a specific realm that they watch over. So you just need to know WHO to call for the various situations of your life. There is a goddess or three for every possible situation that may arise. We've devised this little chart that you can keep on hand.

Quarreling with friends?	Amphityonis
Scared to learn to swim? Scared of the little fishes?	Amphitrite
Questions of love?	Aphrodite
Find a stray dog?	Artemis
Want to cause a little mischief?	Ate
Get back to nature . . . go vegan!	Demeter
Having trouble getting up in the morning?	Eos
Is your period out of whack?	Hera
Family squabbles?	Hestia
Not enjoying your youth enough?	Maia
Need help winning the track tournament?	Nike
Having trouble pulling off those card trix?	Selene
Your jokes not going over well with that cute boy?	Thalia
Is your voice out of tune in choir class?	Polyhymnia
Getting through the longest poetry class ever?	Calliope
Getting through the longest history exam ever?	Clio
Having trouble finding your rhythm on the dance floor?	Terpsichore
Help getting that boy to fall for you?	Io

October 3

You're a star!

hello!

DEAR:

MAKE YOUR VERY OWN STATIONERY

Sure, email is very cool. We love email. And instant messaging. Oh, we love that, too. But there is something to be said about actual letter writing. You know, with paper and pen. It feels more romantic. And more personal. And even (a little) more friendly.

So we think you should, as the Boy Scouts say, always be prepared. With letter gunk. By having stationery and a favorite pen and a couple of stamps lying around.

You can buy stationery that fits your personality. Cool Japanese cartoon pads of paper or scented linen sheets from some store with the French word for paper in its name. Or you can make your own. Take a favorite picture and shrink it down. Put it in the corner of the paper and copy. Or take an illustration you did. Or your boy did. Or your best gal pal did. And copy it onto cool paper. Or plain paper. Or lined paper.

If you have access to a scanner, you can scan in any photo or drawing and screen it back so it only shows up lightly across the whole page. Print lots of sheets. Or you can skip the scanner, skip the copy shop and make each and every sheet totally personal. Got an hour to kill? Start decorating the margins of your plain ol' paper. Store your new gorgeous stationery in your desk. So it's ready-freddy next time you get the urge to purge those words. (We love to talk in rhymes!)

And make sure you have envelopes, too. But if you don't, here's a secret you might already know. You can fold any piece o' paper into an envelope. Pretend you're wrapping a very thin present and go for it. Add stamp.

So get a-crackin'. Find a quiet place away from the noise. (Or bring on the noise—we like to write to music.) Write a letter to your aunty Jane. Or your email pal in New Orleans. (Hi, Lisa). Or us (Hi, us).

Worry Dolls

Worry Dolls are teeny-tiny little figurines made of cloth and a bit of sand for hair. Little Indian children in Guatemala were encouraged to "tell a worry, a single worry" to each doll. Then they placed the doll under their pillows at night when they went to sleep. In the morning, their worries were whisked away. Superstitious? You betcha. Magical? Maybe. But we think they're cute, and when stored in their little wood box, they make a fabulous noise when shaken. Or you could intoduce them to the little green army men of Armed Forces Day and have a party. Yay!

October 5

How cool to send secret messages!!!

Think about something you wanna say to the world, to an unknown person who may find the balloon (or balloons)—a statement you want to make, a secret you want to release. OK, got it? Got it! Good.

Now take a smallish piece of paper and write down what you want to say. Now go get a helium balloon and tie the piece of paper to the string. Now find a cool spot to release your balloon and on the count of three...

3, 2, 1...good-bye and good luck to the balloon!

Message in a bottle . . . we mean Balloon!

imagine you are Royalty

PUPPETS ARE MORE FUN

than you might be thinking. Puppets don't have to be about old socks and buttons either (although those kinds are nice). Clea's aunt Cele used to make these kinds of puppets for her and her brother when they were younger.

WHAT YOU NEED

Little cereal boxes (one for every puppet you desire to make) • Scissors • Glue • Photos and/or pictures from magazines, preferably of famous people and preferably quite large (you're looking for heads about three inches tall.)

WHAT YOU DO

Stand the cereal box right side up, with the front of the box facing you. You want to cut horizontally THREE SIDES of the box, leaving the back side UNCUT. Fold over the uncut side. You now have a puppet shape. Make your faceless puppet talk in a funny voice. Now cut out the head of a star. Leave his/her neck and shoulders behind.

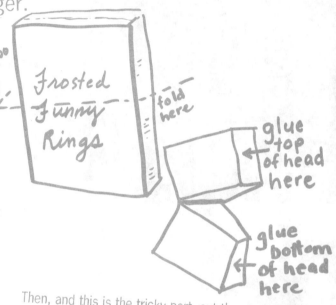

cut this side, too

Frosted Funny Rings

fold here

glue top of head here

glue bottom of head here

Then, and this is the tricky part, cut the star's head in two pieces horizontally through the lips. Yes, the top half of the head should go from top lip on up and the bottom half should go from lower lip on down. You know what to do now. Glue the top half of the head onto the top part of the puppet and then do the same for the lower half. You now have a celebrity puppet. You can make it hats if you like.

Make at least four puppets so tomorrow, in honor of Columbus Day, you can act out a little "How Columbus Plundered America" puppet show. C'mon, it will be fun. We suggest a Heather Locklear puppet as the queen of Spain and Leonardo DiCaprio as Columbus. You'll also need a couple of puppets to be the Indians.

YOU'LL NEED SEVERAL OF YOUR CEREAL BOX PUPPETS TO PERFORM THIS HISTORICAL DRAMA. HERE'S THE BASIC SCRIPT—YOU CAN ADD YOUR OWN HISTORICAL KNOWLEDGE TO THE PROCEEDINGS.

Columbus: (stepping foot on Caribbean soil) Ar, matey. Me hopes we find some gold on this here land. Me needs gold to put me in good favor with King Ferdinand and Queen Isabella of Spain. Well, even if there is no gold, I discovered this new place. I am a great Discoverer.

Indians: Greetings. Would you like some food?

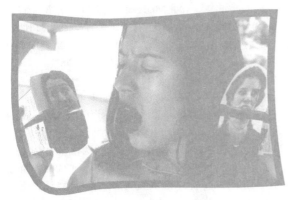

Columbus: Why, hello. Well, yes. Thanks. I am Christopher Columbus and I discovered this here place.

Indians: But we were here already. And besides, you're not even the first people to visit us. Oh, gosh, some Vikings were by in 1000 A.D.

Columbus: Oh. So is there gold?

Indians: Nope.

Columbus: Well then, I need something to take back to the king and queen. You guys dress kinda cute. I wonder if they'd like you.

Indians: Um, no thanks.

Columbus: Too bad.

And then they fight. Columbus goes back to Spain with several Indians. Some of his crew stay behind in the Caribbean. They get killed by the Indians who are understandably very miffed. Over the next few years, Columbus returns and takes more Indians and more. Between the slave labor on the Indians' continent, the slave labor in Spain and the random killings and disease, Columbus almost singlehandedly wipes out the whole Arawak Indian tribe of Haiti. That's right, he wasn't even in America, but you knew that already, didn't you? *the end*

So why do we celebrate Columbus Day anyway? Do you see anything redeeming about it? Do you think the holiday should be rewritten? Maybe now it should be about tolerance and living together peacefully, even though you have different beliefs from your neighbors. What do you think?

MEDITATE

Meditating is great when you're stressed, depressed, vexed or perplexed. Meditation doesn't mean you're a Buddhist or a New Age guru or any such thing as that. It means taking a quiet time-out to even yourself out. To reflect. And to relax.

First thing to do is find a mantra. A mantra is a word or a phrase or even just a sound that you will repeat to yourself. A lot of people think mantras should be just simple noises with no apparent meaning, that way you don't focus on one thing but rather let your mind wander. But really, this part is up to you. So pick a word or a sound. We like "Hee Haw," like that old country show. You can say "Hee" on inhalation and "Haw" on exhalation. Or "Digga Me" is good.

Now to begin. Find a comfortable, quiet spot and sit in an easy position. Close your eyes. Breathe naturally. Before concentrating on your mantra, try to just sit quietly and breathe. This should slow your breathing down a tad and get you in the mode. Slowly begin to focus on your breaths. As you do this, start focusing on your mantra. But don't force it. Let it come. Inhale. Exhale. Hee. Haw.

If your thoughts wander off the mantra, just go with them, but don't control them. If you get off-line, so to speak, just go back to the mantra. Hee. Haw.

Do this for 20 minutes or so, but don't use a timer. Just feel the time. (Unless, of course, you have to be at school or work soon, then by all means, use a timer. But maybe set your alarm clock on music instead of that awful buzzing noise.) And you are allowed to look at a clock from time to time. No hard-fast rules in the world of meditation.

You can do this anytime, but it is especially good after a hard day or a long day or just a day day.

Fondue. It's like the hip chic version of chips and dip.

For centuries, fondue had simmered along as part and parcel of the peasant cooking tradition of Switzerland. The name is nothing more than a noun adapted from the French verb "fondre," meaning "to melt." And for peasants who did much of their cooking in a single pot, that's exactly what fondue was—a pot full of melted cheese, often perked up a bit with a dash or two of cherry brandy. (But, hey, no liquor allowed here, plus we think it ruins the mmm-mmm cheese.) Put on your party dress and apron and get thee to the kitchen.

Ingredients:

You'll need: 1 garlic clove, peeled and cut in half • 1 pound Swiss cheese, shredded • 1/4 cup flour • 1/4 teaspoon salt • pepper • 1/4 teaspoon ground nutmeg • 1 1/2 cups dry white wine (The alcohol cooks out, but still if your folks aren't going for it, use milk or water even.) • French bread, cut into 1-inch cubes.

Let's fondue!

HOW TO:

Rub with garlic the inside and bottom of a deep, heat-resistant, nonmetallic casserole or heat-resistant, nonmetallic fondue pot. Discard garlic. Combine cheese, flour, wine or other liquid, salt, pepper and nutmeg in the prepared pot and mix well.

Heat, covered, in microwave oven six minutes, stirring a couple times. Stop the microwave and stir, restart. If cheese is not completely melted, heat an additional 30 to 60 seconds. (Or cook over low to medium heat, stirring.)

Spear squares of French bread with fondue forks or regular forks and dip in fondue.

A HOT TIP:
°Put the pot on the warmer stand and it will stay warm. You can spear other things, like apples or red pepper. Or make chocolate fondue and dip cake, strawberries and more.

As Madonna says, express yourself.

Pick up the magazine nearest to you. Search for words that describe how you feel right now. STRONG. DORK. COOL. FRIEND. COLORFUL. GREAT. OK. Cut them out.

Now get that glue stick. Pick out half of them and glue each one to a separate little piece of paper (construction, colored is good). Trim around it. Glue the other half of the words to the opposite sides of your pieces of paper. Instant "charms." Coat them in clear nail polish, it will make them hard. Make a hole in each one with a big sewing needle or use a hole punch. Get a piece of nylon cord or string or even a chain bracelet the size of your wrist and string the new "charms" on. Wear. Be admired for your creativity. Take compliments gracefully.

LiPPY GLOSS

Unhappy with that new shade of lippy gloss you just bought? Just can't seem to buy the right shade? Or maybe you're just broke. We're here to tell you just how to make your very own, very personal, very cheap lip gloss. You need some petroleum jelly. There has to be some lying around the house somewhere, right? And you need the ends of some old lipstick. Ask Mom if she has any that are broken or almost used up. The more colors, the more you can experiment, but even just one will work and work well.

apply with fingertips. it's pretty.

Put a glob (you know, a big tablespoon or so) of petroleum jelly in a glass bowl and add a touch of old lipstick (or lipsticks). Stir with wooden spoon.
The more petroleum jelly you add, the sheerer your gloss will be. Don oven mitts (if this stuff spills on you it will hurt). Nuke it on high for 30 seconds. If it's not melted yet, go for another 30 seconds. Once it is all melted together, CAREFULLY pour into little container. Let cool.

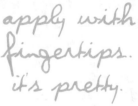

October 13

Elvis? VS. James Dean?

Clea: Some. And some get bald. I like balding men, did you know that about me? I mean, I like it if it looks like they will have a receding hairline when they get older. It's charming.

keva: yes, i agree.

Clea: Do you like pistachios?

keva: salted and with that funny red stuff. what is that funny red stuff?

Clea: Chemicals for people who prefer red things, like me.

Clea: Elvis was cute when he was young, but personally, I am a big fan of the bigger, more obese, fried food-loving Elvis. I love jumpsuits— the more studs and glitter, the better.

keva: so if you had a choice between making out with the skinny super fine elvis or the sorry, drugged-out, sweaty, burping elvis, which would it be?

Clea: I don't wanna make out with Elvis. Nope. But who would I like to invite to a dinner party? Fat Elvis.

keva: i'd like to make out with james dean.

Clea: Ah, the loner bad boy guy. If he were alive, though, he'd be like 50 and prolly he would be super duper fat just like Elvis was in his later years...

keva: do guys get fat as they get older?

Discussion questions:

Whom do you prefer, skinny Elvis, chubby Elvis or dead Elvis? Could you even imagine making out with any Elvis? How about James Dean? How do you feel about crushes on dead actor guys? What is that red stuff on pistachios? Do you, like Clea, prefer red things? Discuss.

DO YOU CROCHET?

Keva says the crochet queen is her nana. Keva's nana taught her to crochet when she was 10. She made granny squares; that was her thing. Keva once crocheted a whole blanket for her then-boyfriend. Um, hello? A whole blanket! Granny squares look like this. You can make a bunch and stitch together with yarn and make a cute beanie!

Go directly to your own nana, or the neighborhood nana or the local craft store, and beg and plead. Ask, "Will you please teach me to crochet?" Start with granny squares. It's not too hard once you get going, and the list of things that you can make is endless.

In fact, Keva has a friend named Clare Crespo who is a genuine artiste. She crafts food out of crochet. She makes crochet hamburgers and french fries and sushi. Let your mind wander. You can make a lot of things out of yarn, your hands and a bit of your own oddly skewed imagination.

keva made clea the purse in the background. cute, huh?

DRUGS ARE BAD. WE MEAN SAD.

Do you really know what they're made of and what they do to you? It's kinda gross and scary. We thought you might like to know more (and even if you don't, tuff) so here's a few words on nitrous oxide. You know, laughing gas. You know, that stuff that ravers do in cars. N_2O, or nitrous oxide, is a weak anesthetic gas that has been in use since the late 18th century for various sorts of medical stuff. Nitrous is also used in the dairy industry as a mixing and foaming agent (whipped crème cans) and it stops the growth of bacterias. It's used in race cars to speed engines. It has no taste and no smell. When you breathe it in, you become intoxicated, really dumblike (yep, it dulls even your sassy senses) and really dizzy. If you are caught with a nitrous tank in your possession, it's a misdemeanor. With each nitrous breath you get more and more deprived of your body's oxygen. That makes you a candidate for suffocation. You may get frostbite, nausea even, and you can forget about the motor skills you once had. Oh, and the B_{12} is leaked out of you and even your precious folic acid may be attacked, and while you're sitting there getting stupider by the second because your brain cells are being killed at a rapid rate, you might throw up. Yuck. Hate that. So, if you think you like the feeling of pins and needles all over your body, spin around a bunch. There. That's what it's like, only you don't get dumb or, like, die.

Door-to-Door Dinners

Free day, free day, bee day. OK, here's an idea we stole from Keva's sister, Aimee. She and her funny friends used to play this game when they were bored, licenseless and broke. Here's da scoop:

Figure out what ya'll wanna eat. Write down all the necessary ingredients. Keep it simple. Don't be picking anything like chicken cordon bleu! Then find pictures of all the ingredients. Look in mags. Online. Or hand draw.

Everyone takes a few pictures, then you start going door to door. No more than two of you can go to one house.

When someone answers the door, say, "Hi, we're part of a school scavenger hunt and to make the points, we need [the ingredient on your card, like a cup of flour or a pinch of salt]." And so forth until you have everything you need. Or until you get in trouble! And be nice.

Then go home and cook up your free meal!

** You can do it only once per neighborhood, so play carefully.

October 17

Future Files: Cars

Are you driving yet? Do you dream of the day? Heck, maybe you don't care. Clea's brother still doesn't drive, just has no desire. He likes city transportation. Anyhow, we doubt you're like Clea's brother. He's lovable, but odd. And, well, he's a boy. And you're likely, well, not.

In Keva's Future Files:
Mercedes A-Class in hot pink, old cop car with Elvis black-velvet painting and fringe and Xmas lights, Land Rover and Saab.

In Clea's Future Files:
'67 Jeepster (that's my car!!), '61 Dodge Polara convertible, '71 Dodge Demon 340 (in panther pink) and '71 Challenger!

So say it with us, Future Files. That's right, today you shall create a file, record jacket or shoe box dedicated to cars. Any cars you dream of, cars you desire, cars you want, need, must have. Throw the pictures in your file. Now, you know we prefer the old junkers to brand-new cars. It's just a style thing. But if it's new cars you crave, why not go online to the car makers' websites and send away for catalogs. (Or just call local dealers and ask them to send you one. They will.) Catalogs are filled with great info (like the paint colors they offer, interiors, stereo options and such). After you're done reading through them, file them away in your FUTURE FILES marked "cars" (or "Put-Put" or "junker" or whatever). You can also look through ancient magazines that you see at thrift stores for old car advertisements if it's vintage cars you admire. Or peruse the shelves of used bookstores for cheap books about types of cars like muscle cars (Clea's favorite) or fifties convertibles or old pickup trucks. And even if you already have a car, you probably don't have your exact dream car, so start planning now. And if you do drive your dream car, congratulations, we're jealous.

Caramel Apples are delicious!

yummy!

4 medium apples, washed and dried • 2 cups sugar • 1 tablespoon corn syrup • 1/2 cup water • 1 cup (2 sticks) unsalted butter, cut into pieces, room temperature • 1 cup heavy cream • Pinch of salt • Sticks for the apples

> **Keva:** *Do a little dance, make a little romance. Cackle, cackle.*
> **Clea:** What the heck is that?
> **Keva:** *That's the chant for the caramel apples.*
> **Clea:** Um, OK, Keva.
> **Keva:** *What?*
> **Clea:** I think I better finish these. You're acting weird.

Fill an oven-proof bowl with water. This is so you can submerge the bottom of your saucepan in water if the caramel starts to burn. Insert a small stick into the stem end of each apple. Set ye apples aside on lightly buttered parchment paper (or wax paper). Place sugar, corn syrup and water in heavy-bottom, medium-size saucepan with high sides. Stir once with wooden spoon to combine. Cook over medium heat. Don't stir again until the syrup becomes a deep golden amber. Remove from heat. Using a clean wooden spoon, beat in butter. Then stir in cream. Add salt. Dip apples in caramel, swirling and tilting pan around so apples are coated completely. Return apples to paper to cool and harden.

Once hard, eat. And share. Man, these are good.

"One time I bit down on a caramel apple and my loose tooth came out." – Keva

October 19

But what about hockey?

We know, we know, we know. You still have a pressing desire to know and understand how to read the hockey scores in the newspaper. We're here to explain it to you. Because we know, you needed to know this.

Turn to the hockey pages of a newspaper's sports section and follow along.

At the top, in bold, are the names of the teams and the final score of the game.

This is the numerical recap of goals scored during each of the three periods (yes, there are three periods in hockey) and, if necessary, overtime.

At the very bottom of the box score is a list of the goalies. Next to their names (in parentheses) you can find how many shots they stopped compared with how many they saved.

Nova (13-10-2) vs. Flash (13-11-1) 6-5
Nova 1   1   1 -   3
Flash 0   2   2 -   4
1st p - 1, NVA, C Hantman (K Marie) 7:32. Penalties - K Marie, NVA (TRIPPING) 12:41; J Motch FLH (INTERFERENCE) 12:55.
2nd p - 2, NVA, M Hepler (K Haze) 00:32. 3, FLH, K York (J Motch) 2:35. 4, FLH, J Oakes (K Mais) 6:47. Penalties - A Devers, FLH (HIGH STICKING) 7:48; K Dunn, NVA (ROUGHING) 11:12.
3rd p - 5, FLH, K York (J Motch) 4:10. 6, NVA, F Crossley (P Obeirne), 5:23. 7, FLH, M Hall (M Adkins), 11:54. Penalties - S Halle, NVA (CROSS-CHECKING) 6:42. Goalies - NVA, R Fairbanks (13-10-2) (22 shots-18 saves); FLH, T Rutherford (13-11-1) (19-16).

Short paragraphs then report details of the goals for each period. This is listed as follows: name of team, name of player who scored the goal, the skater(s) who passed the scorer the puck (in parentheses) and the time of the period this happened.

At the bottom of each paragraph is a report on penalties, listed as follows: name of player, name of team, the violation committed (in parentheses) and the time it happened.

If in fact you had no need whatsoever to know this, but you are now so full of knowledge, so brimming with this incredibly important information that you can't thank us enough, well then, don't mention it.

You need a cake recipe and you need it to be special.
This is one of our favorites. Why? Because it looks like...

KITTY LITTER!

You'll need: 1 package spice cake mix • 1 package white cake mix • 1 package white sandwich cookies • green food coloring • 12 small Tootsie Rolls (you know what they're for, don't you?) • 1 package vanilla pudding mix • 1 new (small) kitty litter box • 1 new pooper scooper (we said NEW!)

Prepare cake mixes and bake according to directions. Let cool. Prepare pudding mix and chill. Crumble the cookies in small batches in blender or food processor. You wanna get the cookies down to uneven crumb size. Set aside all but about 1/4 cup. To the 1/4 cup cookie crumbs, add about 10 drops green food coloring and mix using a fork. (This is supposed to look like chlorophyll, the stuff that comes in kitty litter, and it does!) Crumble the cooled cakes into a large bowl. Toss with half the remaining cookie crumbs and the chilled pudding. Gently combine. Now line the new, clean kitty litter box with cellophane wrap. Put mixture into litter box. It looks good, huh? Put three unwrapped Tootsie Rolls in a microwave-safe dish and heat until soft (like just 10 seconds). Shape to look like cat poo. Repeat with three more Tootsie rolls. And three more again.

Put a couple on top and then bury the others in the mixture. Bury a lot so that every one of your friends gets a special chocolate poo. Sprinkle the other half of cookie crumbs over top. Scatter the green cookie crumbs lightly over the top. Put a few more extra-mushy Tootsie Rolls on top, sprinkled with cookie crumbs. Serve with your brand new pooper scooper. Serves 18—that is, if you can find 18 people to eat it!

October 21

Find a tee shirt in your wardrobe that you don't really wear much anymore. We're just gonna write right over that old picture of Ziggy.

Keva: Nooooooooo!
Clea: Yes.

1. What should be all over your shirt? That's up to you. Since it's almost United Nations Day, you could start with the flag of the country your family hails from. Or its national fruit.

2. We said rock star, right? Well, here's how we'd do it. Markers. As in permanent. Just draw the symbol or the saying or the fruit directly on the tee shirt. If this just isn't your way of doing things, you could get that fabric paint stuff, we suppose.

3. Now, grab needle and thread. Adorn the drawing and words with random beadwork. Just sew those beads on. And maybe even add glitter paint. The kind that's washable. And if you're feeling especially crafty (and who isn't?) you could actually appliqué some fabric on the tee.

4. But you don't have to go that route. You can pick a slogan or saying that you and your friends use way too much.

5. It doesn't have to be perfect. It's rock star. And it's a good reminder that no one, NO ONE, is perfect. But us crafty girls are pretty darn close.

Grandmas

This is clea and her grandma, way back when, before her grandma took flying lessons.

My grandma called the other day and left a message on my phone. A modern concept she hasn't mastered yet. There was a silence on the machine for the first few seconds, so I knew it was her even before I heard her voice. Then from the brisk silence came a gurgling yell, "...I found this coupon in the paper, so I thought what the hell and it was the most exciting thing, Clea, dear, oh, my gawd, you cannot imagine how amazing it is to fly a plane. I felt so connected to the world and to your grandpa and, well, I don't know if I will make it all the way through for my license but I have another lesson on Tuesday." Then came another silent pause. Another gurgle. And then in a clear confident voice, she finished her conversation with my machine: "See you 'round, kid." Grandmas are the greatest, and not just my own kooky, flying, 78-year-old one. Grandmas (and nanas, too) have seen the world, they've been through intense times and sheer pleasurable times and they've come out of it all with this all-knowing kind of intelligence. They are women of the highest order, the grand poo-bahs of chicks, the very essence of feminine wit and charm. Even if you see your grandma as a white-haired bitty or an uptight old lady, relax. Let her tell a story or two. Let your grandma surprise you. We guarantee she will. And if you are sad right now because Grams has passed on to another place, borrow a grandma. Your friend's, your boyfriend's, your next door neighbor. Borrowed grandmas are really almost as good as your own. Grandmas rock.

October 23
IT IS PEANUT BRITTLE DAY

It's fast and easy and mmm... good as heck. And it makes a super rad present when broken into cute pieces and put into a box with tissue. Hooray, let's make peanut brittle today!

If right now you're saying, "Peanut Brittle Day?! Well, that doesn't hold much meaning. It's so very superficial," you'd be wrong. See, peanut brittle is serious comfort candy. It's like the mom of candies. Also, there is great reverence in the making of peanut brittle. Grandmas have made this stuff for years and years. So by making this recipe (and possibly starting a tradition, hint, hint) you are participating in a long historical line of candy making of the most delicious kind. Now let's get it on.

You will need a candy thermometer.
(They have them at the grocery store.)
Do not use a people one. That would be bad.

1 cup white corn syrup
2 cups sugar
1/2 cup water
1 pound Spanish peanuts, raw
2 tablespoons butter
2 teaspoons vanilla extract
2 teaspoons baking soda
1/2 teaspoon salt

Makes 1 to 1 1/2 pounds.
Make sure to give some away.
It's good karma.

Combine syrup, sugar and water in saucepan. Heat slowly until mixture registers 230 degrees on a candy thermometer. Add peanuts and continue to cook to 300 degrees. Remove from heat. Add butter, vanilla, soda and salt. Stir until blended. Pour into well-buttered 15 1/2" x 10 1/2" (or whatever size you got that's close) pan. Now let it cool. Till it's good and hard. Then break into pieces.

wITCH MOVIES

Be bad. Be dark. Be dangerous.

TONIGHT IS THE NIGHT TO GET WITCHY, IF YOU'RE IN A $%#@!! MOOD, YOU WILL ESPECIALLY LIKE THIS DAY. SO GRAB THE BROOM AND DON YOUR BLACK GARB AND GET DOWN WITH YOUR BAD SELF.

MOVIES TO CACKLE WITH:

"THE CRAFT"; WITCHY POWERS GET OUT OF CONTROL IN THIS GOOD GIRL VS. VERY BAD GIRLS SCREAMFEST. HAVING SECOND THOUGHTS ABOUT PLAYING WITH THAT OUIJA BOARD YET?

"THE WITCHES OF EASTWICK"; OK, SO WITCHCRAFT IS THE ONLY WAY TO EXPLAIN HOW SCARY OLD JACK NICHOLSON GETS LUCKY WITH CHER, MICHELLE PFEIFFER AND SUSAN SARANDON. P.S. THE MOVIE IS BASED ON THE SUPER RAD BOOK BY JOHN UPDIKE. GET IT!

"CARRIE"; THE ORIGINAL. IF YOU ARE SUPER POPULAR YOU MIGHT WANT TO CHECK THIS OUT AS A WARNING TO BE NICER TO GIRLS YA DON'T THINK ARE AS COOL. AND IF YOU'RE A FIREBALL TRAPPED IN A FRUSTRATING BODY, THIS IS YOUR REVENGE FLICK, BABY.

"FOUR ROOMS"; LOTS OF HIPSTER ACTRESSES CAST SPELLS AS A COVEN OF WITCHES IN AN AWESOME HOLLYWOOD HOTEL. MADONNA IS ONE OF THEM. 'NUFF SAID. OH, AND HER GIRLFRIEND/SLAVE GIRL IS NAMED KEVA AND SHE HAS BLACK-TAPE XS ON HER BOOBS. EEK.

**Disclaimer: Your basic witch doesn't worship the devil or ride on broomsticks (to our knowledge). They worship nature and don't generally get into casting bad spells on folks. We think that's cool. Although neither of us is in fact, a witch.

October 25

Clea dressed as a Girl Scout for Halloween for four years straight.

HELP HAS ARRIVED.
HERE IS THE KEVA & CLEA GUIDE TO COSTUMING FOR HALLOWEEN.

In the interest of sparking your imagination this hallowed holiday season we have listed some of our favorite costumes. We've also denoted some specifics with our handy dandy chart system, below. Take notes, there will be a test.

THE CHART
CHEAP & EASY = $
UNDER FIVE MINUTES = @
GOOD FOR GROUP EFFORTS = &
CLEA WAS ONCE = C
KEVA WAS ONCE = K

MODERN ART (with body paints and cheap frame)	$C
STINKY BIG OL' FLY	K
PIPPI LONGSTOCKING	
AN OREO COOKIE	
SNAP, CRACKLE AND POP	&
CHRISTMAS PRESENTS	$@C
MADONNA	$
BIRTHDAY CAKE	
EASTER BUNNY	
AN ANNE RICE CHARACTER	
A FAVORITE COOL GIRL	$

ONE OF YOUR FRIENDS	$@
A PARTY (attach balloons to dress)	$@
THE SAD LONER STONER KID	$@
THE GO-GO'S	&
OR A RANDOM ROCK BAND	CK&
A LAMP	$@
TARZAN AND JANE	&
ROLLER DERBY TEAM	C&
CHARLIE'S ANGELS	&
TOOTH FAIRY	$
BONNIE AND CLYDE	&

Spider webs are spooky.

Halloween is the perfect opportunity to master your spider web collecting skills. And once you've collected several you can display them on the front door of your house in time for the 31st. Afterward you can frame them and keep them in your room.

First, wait for the spider to go away. Or talk the spider into leaving for a while. Spiders like sweet talk. Don't touch it because some spiders do bite. You can tickle the little guy with a long stick, if the sweet talk ain't working.

You will need a rag or two, some newspaper for spillage, enamel spray paint in white, some sturdy construction paper and scissors. Don't do this if it's super windy out—you will have a really hard time getting the web to stay as one piece.

Spread out your newspaper on the ground below your newfound web. Now grab your enamel and (with the wind) spray short gentle bursts of paint on one side of the web from an angle and then try to do the other side as well. You don't want to spray head-on, it might cause the web to break. And don't get downwind of the paint. Ick.

When all the threads are lightly coated in paint, stick the piece of construction paper carefully behind or under the web and with one fell swoop try to touch the paper to the whole web. Keep your hand steady and just go for it.

Once you're sure the whole web is stuck to the paper, carefully cut the spider web threads that are holding it to the tree, shrub or fence. And set down to dry.

Look at how incredibly intricate the pattern is. The spider starts by constructing a frame and then builds a radial inside the frame. The spider creates the primary spiral after that. Then the little one adds sticky threads for catching prey. It's just bizarrely complicated. And oh so beautiful. And if you're worried about taking away spiders' homes, remember that they create these things in like 30 minutes and after hanging out for a while, they move on to make a new home. So don't feel too bad.

October 27

PET MASKS

OK, fine. Some people don't like dressing up for Halloween (we don't know any of those people, but we hear they're out there). So in the interest of those of you who don't like to get into the spirit, we've crafted an easy, breezy mask that will allow you to participate but in a marginal, noncommittal way. And if you do like to dress up, then by all means take this idea a step further, creating a full costume to go with your mask. Or, even better, make masks like these for year-round use.

You know that pet you love? The one with the droopy eyes and stinky butt? Well, get your favorite picture of said pet and head directly to the copy shop. Have the copy gal make you a color photocopy enlargement of your pet's face. You want it as big as your own. Yes, that big.

Cut out around your pet's giant face. Laugh at how silly it looks.

Now, find an old box or a stray piece of cardboard. Place the pic of your pet down on the cardboard and trace around the silhouette. Now grab an X-Acto knife (and please be careful) and cut the shape out of the cardboard. Glue pic to cardboard.

Now take that X-Acto knife and cut out two little holes in the eyes. Don't cut out the whole eye unless you want to be a pet-zombie for Halloween. Just big enough to see through. You're almost done. You need a stick.

Get a twig. Or a BBQ skewer. Or a Popsicle stick. And tape it to the back of your mask. Now hold mask in front of face and make appropriate pet sound. Practice saying "Trick or treat" in your dog or cat voice.

Yep, that's the fabulous George, represented in a Halloween mask. Ruff or Reat!

DAY OF THE DEAD

A VERY COOL MEXICAN HOLIDAY

How would you feel if your mom called you up and said, **"Oh, great-grandpa's coming to visit you next week,"** but you knew your great-grandpa died like 20 years ago? Well, if you were Mexican you would probably understand that it's almost **Dia de los Muertos.** El Dia de los Muertos, or the Day or the Dead, is a very big holiday in Mexico, and while it coincides with Halloween and has the whole skeleton thing in common, **Day of the Dead** ain't meant to be scary. It celebrates the whole life cycle (including death) that is part of just being. It's not a sad holiday at all, but it is a time to reflect and remember your ancestors. It is believed by many that during the month of October, the spirits come and visit earth. Hence Great-grandpa's visit. And hence, the **"ofrendas"** or altars with offerings for the dead. What do people offer? Well, food, of course. Lots and lots of **yummy food** and delicious Mexican drinks and sugar skulls and other candy. And unlike Halloween, the colors aren't limited to orange and black. In fact, the more color the better for Day of the Dead celebrations. **La Catrina,** a female skeleton in a big, bright flowery-party hat, is sort of the symbol of Day of the Dead. So to celebrate this very cool day make **big papier-mâché Day-Glo skulls** and hang up streamers and cook. You must cook. Since the holiday has a lot to do with food, there is plenty of cooking. And there is lots of giving. It is traditional to exchange **sugar skulls** with your loved ones. So if you have access to a Mexican community in your town, get down there and check it out. Some people actually go down to the **cemeteries,** bringing food and marigolds to leave on the graves. They bring hot chocolate (spiked with cinnamon) to stay warm. And they try to remember the good lives of the people they have lost. **No depression allowed!**

October 29

To carry around door-to-door. And if you think you're too old to trick-or-treat, well, we have nothing to say to you. Sure, pillowcases work. So do backpacks (but they're tacky on Halloween). You can decorate a paper grocery bag. Or you can get a metal bucket and decoupage! Clea's definition: Decoupage is the art of gluing paper things in a collagelike manner to something, anything. In this case, a metal bucket. It couldn't be easier. That art store we keep sending you to, go there again and get matte medium. It's a glue, sort of. And it's clear. And it's great for decoupage.

Now grab pictures and words and anything thin and papery that you want on your very own candy bucket. (You can even use candy wrappers and work the whole Halloween theme.)

YOU NEED SOMETHING TO HOLD ALL THAT CANDY.

Now paint a little matte medium on the bucket and then lay down your art. Keep doing this till the whole bucket is covered. Then paint a thin coat of matte medium OVER your masterpiece, all over the bucket. This will seal it in, making it last for many Halloweens to come.

October 30

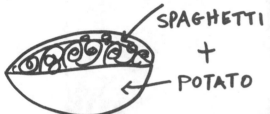

THROW A GROSS·OUT DINNER PARTY...

Cook up a scary, ghoulish meal for friends & family in honor of Halloweenie. Make invites. Turn the lights down low. Light candles. Serve these deliciously devilish and frighteningly fun foods...

SPAGHETTI
+
POTATO

OPEN FACED BRAINS
3 medium-size potatoes, baked
1 8-ounce package thin spaghetti, prepared
1 14-ounce jar spaghetti sauce, heated

Scoop out the innards of the potato, leaving just the skins. Now pile the cooked spaghetti inside the potatoes. Place them on a platter. Now take the red spaghetti sauce (remember, it's hot, be careful) and gently splatter it over the "brains." Serve more blood on the side. Makes 6 brains.

PLASTIC GLOVE +
WATER +
FREEZER =

DEAD, COLD FLOATING HAND!

A FROZEN HAND FOR YOUR FAVORITE PUNCH
Red, blue or green food coloring and water
A new disposable plastic or rubber glove
(the kind of gloves without the powdery coating inside)

Add food coloring to some water until you get a good dead-flesh color. Fill glove with the colored water and fasten the end with a rubber band. Hang glove from a shelf in the freezer, fingers down, with the help of a clothespin. Freeze overnight. Just before your guests arrive, take the glove off the giant hand ice cube and float in punch.

APPLES +
GUMMY WORMS =
GROSS BUT
YUMMY DESSERT!

And for dessert? Why, old apples with worms!
12 large apples, boysenberry jam
4 tablespoons butter, 12 gummy worms

Core each apple, but don't go all the way through. Leave the bottom in so the apple goo won't leak out. Mix together the butter & jam. Stuff each hole with the mix. Place on a baking pan (with sides so it holds the juices in) and bake uncovered for 35–45 minutes at 350 degrees. Let apples cool for 15 minutes. Set each apple in a bowl and spoon the leftover syrup around it. Insert a gummy worm or two in the hole and let it hang out the side.

October 31 — IT'S HALLOWEEN!!

You shouldn't even be reading today. Hello? It's like the best day of the year. Halloween. We say get your butt out there and beg for candy. Oh, but before you go, here is our ever so humble list of the best and worst candy of Halloween.

the BEST candy   the WORST candy

BUTTERFINGER

Gummi Bears

Chupa Pops

Starburst

Reese's peanut butter

Bit-o-honey

Mixed Fruit Mentos

LIK-M-AID cherry grape lemon

Chick-O-Stick

← SNOT CANDY those Pot o' Gold fake Reese's

Mint Mentos

← chocolate covered raisins!

Rocky Road

yum Granola!

← salted plums!

Charleston chewwwwww

Mounds (dark chocolate AND you don't even get the nut)

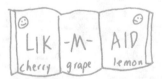

NOVEMBER

it is a month for celebrating. yippee.

MAKE GIFTS!

We recently saw a news clip wherein the bubble-haired anchorwoman took to the streets and asked the public what their best friend gave them for Christmas last year. You know what? Out of dozens of people asked, only three could remember. You know what those three people got from their best friend? Homemade gifts.

Sure, you can spend loads of cash on glitzy presents that will wow your friends...for all of a week. But come next year, most won't remember that glitzy gift. It's a proven fact. So we urge you to come up with gifts from the heart and from your hands. We'll give you some inspirational ideas for things to make, sure, but when crafting them, channel the powerful energy of your friend or family member, bring them into the effort spiritually and create presents that aren't just about spending or buying or even giving. Create presents that are about your relationship with this person. Celebratory little bits of a glorious friendship.

P.S. Stay tuned for gift ideas, but meanwhile compose a list of all the people you want to share your fabulous talents with, all the folks you want to make gifts for.

CARD TRIX.

Every girl should have a few card tricks up her sleeve. It's just plain common-sense resourcefulness, like always having a quarter to call home. So in the interest of common sense and decency, here's a great one.

IT'S CALLED THE NICE AND EASY.

Because it is. Shuffle your deck of cards. Let your fool choose a card. Tell him or her to memorize it and place it facedown on top of the deck. Put the deck behind your back and utter a few magical words. Incant the names of a few goddesses. Hecate. Aphrodite. Cassiopeia. Meanwhile, behind your back just flip that top card over so that it is faceup. But don't let the fool see you do it. Bring the cards back and hold the deck upright, showing your fool the bottom of the deck. Ask him or her if that is the card. (It isn't because the card is now facing you. Remember the card.) Look ashamed. Put the deck behind your back. Say a few more goddesses' names. Helena. Minerva. Thalia. Meanwhile, behind your back, flip the card over again, stick it anywhere in the deck and bring out the cards again. Turn the deck faceup. Spread them out. Pick out the fool's card. **And make sure to say, "Ta da!" Watch the fool be amazed at your skill.**

November 3
It's Culture Day!

On this holiday schools and the government award certain people prizes for their special cultural activities. Since America has no such holiday or ceremony, the responsibility to praise those that have done wonderful cultural things is now on your shoulders. Look around you. Who is brilliantly artistic and uses their talents for good and not evil? Who has helped out in the community to make it a better (and more fun) place to be? Make a list of all the people you want to thank and then come up with an award specifically for them.

✱ Mas Especial ✱

You Rock!

chlöe   dad   tricia
lisa   Susannah   Clea
lauren   bee   alfie
aimée   Pete   Mom
Kim   tim

looks like clea needs an award!

You can pick up old baseball or tennis trophies at the thrift store. Make stickers with the new award name and tape it over the original engraving. Who cares that the trophy has an ice skater on it and your best friend can't skate? That's part of the beauty of the whole experience. Because it's Culture Day, you're celebrating everyone's creativity. So your awards should be equally, um, creative.

Like say your brother's band played at the ice cream social for free. And OK, they weren't amazing but, hello, they did it for free. They can win the "You Rocked for Free" award. Or perhaps your teacher arranged for the class to beautify the ugly concrete wall outside your school with original paintings and now it looks stunning, and you think she didn't get enough recognition for her ideas and efforts. Make her a "You've Created a Legacy" award to let her know you appreciate her. Maybe your best friend has been studying Spanish because she really wants to go to Cuba one day (and she's not even Cuban!). Make her a "Mas Especial" award.

This month you may be visiting a relative or staying with a friend's family during the impending holidays. We're here today to remind you to be a fair and generous houseguest. Sure, it may seem like common sense, but all too often people get so caught up in their own worlds that they forget to see that the person who has opened his or her home to them and waited on them hand and foot has a life. A life that usually doesn't include you. So, that said, be gracious. We've got a few tips, if you will. If you have recently taken up the cause of veganism, it would be a kind thing to let your future host know this ahead of time. They should respect your new wishes, but make sure you give them enough time to make arrangements. Same goes if, say, you're allergic to something pretty common, like, oh, chicken or butter or peas. Bring a gift. Just a small token of your thanks. A houseplant is nice, and so is stationery or some lovely tea (if your host likes tea, that is)—even flowers will do nicely. Offer to clear the table or run out for milk. Small gestures like this will be appreciated. If your host insists that you relax, then do so. But the next time an opportunity arises for you to pitch in, offer again. Stay out of the way! For instance, if in the morning, you arise earlier than the others, try not to make any noise. If the bathroom line is getting long, wait till everyone else has showered. You should feel comfortable, but not so much so that you overpower the house. Make your bed, keep your luggage neat, your towels folded, that sort of thing. If you borrow a book or a CD, put it back when you're done. Lastly, send a thank-you note! We've already encouraged you to write more letters—now is your chance. And this is the perfect opportunity to hone your handwritten letter skills. Just thank your host for being so cool and accommodating. We guarantee, you will be asked back again.

NOVEMBER 5

It's GUY FAWKES day

Guy Fawkes Day is a holiday in England that has all the mystery of a good novel

...plus fireworks and burning dolls. It's all very sordid and yet very acceptable on this particular day in Britain.

Guy Fawkes was an extremist back in 1605 (by the way, we hear he was actually referred to as Guido back in the day) and he plotted to blow up King James I and the whole Parliament because he was unhappy with the job they were doing. (That's right, they have a holiday named after a terrorist, those silly English!) But the king found out about it and tortured and killed Guido and his friends.

Some historians say that the king framed Guy and in fact knew about the whole thing all along. But who cares? He still tried to blow up the king! And now England celebrates him with bonfires where they throw effigies (crudely made dolls) of Guy Fawkes into the flames.

Almost voodoolike, isn't it?

In fact the holiday is sort of a cross between Halloween and the Fourth of July. They have fireworks. And kids get in the act by making the effigies (little stick dolls made of trash) and wandering the neighborhood asking for "a penny for Guy." The kids keep the money AND get to burn the doll! We find this to be one of the oddest holidays we've ever heard of, and we're experts on holidays!

If you light a bonfire and start throwing boy dolls in the flames after asking people for money, we think you might find yourself in a heap o' trouble so we think this a bad, bad idea. Instead, have a BBQ. Yeah, a BBQ. And thank goodness you're not English (just kidding, some of our best friends are English).

Imagine you have found a magic lantern, complete with a genie, who asks you...

"WHAT ARE YOUR THREE WISHES, MASTER?"

NOVEMBER 7

ELECTION DAY

Today is Election Day. What's that, you say? You don't vote? Not old enough? No reason not to participate in the process. See, this is what we would do.

Come up with some issues that are important to you and your friends. Not stuff like whether they're gonna build an Urban Outfitters in your neighborhood (although, admittedly, that is a very important issue), but environmental issues, neighborhood improvement measures and the like. Grab a piece of paper and a friend or three. Write down the things that are important to you guys that can be helped and/or fixed with the involvement of the government, local or national. Is your school getting rid of the music program because of lack of funding? Do you have metal detectors at your school? What are your thoughts on that? Are your beaches or parks a mess? Anybody dumping cruddy stuff in your water? You don't like the way the zoo treats the animals? Are they turning a local park into a housing development? NOW CREATE A BALLOT. Pass out pieces of paper on which you ask your fellow students what is most important to them. What areas of their school are lacking real funds? Where would they spend the money if they had it? Have them number in importance some of the issues. And then leave a blank space for problems that you didn't address that are of importance to them. Throw in some fun stuff for good measure so people actually fill out the thing. You know, like the Urban Outfitters plea. Collect them all up and then, with some friends, tally the results. What was most important to the people at your school and in your neighborhood? Write it all down and then box up the ballots and your results and send them to your mayor—

or your city council member, or your senator or representative— with a letter that tells them that while you and your friends cannot yet vote, you still have concerns and it won't be long before you and all those other people out there that are your age can indeed vote. Let them know that they should get cracking on your issues now.

Email & snail mail addresses of government officials:
http://www.ifas.org/activist/

NOVEMBER 8

Mom's china simply too precious? There's an easy remedy. Create your own set of dinnerware. No pottery wheel necessary. These make incredibly personal gifts, too.

What you will need is this: magazines or photos, clear glass plates, totally clear glue, a paintbrush, paint (should be nontoxic, although let us say, you will not be eating off the paint side of the plate).

Start with plain glass plates, just plain old clear glass plates. They shouldn't have any ridges or decoration. You can pick them up for like $0.50 to $1.00 at thrift stores or big cheap department store type places like Target or Wal○Mart. Now cut out pictures from magazines of anything you like: movie stars, Hello Kitty, Lynda Barry cartoons, cool clothes from catalogs, you name it. You can even use pictures of you and your friends, but the thinness of magazine paper works a tad better than photos.

Get some newspaper and spread it all around, just in case you make a mess (which is half the fun anyway). Now place the pictures facedown on the back of the plate, so you see the image from the top of the plate. You can tack them down with CLEAR glue or just hold them in place with tape for the time being, but put the tape on loosely, because you'll want to take the tape off before painting. Now take your paint and paint the back of the glass plate, over the back of the pictures. The paint acts as a kind of glue, sealing the photos or pictures in. Do not paint the top of the plate where food goes. We repeat, do not paint the top of the plate where food goes. Just the underside. You might want to do two coats for a truly opaque plate, but wait for the first one to dry before continuing on to coat two. You can also experiment: Paint stripes of different colors or paint shapes or flowers. Let them dry. Now throw yourself a dinner party where the menu is all Tater Tots (see March 19) and the fine china features YOU (or Hello Kitty or Ernie Pook's Comeek or whatever).

P.S. Don't put them in the dishwasher. Just rinse with warm water, suds and your own little hands.

NOVEMBER 9
MAKE PLACEMATS

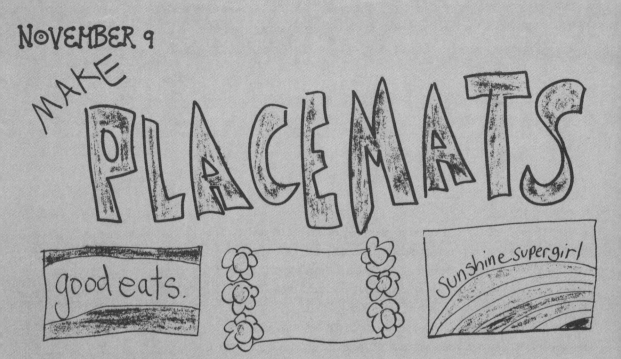

good eats.

Sunshine supergirl

A fantabulous gift for you or your friends? Place mats, of course.
OK, so it sounds boring, but remember, you can make them to match that
dinnerware from yesterday. And these can be truly inviting, spectacular
place mats. In fact, you can make them with anything flat!

Pictures of you and your friends, pictures from magazines,
drawings that you made or your little sister made
(oh, that would be a lovely gift for your mom!),
maps, old postcards, newspaper articles, you name it—
if it's flat, it can be done.

What you need to do is go to either the stationery or office supply place
and get lamination sheets and follow the directions to laminate something
that is about 10" x 18". Or you can take it to one of those friendly
one-stop copy shops and have them do it. It should not cost more than
a buck or two apiece (a pretty cheap holiday present, if we do say
so ourselves, even if you make a set of four). Remember, if the guy
behind the counter wants more money than that, make sure to tell
him he's gouging you, that's very, very wrong, and leave.

Mentos ★

Mentos is like the philosophy king of candy. Those commercials, those 30-second minidramas on TV, attempt (and often succeed) to teach us to nurture our personal desires and overcome obstacles by challenging the everyday conventions of society with a goofy smile and a ridiculous, oft-intrusive gimmick like turning your wet-paint mishap into groovy business stripes.

Today, you should act like you're in a Mentos commercial. Paste that cheesy smile on your face and turn a bad situation into something good. Sing the Mentos song (you know, "Nothing gets to you...") But the main thing is to act in a cheerfully bewildering manner. Get friends in on the act and really perplex a few total strangers. Make a big point of eating a Mentos in front of everyone. And then let it be your guide, empowering you to do things you wouldn't otherwise be able to. Act like mannequins at the mall. Pretend you're a waiter at a restaurant and get your own water. Ask some big football player guy to pick up your car and move it to safety. But make sure you shine your onlookers the "fresh" sign: your pack of Mentos.

**We also suggest working the word "Mentos" into your speech as a sort of semiderogatory remark. Such as "That dude totally mento'd me," meaning he gave you the shaft, honey, but it was OK in the end.

let's talk # HOT WAX!

waxing
kinda,
um,

hurts.

Clea: Um, I have never waxed. Not my legs, not my lip, never. I shave my legs and get horrible bumps and haven't figured out a way to fix it. And I bleach my little lippy hair. And you?

Keva: I not only bleach my lip hairs but I bleach the lip hairs of my sister and all of her friends. They get embarrassed.

Clea: And you don't think she'll be embarrassed that you just told us all that? What about waxing? Done it?

Keva: She doesn't wax. Oh, you mean me?

Clea: Yeah, you.

Keva: Once by this weird scary lady and before she did the rrriiiiiiiiiiiiiiiiippppppppp she said, "No pain, no gain, lady" in a thick accent.

Clea: Ouch. Um, next...

Keva: Right on. Sometimes I shower only once a week and I don't care!

Clea: I never ever wash my hair. Silly is as silly does. Or something like that.

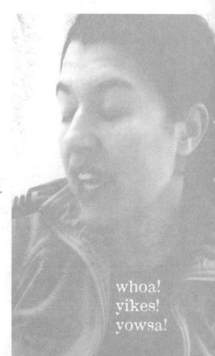

whoa!
yikes!
yowsa!

DISCUSSION QUESTIONS: DO YOU BELIEVE IN WAXING? IN BLEACHING? HAVE YOU EVER FELT THE NEED TO PARTICIPATE IN EITHER RIDICULOUS FEMALE BEAUTY RITUAL? IS BATHING AN IMPORTANT PART OF YOUR DAY? HOW ABOUT WASHING YOUR HAIR? IS SILLY IS, IN FACT, AS SILLY DOES? WHAT DOES THAT MEAN? ANYTHING? OR IS IT JUST, UM, SILLY? DISCUSS.

clea studied political science!
keva studied marketing & art history

woo hoo!!! It's:

CAREER DAY

Yes, today is Career Day. Now, you've already compiled a whole file of potential careers in your Future Files (haven't you?). But have you thought about the link from a specific degree to a cool job? We created this little "chart" of sorts to remind you that you can be whatever you want. You just need to think about the paths and choices and decisions you must make that will lead you to the job that you want, you crave, you need. You already know, if you want to be a doctor, you must go to med school. But what if you want to be something less "obvious"? On the left, seemingly boring college majors. On the right, the excessively cool jobs you can get with those degrees. It's like a game. Play along.

Degree → Excessively cool jobs

Degree	Excessively cool jobs
Chemistry	Makeup creator / Wine expert/wine maker
Business	Owner of own line of girly-clothing catalogs / Record label mogul
Biology	The chick in charge of the seals at the zoo / Owner of Fish and Lizards R Us
English	Famous book author / dEliA's copywriter / Movie reviewer
Computer Science	Master of own website for girls / Private eye (you got to know how to crack the codes)
Philosophy	World-class thinker / Famous feminist activist
Political Science	President / Speech writer for first female president
Art History	Antique appraiser / Art restorer (yes, someone has to fix Michelangelo's works)
Mathematics	Card shark / Poker shark (you know how to count cards)

NOVEMBER 13

Spa Night

GET READY

OK, today's spa night is for those of you who say,

"Eww, moisturizer?! My skin is too oily for moisturizer!"

Moisturizing Spritzer is the lightest moisturizer you can devise. And it will still nourish your skin, but not make you any oilier than you already are. Got it? OK, go to the drugstore and buy one of those plastic spritzer bottles. They come in all sorts of colors. Find one that speaks to you. If all they have is plain ones, plan on decorating it at home with markers and glitter.

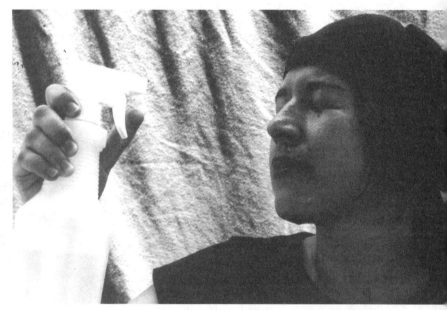

NOW YOU NEED:

1/2 cup distilled water
3 teaspoons glycerin (drugstore)
5 drops lemon essential oil (health food store or Body Shop type place)

Put all three things inside the bottle. Shake well. Close your eyes. Spray on your face. Feel the moisture seep into your skin. When you get back from a long day in the sun or a soccer game, wash your face and then spritz. Before bed, wash your face and then spritz. Before a hot date, wash your face and then spritz. Spritzing can be oh so fun. (Oh, and shake each time before you spritz.)

OOH LA LA

Costume Suitcase

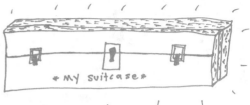

My suitcase

Every gal should have a costume suitcase. "What?" you say. A costume suitcase. It's an old suitcase, maybe from a thrift store, maybe from your parents' basement, maybe from the trash pile, but it's a suitcase and it's old. And then when you see groovy accessories that you must have but, face it, you won't wear everyday, you plop them in your suitcase. The reason this is a fabulous idea (as if it needs explaining) is that say one day you're bored and decide to just put all your most flamboyant, fabulous artifacts on to dazzle the world with your grooviness.

Well, this way, all you have to do is grab your costume suitcase and dive in. Or say you are having a party and it needs some life. Break out the suitcase and make everyone partake of something fabulous. Make Jeff wear the feather boa and Marie wear the butterfly wings and Marcel wear ALL the belts AND the beaded mask.

inside keva's costume suitcase:

Feather boas   Studded belt
Wings from Halloween fly costume
Patent leather miniskirt that was stapled on once   Orange chiffon scarf
Green satin gloves   Leather visor with butterfly etching
Bunny ears, furry ones
Homemade paper bunny ears   Tan rayon gypsy shawl

inside clea's costume suitcase:

Glitter rainbow belt
Not one, not two, but three afro wigs
Glitter rainbow suspenders
Not one, not two, but three tiaras
Good & Plenty scarf
My dog's clown hat (also could fit a very small baby)
KISS makeup kit (white face makeup)

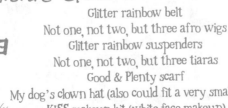

it's time for....

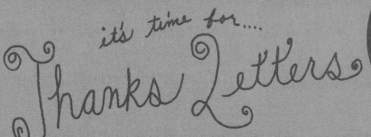

Thanksgiving really kicks off a very busy, very hectic season. So we suggest that today, a week before Thanksgiving, you get your **"thanks letters"** out. Of course, you can write this kind of letter any ol' time throughout the year, but now is an especially good time.

What we mean by **"thanks letters"** is this: sit down with a pretty piece of paper (or a piece of homemade stationery) and make a list of the things you are thankful for. Now, are there people responsible for those thankful things? If so, you should take the time to write them a thanks letter (it's less formal than a thank-you card). It can be casual, it can be frank, it can be addressed to anyone you wish to thank.

Now here is our favorite part. We think they should be rolled up all scroll-like rather than folded in a traditional envelope (of course you can fold traditionally, we will not hold it against you). But our way is better. So either pick up those mailing tubes at the stationery store or make your own with a toilet paper roll. If you do the latter, just stick the rolled up thanks letter inside the empty tube, then wrap the toilet paper tube like you would a present but with plain paper. Then write the address on it and stamp it—the mail people will indeed ship it, we promise. Or you can hand it over to your friend or family member and not mail it (but mailing is so cool).

So get crackin', give thanks and get ready for turkey dinner (or Tofurky dinner, if you are indeed vegan).

The Joy of the Bedazzler

Bedazzler Bedazzler
oh how i love thee
Bedazzler Bedazzler
you add sparkle
you add shine
you are all mine!

GET THEE TO THE CRAFT DEPOT NOW! ASK MRS. JAMESON WHERE THE HECK THE BEDAZZLER IS AND HEAD RIGHT FOR THAT AISLE. GET THE DARNED THING AND GET LIKE TONS OF BAGS OF JEWELS, AKA RHINESTONES AND BACKS. GET MULTICOLORED ONES. GOLD ONES. SILVER ONES. GO NUTS! WHAT'S A BEDAZZLER, YOU SAY?

WHY, IT'S A LITTLE CRAFT GUN THAT SHOOTS DAZZLING STUDS AND RHINESTONES INTO FABRIC, SILLY. GET READY TO BEDAZZLE THINGS. WHAT THINGS?

° **TANK TOPS** °
gold stones look fabu on hot pink tank tops. Line all along the neck and the straps.

° **UNDIES** °
get the kinds with string straps and bedazzle the part at your hips. Ooh la la. Or better yet, bedazzle a silver rhinestone star, front and center.

° **MINISKIRT** °
down the sides
'80s style!

° **GLOVES** °
get some cool green (or black or red or pink or turquoise) Audrey Hepburn style gloves and bedazzle the cuff area.

Your **backpack**, your **pillowcases** (just the ends or else they will leave hickeylike marks on your face), your **socks**, your **Peds**, your **hair ribbons**, your old **Barbie clothes** (punk rock Barbie!), the **family napkins** (did we say that?), **tees, tees and more tees,** your **boyfriend's tees** (oh, yeah!), the **cuffs of your jeans** and more...

HAPPY BEDAZZLING!!

PHILOSOPHY

Today grab a good friend, a great friend, and go on an adventure of sorts. The two of you should go to a café, preferably one you've never been to, and order a decaf cappuccino or a hot chokky or something of that sort. And discuss things you don't normally talk about. Not boys, not fashion, something altogether serious. Like philosophy. Yeah, philosophy. To help get you started we'll tell you a little about **Simone de Beauvoir** and her existential beliefs. Get a load of this. Her whole name was **Simone Lucie-Ernestine-Marie-Bertrand de Beauvoir,** she was born in 1908 in Paris and she died in 1986. She is known primarily for her book "Le Deuxième Sexe," 2 vol. Which translates to The Second Sex. It was a very passionate plea to society to destroy the myth of the (say with thick French accent) "eternal feminine."

clea feels strongly about her existentialist beliefs while keva still struggles with the idea

Beauvoir wrote how in history, women have occupied a secondary position like that of the oppressed minorities. She critiqued how women have been portrayed in literary works and the image women have of their own selves. She was totally groundbreaking on all fronts. **Beauvoir** attended the Sorbonne, where she passed her aggregation (kinda like a master's degree) in philosophy and met Jean-Paul Sartre, another philosopher. They became lifelong friends, colleagues and lovers. In 1945 she and Sartre founded a monthly review (sort of like a French zine of their time), "Le Temps Modernes." She was a modern woman with a fire up her butt. **Simone de Beauvoir** rocked.

1.

You read yesterday's entry and thought, "Yeah, who cares? What is existentialism anyway?" Well, its main focus is on individual existence.

The bulk of philosophers way back since Plato all talked about the ethical good of the universe or of the community. But Kierkegaard, a Danish guy from the 19th century, said, "Whoa, nelly." (OK, he didn't actually say that, but he felt it.)

3.

See, existentialists sort of go against the notion that there is a "community morality" but believe rather, each person has to decide what is right for himself or herself. The punk rock of the '70s was super into existentialism, espousing one of that philosophy's most famous phrases, "Freedom of Choice."

Other famous existentialists were, of course, Sartre but also Albert Camus and Friedrich Nietzsche.

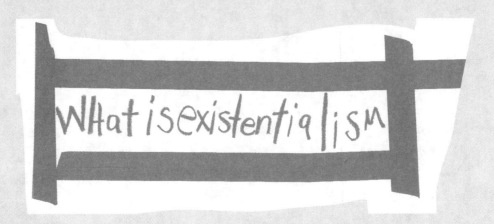

WHat is existentialism

2.

He thought that what is most important is for each individual to find his or her unique calling, which sort of went against previous philosophy that almost always centered around the "common" good.

4.

Now, this is just such a pinpoint tip of an iceberg, so if you're curious about fate vs. choice and the individual's debt and place in society by all means, grab a book or two by Beauvoir and her friends or hit the Web and type in "existentialism." And make sure you have an almond croissant with that coffee.

FUN WITH NUMBERS!

LOTSA FUN WITH NUMBERS. CUTE FUN. NUMBERS HAVEN'T BEEN THIS FUN SINCE FIRST GRADE.

fUN WITH NUMBERS

GET A BLANK PIECE OF PAPER AND PEN. WRITE DOWN THE NUMBERS BELOW AND THEN THE ANSWERS TO OUR QUESTIONS. WHEN WE ASK FOR NAMES, YOU MUST CHOOSE PEOPLE YOU KNOW. NONE OF THIS LEONARDO DiCAPRIO CRAP.

FIRST, WRITE THE NUMBERS 1 THROUGH 11 IN A COLUMN. THEN, BESIDE NUMBERS 1 AND 2, WRITE ANY TWO NUMBERS YOU WANT. BESIDE 3 AND 7, WRITE DOWN THE NAMES OF MEMBERS OF THE OPPOSITE SEX. WRITE ANYONE'S NAME (LIKE FRIENDS OR FAMILY...) IN THE 4TH, 5TH AND 6TH SPOTS. WRITE DOWN FOUR SONG TITLES IN 8, 9, 10 AND 11. FINALLY, MAKE A WISH.

AND 11 IS THE SONG TELLING HOW YOU FEEL ABOUT LIFE!
THE TENTH SPACE IS THE SONG THAT TELLS YOU MOST ABOUT YOUR MIND.
THE TITLE IN NUMBER 9 IS THE SONG FOR THE PERSON IN 7.
WITH THE PERSON IN NUMBER 3.
THE SONG WRITTEN IN NUMBER 8 IS THE SONG THAT MATCHES
THE PERSON YOU NAME IN 6 IS YOUR LUCKY STAR.
THE PERSON YOU NAME IN NUMBER 5 IS THE ONE WHO KNOWS YOU VERY WELL.
YOU CARE MOST ABOUT THE PERSON YOU PUT IN 4.
THE PERSON IN 7 IS THE ONE YOU LIKE BUT THE RELATIONSHIP CAN'T WORK OUT.
THE PERSON IN SPACE 3 IS THE ONE THAT YOU LOVE.
YOU MUST TELL (THE NUMBER IN SPACE 2) PEOPLE ABOUT THIS GAME.

Pele Pele Pele Pele Pele Pele

OK,
of all
the
goddesses we
have checked out
(and we have checked
out a lot), the very best one,
the freakiest, coolest, most crazy-
sneaky cool, is the **Hawaiian
goddess Pele.**
She of volcanic fire and sorcery.

This is how the story goes: Pele went in search of a place
to plant her fire. There was already a volcano god but he was
a cowardly god, and when he heard Pele was coming to town,
he split, lickety quick. Pele found a home in Mt. Kilauea on the
Big Island and planted her magic digging stick into the top,
creating the volcano. When she comes out for a peek, the volcano
erupts its hot liquid. We told you it was kinda sexy-cool.

Pele was one hot chick, no pun intended. She had many lovers and many
rivals, and most of them ended up trapped in misshapen pillars of rock
because she often hurled molten lava at those she was ticked off at. Apparently
you can still see these figures today, dotted all around the mountain's base. It has
also been said that she kept her little sister, who was born from an egg, warm in
her armpit on a long journey to the Hawaiian Islands. That sister, Hi'iaka, grew up
to be the Hawaiian patroness of dance. Pele should be proud. Pele was all about
seducing mortal men and she often got into fights with Poliahu, goddess of snow-
capped mountains. Man, they went at it, often killing the poor men in the process. To this
day, tales of Pele's power continue. People tell tales of Pele's presence on the island all the
time. Many drivers have picked up an old woman dressed all in white accompanied by a little
dog on roads in Hawaii Volcanoes National Park, only to look in the rearview mirror moments
later and find the backseat empty. Pele's face has mysteriously appeared in photographs of
fiery eruptions. People of all religions speak carefully about this ancient goddess. She has, after
all, destroyed more than 100 structures on the Big Island since 1983 and, perhaps even more
awesome than that, added more than 70 acres of land to the island's southeastern coastline.
She's hot, fiery, sexy, woman power. **She's Pele**.

NOVEMBER 21

It's Another Make-A-Present DAY!

PERHAPS YOU WERE CONSIDERING GETTING YOUR MOM OR UNCLE A PRETTY VASE. WELL, THAT IS A GREAT GIFT FOR SOMEONE WHO APPRECIATES CUT FLOWERS.

It's another make a present day!!!

But why not go one step further. Yeah, pick them up a vase (and don't just think new—you can find great vases at the thrift stores) but also hit the floral supply store for some cheap little accessories to fill the vase with:

Things like those metal or plastic frogs that go in the bottom of vases to hold the flowers up (why do they call them frogs anyhow?).

Seeds so they can plant them and always have fresh flowers.

A good pair of flower scissors.

Some flower food. (Makes your flowers last longer.)

Floral clay.

And anything else around the floral store that looks interesting and inexpensive.

NOW PUT EVERYTHING INSIDE THE VASE. WRAP THE VASE IN PRETTY TISSUE PAPER AND TIE A BIG, FAT BOW ON IT. BREATHE A SIGH OF RELIEF. ANOTHER GIFT TAKEN CARE OF.

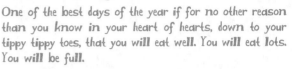

today is thanksgiving

Signature Dish

Keva's famous, garlicky eggplant extraordinaire

One of the best days of the year if for no other reason than you know in your heart of hearts, down to your tippy tippy toes, that you will eat well. You will eat lots. You will be full.

So we think you should create a signature dish that you can contribute to the family Thanksgiving meal every year. You know how at every household around the world families say, "Oh, I hope Aunt Ellen brings her famous apple pie" or "Man, I can't believe Eli didn't make his fabulous Swiss enchiladas this year." Well, let's create a dish that everyone, every year, is hoping you're going to bring.

Now, if you're vegan, this is the perfect opportunity to craft some dish that ensures there will be food you can eat at the table and simultaneously maybe turn someone on to your way of life. Might we suggest Tofurky. (Gosh, we love to say that word. Say it out loud. Food just doesn't get any funnier than that.) Or some meatless main dish that can stand in as an alternative to the always-present turkey. Like green beans in tomato sauce and soy cheese. Yum. Or an Indian casserole made with curried veggie burgers, chickpeas and cauliflower. Double yum.

Even if you're not trying to prove something to your family, you can still devise a dish that is totally your own (but made to share). Like your candied yams with both honey and brown sugar topped with oranges and marshmallows. Or lumpy mashed potatoes with extra cream and roasted garlic and fresh flat parsley with parmesan cheese on top. But whatever it is, go for extra goo.

Now, here is the most important part. You must name it. And include your name in the name. That way it is always associated with you. And every year on Thanksgiving, someone, somewhere, will be saying, "Man, I sure wish we were having Tiffany's Tofu Tettrazzini with Tartar Sauce; it just really isn't Thanksgiving without it."

¡YEAH!
BOARD GAMES

Sometimes you need to slow down. Take a break from the monotony of school, the repetitiveness of your schedule, the tedium of the day. Sure, you could watch *TV*, but that in itself is part of the tedium. Cards are good. You already know we like card games. But here's another suggestion. See, it's, um, now don't laugh...board games. Yeah, board games.

And we don't necessarily mean those new high-tech games that line the aisles of Toys-R-Everywhere. We mean old games. The kind you get at thrift stores and garage sales for $1 or $2. Because the less money spent, the more fun they are.

Play everything from Scrabble (which is a good one to play with your parents in a familial bonding session) to the Legend of Big Foot. A lot of the games from the '70s that are based on *TV* shows like "Charlie's Angels" and "The Bionic Woman" are so bad, they're good. They're unbelievably easy. And the covers themselves are so cool looking that when you're not playing, they make excellent wall décor.

Whenever we need to unwind after a hard day of writing, we break out Kreskin's Game of *ESP* or Home Alone or Sassy: The Board Game (we fight over who has to be Jane), and we open a bag o' chips and a few pops. We grab all the pillows from the house and plop down in the middle of the floor. We sometimes invite over a few friends to join in. It's relaxation at its mindless best.

P.S. amy, our editor, loves loves loves Trival Pursuit!

CLEA IS A QUIRKY GIRL.

say hello to clea and her brother Aesop!

Aesop
clea

I KNOW THIS BECAUSE I SEE HER EVERY DAY, EXCEPT MOST SATURDAYS AND SUNDAYS.

But, hey, five outta seven is pretty much all the time. Still, Clea is a quirky girl with many Clea-isms. That's what makes Clea so great. So great and so very one of a kind. The more Clea-isms I get to witness, the more I love her.

SOME OF MY FAVORITE CLEA-ISMS:

When Clea is happy she gets up and does a weird little dance, all just for me. And if she is really happy she may sing a little ditty to go along with that weird little dance. In fact once, when we were in Los Angeles, driving around, I asked her to sing to me. She did. She sang the theme song to "Three's Company." That's a Clea-ism. And yes, she knew all the words.

When Clea is in a sassy, funny oh-oh wanna-just-get-up-and-grab-you kinda mood or when she is trying to describe something cute like "bunches of little beads," she will put her hands up to her face and scriggle her fingers all out. That's SUCH a Clea-ism.

And when she's mad she gets sad and quiet and sometimes has to go outside and take a walk but then sometimes I'll get her a brownie and that cheers her up. Ahhhh, a toast to Clea and her isms!

is for clea

super clea!

So, you got some isms? Your best friend, I'm sure, has isms, too. Isms are what make people special and fun and it's really important that you take note. So today or next time you are hanging out with yer pal, notice the little things that he or she does and celebrate the isms because that's what makes them, them and you, you.

WOO HOO!

FUTURE FILES...

Ever seen the show "Land of the Lost"? The old one from the '70s? Two kids and their dad travel back in time and encounter the land of dinosaurs. If Clea could go on any adventure, anywhere in the world, defying time and space, she would go to the Land of the Lost. Now, maybe that ain't possible. (Although she hasn't given up all hope.) But you can dream about the action adventures you could have if money was no object and school was not part of your daily life. And of course, if you're gonna dream about the future that means only one thing...time for a new file! Say it aloud: FUTURE FILES. Grab that record jacket, shoe box or file. Write on it with a big black marker:

Action /Adventure Time

Now fill with all the clips you see of adventures you desire to go on.
Even if they are out of the question (like Clea's Land of the Lost silliness).
Who cares? Add it, because dreaming is a good thing.

So, ever thought about hiking through the Grand Canyon?
Bungee jumping in Canada?
Canoeing down the Nile?
Joining the Peace Corps and going to Africa?
Climbing Mount Everest?
Bicycling from San Francisco to Los Angeles?

If anything like this has ever crossed your mind, why not investigate a little?
Go online and look up Grand Canyon tours or the Peace Corps or Mount Everest.
Look for brochures you can send away for and addresses of people who have done these things or who host tours. Write them and ask a few questions you might be curious about (How long did it take you to bike from San Fran to L.A.?).
And when your brochures or letters come, file them away for the future.

In Clea's Action/Adventure File:
Go back in time to Land of the Lost
Drive cross-country, hitting every single
thrift store from San Diego to NYC
Kayak around the inlets
off the coast of Seattle
Learn how to kayak (ha ha)

In Keva's Action/Adventure File:
Be Pussy Galore in James Bond-life
Rollerskate through Legoland
Be Peter Pan and fly
around New York City
Get a big fat Jeep and drive
to Texas with Tim

Dad and Mom have everything they want and need?? Simple You make them something. How does aftershave and bubble bath sound? Well, OK then! Let's go!!!

.oot

gifts. kevin,

clea loves to make

For MOM:

For DAD:

Relaxing-Rejuvenating Bubble Bath

YOU'LL NEED:

2 cups soap flakes
1 gallon water
1/4 - 1/2 cup glycerin (from the drugstore)
2 cups plain nonsmelly shampoo
Essential oil (from a natural food store
or Body Shop type place)

Over low heat melt the soap flakes and the glycerin in the water. Stir. Now add the shampoo and a couple drops of smelly oil. Put in a pretty jar. Tell Mom to add a couple tablespoons to her bath and to enjoy the bubbles. (You can also save some for yourself.)

Awesome Aftershave

YOU'LL NEED:

2 cups rubbing alcohol
1 tablespoon glycerin (drugstore, natch)
1 teaspoon dried rosemary
1 teaspoon ground cloves
1 tablespoon dried lavender (try a natural food store)

Stir it all up and put it in a jar and then in the fridge. Leave it there for about four days but shake every day or so. Strain it, keeping the liquid and throwing away the gunk. Have Dad store it in the fridge. It will feel good on his freshly shaven face AND it will keep for two whole months.

NOVEMBER 27

Free fun. OK, get ready for a cool secret tip.
Every town has a paper, like a local paper, right?
We have the "Reader" in San Diego; L.A. has
the "Weekly." Anyway, in the classifieds of those
papers there are always certain sections where
they let you run an ad for free. You are, of course,
limited to the number of letters you can use
and whatnot, but that's not the point. The point
is that you and your friend can have a free
little friend thing. Yeah, we're talking about
leaving messages for your friends in the paper.
For free! Especially good if your friend goes
to another school and you don't see her very often.
Here's the deal:

HELLO KITTY:
TD? noway. 530
ok for sat?
warning: i'm
wearing red
dress so don't
even think about
it. also good
news. i can
sleep over!

use code names (DUH). compose a poem
together. trade juicy gossip. Declare
your feelings for that boy you love but
it's like a big secret and you would never,
ever say it out loud. But, heck, with a code
name you can do anything → You publish a
secret message, one a week. And your friend
scurries to the classified section to read it.
She reads it, she loves it, she loves you and
she sends her message off to the newspaper
right away. And so on and so forth. and don't tell
each other what you're gonna write. It's best if
they are weekly little surprises.

DEAR SUPERC:
don't forget 2
bring dress up
stuff. my house.
sat 6pm. new crush
on t.d. talk to
j.m. yet? w/b k.

p.s. hey, tricia, 'member this? xo K.

today is... for the love of Eric Stoltz Day

Why? Because sometimes it's great just to have random days devoted to random people. And, well, Eric is hot. He's the only hot redheaded actor guy we can think of. He's been in some really good movies. So that is the very reason we deem today the official "let's hang out and worship Eric Stoltz day." Here's what you need to do: Memorize the below facts and be prepared to preach them to the unaware.

cute red hair

CLEA'S BAD ERIC STOLTZ drawing (he's cuter than this)

FACTOIDS:

* He was in both "Fast Times at Ridgemont High" and "Say Anything."

* He was born in Whittier, California.

* He has dated Ally Sheedy, Jennifer Jason Leigh and Bridget Fonda.

* His dad is a first grade teacher and his mom, who passed away several years ago, was a violinist and also a teacher. We betcha by golly Eric is a pretty smart boy. All them teachers in the family. He's got two sisters.

* He won the Theatre World Award in 1989. We don't know what that is, but, hey, it sounds impressive.

* He went to UCLA where he studied acting with Stella Adler (famous acting teacher) and others.

* Some of his many movies:
"Kicking and Screaming" (1995) *
"Little Women" (1994)
"Bodies, Rest & Motion" (1993) *
"Memphis Belle" (1990)
"Say Anything. . ." (1989)
"Some Kind of Wonderful" (1987) *
"Mask" (1985)
"Fast Times at Ridgemont High" (1982)

* * Three of Keva's favorite movies of all time.

THE BEST GIFT TO GET AND MAKE* YET.

Give the gift of cookie dough. No really. This is better than a fruit basket. Better than a tie. Better than some nasty scarf you picked out at the last minute for Auntie Helen just because you found nothing else.

Simply make your favorite recipe. Look online or in one of Dad's cookbooks if you don't have a favorite. Make extra so you can have cookies, too. Roll it into a log. Wrap it in parchment paper (from cooking stores) or wax paper. Twist the ends. Tie pretty ribbons on each end. Tie a little card with instructions to one end. (You know, things like the oven temperature and the cooking time. Oh, and the fact that it will keep in the freezer for a month or till they are ready to bake 'em up.) And put in the fridge for a few hours before giving so it firms up real nice.

You could also make a few different flavors.
One with nuts. One with white chocolate chips.
And give the gift of cookie dough.

*'Cause you get to eat some, too.

← pickled peppers

Speak German.

GERMAN IS RAD. It's full of phlegm and guttural noises that are so very foreign to Americans. Have a little fun with these German phrases sure to turn any Germanic babe's head.

SO—I HEAR GERMANY IS BEAUTIFUL THIS TIME OF YEAR. So—ich habe gehört, dass Deutschland schön um diese Jahreszeit ist.

I BET NOT AS BEAUTIFUL AS YOU. Bestimmt nicht so schön wie du.

YOU ARE REALLY HANDSOME. Du bist wircklich schön.

BIG, STRONG AND HANDSOME. Gross, stark und schön.

Schlecht ptooey

PETER PIPER PICKED A PECK OF PICKLED PEPPERS. Peter Piper pflückte einen Peck Essigpfeffer.

ARE SMART GIRLS AS POPULAR IN YOUR COUNTRY AS THEY ARE IN AMERICA? Sind intelligente Mädchen in deinem Land auch so beliebt wie in Amerika?

I AM VERY SMART. Ich bin sehr intelligent.

DECEMBER

December 1

paper chains

Twenty-five cheap and fun things to do to get into the holiday spirit.

1. Make lots of Mexican hot chocolate with cream and cinnamon.
2. This year get a pink frosted tree. Even if you don't celebrate Xmas.
3. Spray glitter all over your cards and decorations.
4. Spray snow on all your windows.
5. Make peanut butter and birdseed pinecones.
6. Go thrifting for random stuff to give as gifts.
7. Spray-paint holiday stuff on your Chinese paper lamps.
8. Spray perfume on lightbulbs. (My goodness, there is lots of spraying going on.)
9. Send pretty invites for your party. What party? Have a party.
10. Serve sparkling apple juice.
11. Or apple cider in a large round jug.
12. Or make your own.
13. Listen to Frank Sinatra.
14. Wear fuzzy sweaters and boots. (And pants, too, please.)
15. Make gingerbread cookies.
16. Craft up construction paper chains for the walls.
17. Save the first snowball of the season in your freezer.
18. Make Rice Krispies treats with red and green marshmallows or red and yellow ones, in honor of Kwanza.
19. Paint fingernails red and green. Paint toenails red and green. Or red and yellow all around.
20. Wear red tights.
21. Watch "Miracle on 34th Street."
22. Call up old friends.
23. Or even better...aunts and uncles.
24. Give the Salvation Army Santa some money.
25. Get your picture taken with Santa at the mall, copy it and send to your whole family.

Ring! Ring!

red green red
green
red

These boots are made for walking...

yum!

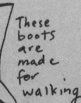

December is the best time of year to decorate your trees. Now this could be a Christmas tree, surely, but it could also be an elm tree, a maple tree, a Chanukah bush, any tree in your yard (or indoors) that you feel like adorning with style.

Dub yourself tree queen from this year forward and take control! Make a promise to yourself to come up with a fabulously cool theme each year and present it to your parents for approval a few weeks prior. Tell them you will take care of the rest (yes, clean up, too!) and then go nuts. Invite your pals to help. Take cute pictures of Sarah stringing the lights. Keep cute pictures forever in album as mementos or make copies and distribute 'round. But remember, whatever you decide to do, make sure to have fun. Because having fun is where it's at.

Decorate a tree...

**Keva: Last year my tree was pink and had pictures of Spice Girls and Spice Girl candy all over it, plus little white lights!

December 3

You need more tiaras in your life. Why? Because they instantaneously make you feel like the princess that you are.

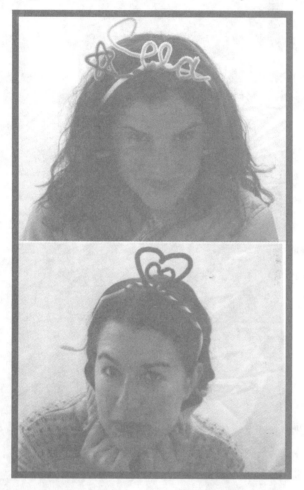

So today, make pipe cleaner tiaras! They're so very cute.

So simple, so chic, so cheap, so very very. Just take a few pipe cleaners.
(Nope, not the ones you just used to clean the pipes. Take a break, plumber princess.)
Craft a headband type shape out of twisted pipe cleaners. It's oh so light as feathers.
A joy to wear on the head. Then adorn with more pipe cleaners.

The best place to wear a tiara: Bowling. The worst place to wear a tiara: Playing soccer.
Oh, and you can get pipe cleaners at the craft store, not the plumber store. Well, you know what we mean.

IMAGINE YOU ARE LUKE SKYWALKER

"Oh my goodness, I am the biggest dork EVER." - Clea

December 5

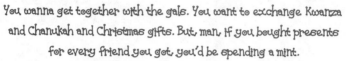

a party + cheap gifts = FUN

You wanna get together with the gals. You want to exchange Kwanza and Chanukah and Christmas gifts. But, man, if you bought presents for every friend you got, you'd be spending a mint.
So here is the answer to your woes.

Invite a whole bunch of friends over. Tell everyone to bring one small present, approximate value: $5 (or $10, it's up to you). It should be wrapped. Set up a gift table where everyone puts their presents when they arrive. Give each a number tag when they arrive, too. Just a sticker with a number on it. Have little scraps of paper that are numbered too and correspond to everyone's tags. Place scraps in a hat. Draw a number. That person then gets to choose a present from the table. He or she opens it in front of everyone. Draw another number. That person can either steal the opened present or open a brand-new one. If he or she steals the present, the person who was stolen from gets to choose another present. And so on and so. Till everyone has a present. It can often take a long time, depending upon how many guests you have. But it's so fun. Especially if people bring funny joke presents. Just more cheap group fun from your pals, Clea and Keva.

TAKE A BREAK FROM THE FABULOUS YOU.

December 6

Are you feeling too cute, too crafty, overwhelmed by the sheer aura of just being you? Do you feel like maybe just sitting around and being dull with some greasy potato chips, a fat couch, ice skating on the telly and, oh, sweatpants. How deluxe. You see, even the crafty overachievers (like YOU!) deserve a day of uncool do nothingness. A few rules to follow and you're on your own. No more from us today... promise!

1 Don't answer the phone. Let the answering machine do its job.
2 Make sure you have ample snax.
3 And ample movies.
4 Locate the remote.
5 Hide away in the guest room if you can.
6 Wear cozy socks and ditch the bra.
7 Grab your wind machine and plug it in.
8 That's it!

December 7

Celebrating Mozart's birthday with those friends who partake in different religious holidays than you do is the perfect alternative to Xmas, Chanukah and Kwanza.

OK, SO IT'S NOT REALLY HIS BIRTHDAY. THAT'S IN JANUARY. BUT WE CAN FUDGE FOR PARTY'S SAKE. AND MOZART WAS PRETTY DARN COOL. FIRST OFF, HIS FIRST NAME WAS WOLFGANG. NOW THAT'S COOL. HE BEGAN COMPOSING MINUETS AT THE AGE OF 5 AND SYMPHONIES BY THE TIME HE WAS 9. WHEN HE WAS 6, HE AND HIS OLDER SISTER, MARIA ANNA, WHO WAS ALSO VERY TALENTED, STARTED TOURING EUROPE AS CHILD PRODIGIES. HE WROTE HIS FIRST OPERA WHEN HE WAS 12. HE TRAVELED ALL OVER, PLAYED FOR KINGS AND QUEENS AND WROTE AND WROTE AND WROTE.

More on Mozart later but you can start the celebration by crafting Mozart Birthday cards for all your friends. Take a walk back in time (well, back in book time) and remember the various crafts we have concocted. Will any of these make excellent Mozart cards? YES, YES AND YES.

You can make paper airplane cards. Or wallpaper cards. You could make a card out of a Polaroid.

Or, since it's Mozart's birthday that you're celebrating, you could make a great mix tape of all your favorite songs (holiday and otherwise), make copies and then decorate the J-card. Happy Mozart!

Happy Mozart's Birthday

Songs for you in celebration of the holidays & the rocking Amadeus!

SONGS

Enjoy.
Listen.
Celebrate!

Rock Me Amadeus.
Dreidel, Dreidel.
Rockin' around the Christmas Tree.
Auld Lang Syne.
Love, American Style.
Couldn't Hurt a Fly.

XOXO Clea + Keva

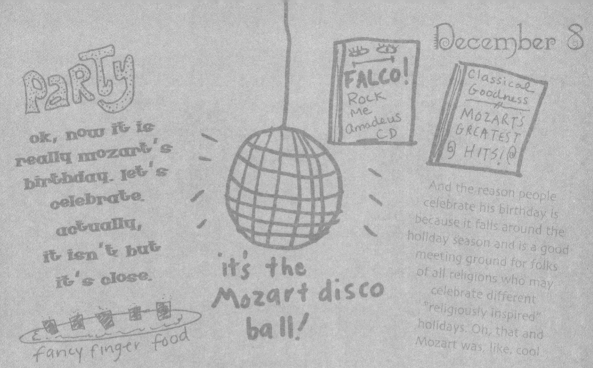

PARTY

ok, now it is really mozart's birthday. let's celebrate. actually, it isn't but it's close.

it's the Mozart disco ball!

fancy finger food

FALCO!
ROCK
ME
Amadeus
CD

Classical Goodness
~
MOZART'S GREATEST HITS!

And the reason people celebrate his birthday is because it falls around the holiday season and is a good meeting ground for folks of all religions who may celebrate different "religiously inspired" holidays. Oh, that and Mozart was, like, cool

Now, you can create your own traditions but here are some of ours. **This isn't a kegger.** This is an elegant holiday party with parlor games. First off you need to rent "Amadeus." Have it on in the background with the sound down on the TV. And play classical music—this is a posh affair, after all. If you just aren't acclimated to Mozart yet, then by all means, mix it up. Maybe put a Mozart CD in the carousel and a Falco CD (**"Rock Me Amadeus"**). And hit shuffle.

Our favorite parlor game involves a poster board. See, you divide it into as many squares as there will be guests, each square at least the size of a **Post-It note**. If you are unsure of the number of guests, guess, but guess high rather than low. Number all the squares 1 through whatever. Get a pack of stickers (like name tags, **"Hello my name is..."**) and number those the same numbers as the squares.

As your guests arrive, give each a number sticker. Now put the poster number chart up someplace that is accessible to all and leave several packets of Post-It notes on a table nearby. Your guests can leave **anonymous notes** for people in their corresponding square. If you see someone you've been crushing on and they're wearing #12, you can then go over and write a **flirtatious note** (nothing too lascivious here, all the party can see) and stick it on square #12. You can choose to do this anonymously or sign it with your number. You can leave **sweet notes**, faux secrets or inside jokes for your friends. Just tell everyone house rules are you can't say anything mean or nasty.

Serve fancy finger food and sparkling apple juice in plastic wine glasses. (Remember to drink out of your chalice.) And don't forget to **sing Mozart "Happy Birthday."**

December 9

Cheese, glorious cheese. Every gal should know 'bout cheese.

Why? It's the cheesiest of foods. Duh. No, see, there is a whole cheese culture and cheese plates are fine eating. Plus, it's just great semiuseless knowledge to have. We all need a little of that in our lives. Now, you can divide cheese into four categories by its texture: Hard, semihard, semisoft and soft. Hard cheeses are things like Asiago (from Italy) and Parmigiano Reggiano, also from Italy. Italians are into that hard cheese thing. Semihard cheeses include Gouda (gouda is good) and Roquefort, which by the way is also known as the "King of Cheeses". Roquefort ripens in a cave. At least that's what we read. Semisoft cheeses are things like yummy Havarti and the beautifully named Brillat-Savarin. It's named after an 18th century French food writer. It too is yummy. Semisoft cheeses rock. Soft cheeses include Brie AKA the "Queen of Cheeses" (that is also a good nickname for your best friend) and Limburger, which is the stinkiest of cheeses.

Cute muscles
My heart aches and giggles
Could it be

Yeah,
maybe you've heard of
haiku in school, but it is a Japanese
poetry form. The word haiku literally
translates to "short verse."

Haiku is cool
it makes use of the senses
tells of living things

OK, that was a haiku. In Japanese, most haiku is 17 syllables total,
with the first line being five, the second seven and the last five. But
because the Japanese language is so very different from English, today's
modern haiku format is expressed in anywhere from 10 to 17 syllables.
It really shouldn't be any longer than the length of a single breath. But
more important is what you write your haiku about.

Think: A fleeting moment.

Whatever you write about, it should be something you
experienced, you thought, you tasted, smelled or heard.

Cherry lollipop
almost burns my tongue
too sticky sweet

pricey silver heels
my feet yearn for you
o sparkle sparkle

Haiku.
Um, bless you.

The father of the haiku was a wandering Zen Buddhist
named Matsuo Basho who lived in the 17th century,
and he saw haiku as quick snapshots of nature. Now,
this doesn't mean all haiku is about leaves and plants
and crud. No, no. Nature can mean all sorts of things,
such as our own five senses. So to write proper haiku
you can think, how does this feel? Or smell? Or taste
like? Or sound like? Or you can forget proper altogether.

December 11

You know those "bombs" you can buy in beauty stores? They're like bath beads but they foam when dropped in water, giving your bath a Sprite-like edge. Well, you can make these for spa night. And they also make excellent gifts. Wrap them individually with a bow or stick a bunch in a coffee mug and plop a big red ribbon on it.

THE DIRECTIONS: Mix the citric acid, cornstarch and baking soda together in an old bowl. Now in another bowl (this one should be glass) mix the olive oil with the essential oil and the food coloring. Now slowly add the oil into the dry mix, stirring constantly so you get no lumps.

Get a piece of wax paper and cut it to the size of your baking sheet. Place it on the baking sheet. Then make walnut-size balls of the gunk and put them on the wax paper. They need to dry for about a day or two. Store in Tupperware or wrap all pretty for gifts.

To use, drop a couple in your bath water. Light candles. And relax. Feel the fizz.

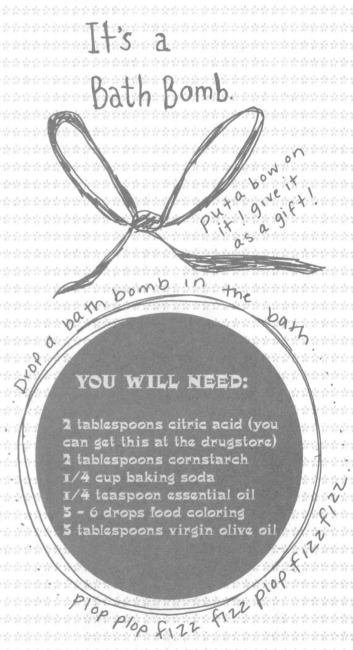

It's a Bath Bomb.

Put a bow on it! give it as a gift!

Drop a bath bomb in the bath

plop plop fizz fizz plop fizz fizz

YOU WILL NEED:

2 tablespoons citric acid (you can get this at the drugstore)
2 tablespoons cornstarch
1/4 cup baking soda
1/4 teaspoon essential oil
5 - 6 drops food coloring
3 tablespoons virgin olive oil

LET'S TALK.
SOME MORE.

Clea: I like being short. I wouldn't trade it for the world. I can't really wear super flat flats, but I can wear platforms galore. I can't get on some rides at Magic Mountain but I can live with that.

Keva: Roller coasters and me are NOT best friends.

Clea: Ooh, something we have in common! I get so nervous-sick that I puke before we even go up! What do you do at Disneyland? Do you go even though you don't like it or do you stay behind by your lonesome?

Keva: I go and buy lots of stickers and rock candy and those sticks of candy in all those flavors like root beer, what are those called...and everyone thinks I'm being lame when really I just wanna eat candy.

Clea: OH, MY GOD! ME, TOO! I love those root beer stick things, what are they called? Like penny candy even though they aren't even a penny. I love that people think you are lame. They are so wrong. Hello, you just like candy.

Keva: Hooray! I'm not lame!

Clea: No, no, and I am the arbiter of all that is lame.

Keva: Disco or rock?

Clea: Um, neither. Pseudo-alt-dance-Jamaican-country sung in French with a good back beat. Now that's the groove, baby. I am just so fresh.

Keva: Do you think that MP3 is gonna ruin the music industry?

Clea: No way, Jose. You know how indie bands got slurped up by big major labels and there are less and less independent record labels and people just doing it in their garages? Well, now small people can soon record their own music and put it on the Web for all the world to hear and that is zippy cool. Besides, did VCRs kill the movie bizness, did video kill the radio star?

Keva: Oh, yes. Yes, yes, yes. I think I'll go there right now and play some hip hop.

DISCUSSION QUESTIONS✤ *What is your opinion of roller coasters? Do you think either Clea or Keva are lame due to their love of candy and hatred of roller coasters? Do you think Clea really is the arbiter of all things lame? Rock and roll or disco? Or Jamaican country dance? And your opinion of MP3? Do you think that video killed the radio star?*

December 13   Snow globes are boss.
Mighty mighty boss.

The water and glitter combo is mesmerizing. Make your own snow globes just in time for the holidays. These are especially good as gifts for people who collect snow globes.

The how-to:

Now, you start by gluing small trinkets to the inside of the jar's lid. Make sure you can secure the lid to the jar before proceeding.

Add some glitter & beads to the jar. Then fill with equal parts water & corn syrup. You could add a drop of blue food coloring for a pastel blue tint, but that's totally optional.

Now put glue all around the mouth of the jar and around the screw part of the lid. Now screw the lid on and let dry. Once it's all dry, you can turn the jar upside down so that the lid is on the bottom and your trinket is right side up. Shake to get the glitter or beads floating around.

Sit, watching, mesmerized.

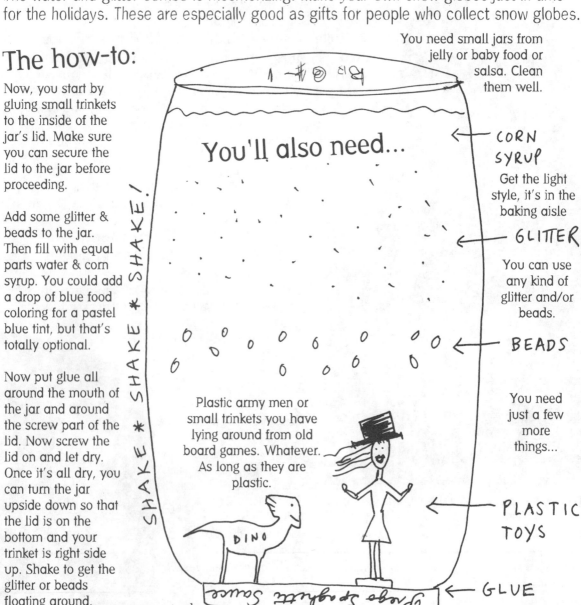

You need small jars from jelly or baby food or salsa. Clean them well.

You'll also need...

CORN SYRUP
Get the light style, it's in the baking aisle

GLITTER
You can use any kind of glitter and/or beads.

BEADS

Plastic army men or small trinkets you have lying around from old board games. Whatever. As long as they are plastic.

You need just a few more things...

PLASTIC TOYS

DINO

GLUE
Watertight kind.

SHAKE * SHAKE * SHAKE * SHAKE!

FRUITCAKE

INGREDIENTS: 4 eggs, 1½ cups flour, ½ teaspoon salt, ½ teaspoon baking soda, 1 cup butter, 1 cup brown sugar.

Things you can add (and don't stop here, use your imagination):

Those nuclear red bottled cherries; walnuts, pecans, pine nuts, peanuts, almonds, any and all nuts; any and all flavors of jam; spices like nutmeg, cinnamon, cardamom, ginger; dried fruit like pears, apricots, figs, dates, apples; raisins, both yellow and black; marzipan (pasty almond candy that's so sweet your lips pucker); chocolate chips, peanut butter chips, white choco chips; Gummi Bears; Milk Duds; Sugar Babies and other small candies; yogurt-covered pretzels; crushed trail mix; coconut.

DIRECTIONS: Butter two loaf pans. Line them with wax paper and butter that, too. Sift the flour together with the salt, baking powder and any spices you might use. Set aside. With an electric mixer cream together butter and sugar. And then add the eggs, one at a time. Now mix in the flour mixture, a little at a time. Then add any of the candy·nut·fruit accessories you plan to use. Stir with wooden spoon till all combined. Pour into loaf pans. Bake at 325 degrees till firm (put a knife or skewer in center and pull out—when it's clean, the cake is done). It should bake about 1 hour and 15 minutes. Maybe a few minutes more, depending upon what you put in your personal fruit cake. When it's done, get them out of their pans and let them cool on racks. Once cool, wrap in plastic and let sit all day at room temperature. Then store in the fridge or eat it. It will last two weeks (not a lifetime like other fruitcakes—this one is homemade, baby).

Does someone in your family have a fruitcake recipe that they make every year? Hopefully not. Because today you shall devise your very own fruitcake recipe and write it down to be saved and cherished forever and eternity. We will give you the basic ingredients, the must-haves like the flour, butter and eggs. You come up with the rest.

gummy worms

almonds

apricots

chocolate covered raisins

Don't forget to name the recipe. Something truly goofy. Like, the Hundred Year Old Fruitcake. Or Cherry-Oh-Baby Fruit cake. Or We Had Joy, We Had Fun, We Had Raisins in the Sun Fruitcake.

December 15

When things get a little boring and you got no car and no money...

Grab the phone book!!

The big fat yellow one. And a pen. A ball point.
That's for sure.
The last thing you want is for your writing to bleed through the pages, right?

OK, so you got the phone book? You got a pen? You are comfy and have snax and drinks nearby? Nice warm sox on? And the phone? You need the phone.

Open up the book. Anywhere. Wherever. Scan the page. Find a job. The first job you lay your eyes on. Say, "carpet cleaner"— now circle it. Imagine yourself a carpet cleaner. Imagine yourself a carpet cleaner with $8,000 to start your bizness. Call the carpet cleaner guy. Ask him how much he charges and write it next to his ad. Wow, that's how much you make. Now think: What do I need? Will I need a truck? New clothes? Cool boots? Billboard ads? Now hunt through the phone book for all those things. Call a company that has each thing and find out how much supplies cost. Tell them you are starting a carpet cleaning bizness and see if they will send you brochures.

Now, once you get the hang of this pick a way better profession. Like female mud wrestler. And go nuts. We mean, you're only dreaming, so the sky is the limit.

Check out the clowns!!!

**Also a good learning experience.

SNOWMEN
are too
COOL

Do you have a gal pal who is aching over a disastrous, unrequited crush? Give her the gift of a fake boy, one who does not talk or walk away, one made of snow. OK, even the gloomiest of gals can dig a snowman, right?

And if you live someplace where it doesn't snow, then this is a great reminder to a friend in a colder region to not take the snow for granted. Pack this up and mail it off with a note that says, "Make a snowman for me."

So how do you "give" a snowman? Well, you don't exactly. You give a snowman kit. Call it the "Build a Better Boy Snowman Kit."

Take the orange clay and mold it into the shape of a carrot. You could even draw carrotlike lines on it with a fork. Flatten the big fat end and push a stick in one-third of the way. That's his nose. The stick makes it easy to attach to your snow guy. (You can just shove the stick in the packed snow head and it will stay miraculously.) Put it in the box.

The black clay is for his eyes and buttons. Make five buttons—just roll black clay into five balls and flatten. Insert a stick in each one. Do the same for his eyes, but make them a little larger. Make his mouth by rolling out what's left of the black clay into a snake shape about $2^1/2$ inches long. Flatten a little. Add stick. Add it all to box.

The yellow clay is for his corncob pipe. (Even though we don't like dating boys who smoke, we'll make an exception this time because he doesn't ever light up.) Shape some yellow clay into a ball (about two inches wide) and then stick your thumb in the center, creating a minibowl. Stick this on the end of a stick. You can take the straw and lightly and repeatedly press an end into the yellow clay to make it look like a corncob, if you wanna get fancy. Add to your box.

YOU WILL NEED: Ten sticks, each about three inches long. You could use popsicle sticks. Or sturdy twigs from around the neighborhood. Clay from the craft store. A pack of orange, black and yellow. A straw you got from the local burger place. A box to put this all in. It should be rather large. And line it with cotton balls. You can also find a cheap thrift store scarf and roll it up and add it to the box.

Lastly, you need to make a card out of construction paper and draw a picture of a snowman, illustrating how each piece is utilized. Toss in a handful of confetti in the box and you're done.

December 17

OK, so another cool and crafty thing to make for a pal for the holidays is...

A HOMEGIRL-STYLE PHOTO ALBUM.

Clea and her tall friend, Laura.

Take two pieces of cardboard from an old record cover and cut them both the same size (like you did for notebooks way back when). Now cut out a square, just a hair smaller than one of your photos, from the top piece, making like a "window." Place the best photo, one of you and your friend where you both look great, behind the hole so it's now sort of "framed." Tape it down from behind. Then glue the back piece of cardboard to the front piece, enclosing your picture completely. Punch a hole in the upper corner. Put that aside for now.

Get some sheets of heavy card stock paper. Cut them a bit smaller than the cover of your album and make sure you have enough pages for all your pictures. Punch a hole in each piece of paper in the same corner as the cover.

Secure these pages and the cover together by putting one of those metal rings (called D-rings) from office supply stores through all the holes. Voila! A grand photo album. It will be loose and more like a big key chain than a traditional album, but who needs tradition on December 17?

You'd be all done, except it doesn't have any pictures in it yet. Grab your photos and either a glue stick, rubber cement or those classy little black photo corners you get at the art store. Cover the pages in photos and take a moment to reminisce. Add a personalized touch and write something sweet. Date the book, wrap in tissue and present. It's one of the most personal gifts you can give.

Imagine you were given
5 *MILLION* DOLLARS
from a secret person who
ooh hh secret.....
told you that the *money
may be used only to HELP
people. What would you do?

December 19

"Chestnuts roasting on an open fire....," goes the song, but if you don't know how to roast them, you'll cast them back into the coals in disgust.

And how terrible to spoil such a sweater-wearing, fire-roaring, romantic moment. Geez. So here's the dealio.

At the store you will probably find two kinds of chestnuts: Castagne, run-of-the-mill chestnuts; and marroni, larger, gloriously meaty chestnuts that can be an inch or more across. You want the second kind. Do not settle for castagnes. No way.

Pick them over carefully, taking only those that are firm and whose skins are a rich, glowing brown.

If they smell moldy, look blotchy, feel light or have pinholes, pass them by. Leave them hanging. It's OK, they know they're bad. Before roasting the chestnuts, make a cut in the round side of each to keep them from exploding. (No kidding, we knew a guy who lost his right eye because of that. Don't let it happen to you.)

Since you are doing them over the stove or maybe over an open fire, you really will want a chestnut-roasting pan, which looks like a skillet with holes punched in its bottom.

If need be, you can make a pan yourself. Take a cheap pie tin and punch holes in the bottom with a fork.

Go, girls. Put the chestnuts in the pan, sprinkle them with water, cover them, and set the pan over a medium flame. Shake the pan frequently (kinda like homemade popcorn) and continue roasting until the skins are blackened and have pulled back from the meat where you cut into them.

This should take 5 to 10 minutes. Wrap the hot chestnuts in an old towel, squeeze them hard to crush the skins, and let them sit wrapped for five minutes. Open the towel and enjoy: The nut meat will be deliciously soft and sweet.

PIE PLATE

POKED WITH A FORK

(OK, that thing about the guy losing his eye was a blatant lie, but still, be careful.)

One of the most signficant meanings of Chanukah is that it is in memory of a war fought for a principle, not land or greed. It was fought for the freedom to practice one's beliefs.

In the year 168 B.C., Antiochus the IV, ruler of Syria, wanted the Jewish people of Israel to worship his gods and pay homage to the statues that he erected. The Jews would not worship what they considered to be false idols, nor were they willing to give up their beliefs. So Antiochus had many of the Jews slaughtered, and many more were sold as slaves.

CHANUKAH

by grandma ruthie

This continued until a man named Mattathias and his five sons, Yohanan, Simon, Judiah, Elleazar and Jonathan, led the Jewish people to fight for their freedom and their religion.

There were many battles and many versions of the tales, but the Jewish people prevailed and chased Antiochus into the sea. The aftermath left their temple in shambles. The Jewish people began to resurrect their crumbling temple.

Judiah wanted to rededicate the temple by lighting the lamps of the menorah, but there was only oil for one day. In spite of this, the lamps burned on for eight full days. This is the miracle that is celebrated on Chanukah. For me, the miracle was the beginning of man's understanding of the freedom of thought and religion. History, and the news of the day, inform us of the conflicts between Jews and Arabs, Catholics and Protestants, whites and blacks, religious and nonreligious, cat lovers and dog lovers, and so on. I think in celebrating Chanukah, we should celebrate the miracle of our differences and honor the uniqueness of man. Let each candle represent those differences and light our way to tolerance and understanding.

*One last thing. On Chanukah, we often eat potato latkes, delicious potato pancakes. Why potato latkes? Who knows, but I love the smell, the taste and the fun of group cooking. You can chop the onions, I'll grate the potatoes.

WINTER

see the rosy glow?

It's the first day of winter. We like spring (for the boy fever), summer (for the sunshine) and fall (for the breezes), but winter isn't bad. It does, after all, house the major holidays. It's just the least appealing of all seasons. Still, it has its very own accoutrements, many of which are rather fun. So...bake something. And if you have never baked anything, now is the time to learn. The smell of baking apples and cinnamon-anything makes winter worthwhile. Tights, tights and more tights. Look for pairs with stuff on them, like little ladybugs or flowers or the Mona Lisa. Tights make winter bearable. Oh, and woolly scarves, too. Make sure you have plenty of hot chokky on hand. Stay in and rent wintery movies with snow storm scenes. Like "Dr. Zhivago." Crochet your dog or cat a warm beanie to keep its little head cozy. If you have snow, grab some that looks extra white (none of that yellow snow, ha ha) and put it in a bowl. Pour maple syrup (REAL maple syrup) over it and eat. Yum. Be happy you live where there is snow. Enjoy the pink glow you get from the cold air. It's au naturel blush and lip tint, winter style.

One last thing: SNOW BOARDING!!!

apple pie

hot chocolate

← beanie

maple syrup

Now, before you start getting all huffy and hurl this book across the room, let us explain. These aren't your ordinary magnets. These are glittery fantastical magnets. These are made special, by your little hands, each one crafted specifically by the giver for the givee (you're the giver).

You'll need:

Those thin sheets of magnet. They are found in stationery stores. They are cheap.

Glue.

Glitter, sequins and·or beads.

A photo: of the givee, of you and the givee, of the givee's friends or of the object of the givee's worship (i.e., Scott Wolf, Tori Amos, etc.).

Glue the photo down on the magnet sheet. Cut around the photo. Start beading and glittering and sequining the "frame" around the picture. A couple drops o' glue, a couple sequins. Some more glue, a little glitter. You get the drift. Now, if there is anything on the picture that needs embellishment, by all means, add more glitter. What we mean is this: If the photo is of you, why not make your lips sparkle with unnaturally red glitter "lipstick"?

How to make a cool present for anyone, for any occasion.

What could this versatile crafty gift be?

Why, magnets, of course.

Could this magnet be any uglier? Yikes!!

Wrap up in a cute little box with more glitter inside and you have yourself a fabulous, special gift.

December 23

Oh, the end of the year is near. Make cookies and play cheery music and dress the part. Oh, and don't forget about eggnog.

1/2 shaker full of broken ICE
1 teaspoon SUGAR
1 EGG (must be oh so fresh or forget about it)
1 CHERRY
a coffee cup full of MILK
1 dash grated NUTMEG

The only good nog is Eggnog

Add your sugar to the shaker with the broken ice. Then add the egg and milk. Shake well and pass through a strainer into a tumbler. Serve with a dash of nutmeg and a cherry. Yummy!

CHRISTMAS EVE IS A FABULOUS DAY

...EVEN IF YOU DON'T CELEBRATE CHRISTMAS (AND A LOT OF
PEOPLE DON'T). BECAUSE EVERYTHING SHUTS DOWN. IT'S FORCED
QUIET TIME. AND THAT CAN BE A GOOD THING. HERE'S
A PROJECT. IT'S A BIG ONE (AND YOU COULD CARRY IT OVER TO
TOMORROW AS WELL, ANOTHER FORCED QUIET DAY).

MAKE A CALENDAR FOR NEXT YEAR. GO THROUGH YOUR PHOTOS
OR YOUR DRAWINGS FROM THIS YEAR AND FIGURE OUT WHAT
MONTH THEY CAME FROM. THEN FOR EACH MONTH, CREATE A
COLLAGE OR SIMPLY USE ONE PHOTO OR DRAWING. MAKE ONE PAGE
FOR EVERY MONTH. YOU CAN MAKE A GRID FOR THE DAYS OF THE
MONTH BY HAND, OR YOU CAN DO IT ON THE COMPUTER. MAKE
SURE TO ADD IN EVERYONE'S BIRTHDAYS (YOU CAN EVEN PUT A
PICTURE OF YOUR DAD IN THE SQUARE THAT REPRESENTS HIS
BIRTHDAY AND ONE OF YOUR MOM ON HER BIRTHDAY AND SO ON).
YOU CAN MAKE A ONE-OF-A-KIND CALENDAR OR YOU CAN TAKE IT
TO THE COPY SHOP (WHEN THEY REOPEN) AND HAVE THEM COLOR
COPY THE WHOLE THING AND BIND IT. GIVE THE CALENDAR TO
ALL YOUR RELATIVES OR FRIENDS.

CHRISTMAS DAY IS ONE OF THE GREAT TRADITIONS AND FUN AND GOOD FOR YEAR-END SOUL SEARCHING.

If you do celebrate Christmas, your family probably has all sorts of traditions and activities. If you don't, then today is the very best day of the year to see a movie. Something frivolous yet uplifting. Silly and sappy.

Or you can rent the best nonholiday movie ever, "Willy Wonka and the Chocolate Factory." It is tradition in Clea's house that every Christmas Day they watch it at least three times while snacking on tidbits of food. They never get dressed. They stay wrapped up in blankets from morning till night. And if you have pajamas with feet in them, today is the day to break 'em out.

In other words, relax. You must reserve all strength for the upcoming New Year celebration. Not to mention the whole NEW YEAR that is just around the corner.

Boxing Day. It's a holiday in England. Keva was going to ask her boyfriend Tim, who is English, what he did on this particular day as a little boy in England but she never got around to it. (They were too busy kissing.) So we've decided to make Boxing Day the day of boxing. As in Muhammad Ali and Sugar Ray. Hooray! First of all, boxers have really hot names like the aforementioned Sugar Ray Leonard and Muhammad Ali, plus ones like Ray "Boom Boom" Mancini, so we think you should, too. Have a boxing name.

Boxing Day

Give yourself a boxing name right now.

P.S. This was much better than another holiday thing, huh?

"Keva THE DIVA Marie"
"SUPER Clea"

Get the gist?

Now boxing and kick boxing have gotten more popular as a great cardio workout lately and we think that you should think about hooking your bad self up with some lessons. If you think you kicked bootie before just wait till you do this. Now get the local paper and look up kick boxing. Call your local YMCA or community college. Find out how much. Find kick boxing classes and sign up. Next, you need to get an outfit together. We think it's hot to wear baggy red satin shorts but whatever. Go about your room and gather up one kick-butt ensemble and wear that to your first class. Imagine the feel of the gloves. Practice a little hop, hop punch punch in your room. And just think: You'll soon be prepared to defend yourself in any situation, any time. Oh, and Boxing Day is really the day you would pack up your boxes from Christmas and clean. Boring.

FUTURE FILES

You know how all year long we bugged you about collecting your Future Files stuff? And you wondered aloud many times, "Why?" Well, the real reason is because minds and memories sometimes need to be coaxed. When you have a flash of brilliance or creativity or desire, you need to capitalize on it, grasp it and never let it go. It's those moments, those flashes, that will propel you to do great things in the future.

Today you need to crack open those files. Spread them out all over your room. For each section, each file, take the things that still mean something to you and cut and paste in a page of a new, unused journal. Or two pages. Or five pages. Or fifty pages. However many pages it takes to get all of them down. You're going to make a book or zine of your future. Or rather of the things you desire and crave and see in your future. Go through and do this for every folder of junk you've saved. You don't have to do it all in one day either, you can spread this out over time. But the finished result, a book or zine that's all about you and your dreams, becomes sacred document #1. Never to be forgotten. Never to be thrown away. Never to be left behind. Keep it with you always. And in the future, when you feel cruddy or stupid or lost or stuck, you grab it and you read it. And we promise you with all of our deep gut-busting souls, it will make you feel better. Sappy, but oh so true.

TALK TALK TALK TALK TALK TALK

OK, so we know that Felicity does this on the TV show but still.

Making a tape and sending it to your faraway pal or stashing it away as an audio diary is still extremely cool. In fact, it can even be treated as an exercise to getting over whatshisname or recovering from a trauma that has been hard to talk about, regular style.

When you go out for meditative, introspective thinking walks, bring along the tape recorder and talk about the things you see, the thoughts you have. (And if people stare at you, tough.)

If you have to try out for the school play, this is a great way to practice.

Or maybe you are just dying to reinvent your voice. Like, you heard it on your best friend's answering machine and freaked...you had no idea it was so high. Practice on your tape recorder.

We say get a mini–tape recorder. Think cheap, try Radio Shack or something like that, but don't spend big bucks. Get some minitapes. And start talking.

December 29

Imagine you can redo 12 things. Change the fates, go back in time. What would those 12 things be? Quick, before you think of something else, grab paper and pen and write down the first 12 things that come to mind.

Once your list is done, study it. Read it over, let the words sink into that brain of yours and ask yourself: "Would I be the same person or a better person if I had done these things they way I should have?" If the answer is "No", well then, our little exercise has done its job. No regrets. But if the answer is "Yes, I would be better", then think about how you can affect those same decisions today. How can you change your life for the better right now. Yes, TODAY! Because as you have heard before, sometimes it's better late than never.

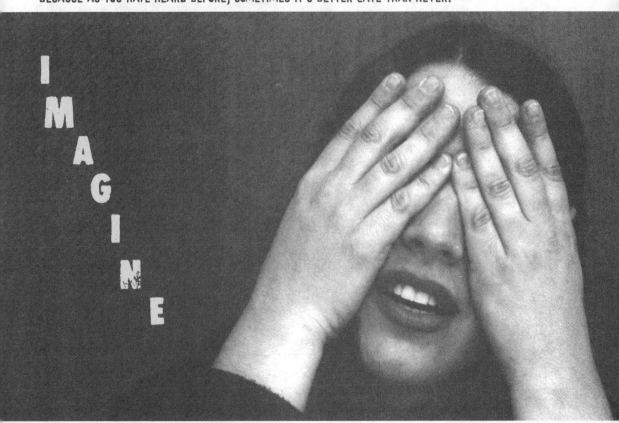

New Year's is a fantabulous holiday. It's all about new beginnings and new chances and new opportunities and, well, a new year. There are so many traditions that surround this day (and night) that we think you should just try to cram as many of them into your day as possible. And if you want to have celebrations all day, just set one of your clocks back so it strikes midnight long before your time zone's bewitching hour. Just tell folks you're celebrating New Year's Day in Ireland or Spain.

New Years Traditions

Black-Eyed Peas

Eat black-eyed peas! (And if you're not vegan, add bacon!) Lore says that each pea you eat is another dollar you get in the new year. You better start eating.

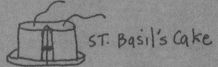

ST. Basil's Cake

Make a Saint Basil's Cake. (No, not a basil cake, as in the herb—that would be gross.) A Greek tradition, it involves baking a cake with a gold or silver coin in the middle (or a charm). When you cut the cake, you cut a piece for Saint Basil, a piece for the house (for good luck), a piece for the poor people (figuratively) and then a piece for everyone at your party. Whoever gets the piece with the coin or charm will have good luck.

Make your own noise shakers. Take two clear plastic cups. Fill one with beads or beans or buttons. Place the other on top. Tape together. And don't shake till the hour of midnight. Another option? Confetti balloons, popped at midnight. Fill un-blown up balloons with confetti (hole puncher + colored paper = confetti) with the help of a funnel. You can even add fortunes in your balloons. Then blow up and knot. Give everyone a balloon and pin at midnight. Pop! Pop! Pop!

noise shakers

12 Grapes

In Spain they say you'll have good luck if at the stroke of midnight you eat 12 grapes as fast as you can. We say it's worth a try. (Hey, we're superstitious.)

Fortune Tree Time. Write a bunch of fortunes on pieces of brightly colored paper. Make them fun. You could even have everyone in your family and circle of friends write a fortune. Then wrap them up like little presents with wrapping paper and punch a hole through them. String a ribbon through the hole and hang them all on a tree in your yard. At midnight, everyone goes outside and pulls a fortune from the tree.

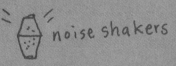

fortune tree

Now go out and have yourself the very best New Year you've ever had. Good luck....

December 31

SOMEWHERE, BACK WHEN WHO KNOWS WHEN, SOMEONE DECLARED TODAY, DECEMBER 31, THE DAY TO START ANEW, TO RETHINK SOME OF OUR OLD HABITS AND MAYBE CREATE A FEW NEW ONES. BUT THE FACT IS, THAT PROCESS SHOULD CONTINUE, EVERY DAY. OR AT LEAST OFTEN. NOT JUST ONCE A YEAR. BY NOW, YOU MAY HAVE FIGURED OUT THAT EXPLORING NEW THINGS AND TRYING TO JUST BE REAL IS OUR SCHTICK, 365 DAYS A YEAR. WE ARE FAR FROM PERFECT. IN FACT, CLEA IS REAL FAR, BUT WE KEEP TRYING TO HAVE A GOOD TIME, LEARN MORE AND BE HONEST WITH OURSELVES. THAT SAID, DECEMBER 31ST IS A FINE DAY TO MAKE SOME RESOLUTIONS. SO IS JANUARY 8TH, MARCH 23RD AND OCTOBER 16TH, JUST FOR STARTERS.

OUR RESOLUTIONS

Keva

Work that body! Less gossiping. More yoga. More holding hands with Tim. More patience for my sister. Less talking on the cell phone. And definitely fewer shoes!!

More yoga, more meditating and more all-around calmness. Appreciate those I love. Less shopping. Less Slurpees. More pink, I need more pink in my life. And lastly, keep on writing...

Clea